THE
NEW
POLITICS:
MOOD
OR
MOVEMENT?

THE

NEW

POLITICS:

MOOD

OR

MOVEMENT?

Edited by

James A. Burkhart
Stephens College

Frank J. Kendrick
Drury College

Prentice-Hall, Inc., *Englewood Cliffs, N. J.*

Current printing (last number):

10   9   8   7   6   5   4   3   2   1

C-13-615211-2

P-13-615203-1

Library of Congress Catalog Card Number: 75-149026

Printed in the United States of America

PRENTICE-HALL INTERNATIONAL, INC., *London*
PRENTICE-HALL OF AUSTRALIA, PTY., LTD., *Sydney*
PRENTICE-HALL OF CANADA, LTD., *Toronto*
PRENTICE-HALL OF INDIA PRIVATE LIMITED, *New Delhi*
PRENTICE-HALL OF JAPAN, INC., *Tokyo*

PREFACE

The myriad of books, magazine articles, and newspaper feature stories which identify, and to varying degrees explain, current trends in American politics, are almost as numerous as the stirrings, moods, and socio-political movements that are characteristic of our era. Many of the commentaries are brilliantly written. In fact, *The New Politics: Mood or Movement?* could not have been written without the benefit of their wisdom. However, with few exceptions, these writings each deal with only one aspect of a movement or a specific problem or issue. Thus, the book's purpose is to synthesize the many current political moods, movements, and trends, and hopefully to provide some insight into their nature.

This book attempts to give expression to as many different and conflicting points of view as possible. Since the final judgment on the new politics is yet to be made, the editors have tried to refrain from drawing conclusions. Rather, it is their intent to raise questions and not to provide answers, and to suggest directions and alternatives and not to submit solutions.

Every book is the product of many people's efforts. The editors wish to express their gratitude to the following individuals who have been so generous with their time, patience, and knowledge: Gene Schmiditlen, Stephens College; Raymond Lee, Indiana University of Pennsylvania; members of the Political Science Department of the University of Missouri; and David Lindquist, Steve Meyerkord and the students of "Politics, Parties, and Pressure Groups," at Drury College in the Fall Semester, 1970. It must be stressed that these individuals deserve credit for any success which the book might enjoy. Moreover, they are most certainly absolved from any errors or inadequacies—these are solely the fault of the editors. Needless to say, the writers whose selections make up the bulk of this book are in a real sense the authors. The editors are also indebted to Emerson, Thoreau, and Freud whose pointed observations concerning man's dilemmas are probably more pertinent today than when they were written.

James A. Burkhart

Frank J. Kendrick

CONTENTS

THE
NEW
POLITICS:
MOOD
OR
MOVEMENT?

THE NEW POLITICS:

MOOD OR MOVEMENT?

Like every evolving and dynamic concept, the term "new politics" tends to defy definition. Attempts at definition are a study in semantics, if not ambiguity. All too often the meaning depends upon the user. As Arthur Schlesinger, Jr. remarked, "This phrase [the new politics] in recent months has been more uttered than understood." An enthusiastic advocate asserts that a new politics is our only hope, and a former governor says, "There's no such thing as the new politics. It's just a lot of people who have nothing to offer so they call it new."

The range of viewpoints on just what constitutes the new politics is revealing. One political commentator notes, "The New Politics is a ground breaking enterprise for the politics of disestablishment in the Seventies." Another suggests, "The New Politics is a form of populism, with vaguely defined goals, representing a call for various kinds of action to make the American political system more responsive to popular demands. It is a call for action by groups which, for various reasons, feel ignored or excluded by the old politics."

Carey McWilliams, the editor of *The Nation*, was one of the first to use the term "new politics," in 1962. McWilliams argued that American politics was "in a shambles—confused, absurd, irrelevant." As McWilliams saw it, new forces were coming into existence outside the traditional boundary lines of established politics. These new forces and new faces included people involved in the peace and civil rights action groups, middle-class housewives, students, Blacks, the poor, and many others. As editor McWilliams described the situation, "What characterizes the "new arrivals" is their sense that we need a new politics; that is, new political ideas and issues if not new parties. Instinctively they [the new arrivals] hold the classic view that the pursuit of the common good is the purpose of politics—not the acquisition of power, the endless buildup of arms and armaments. They sense, too, that this new politics should logically arise in this country where the first fully matured industrial, mass consumption society has emerged—a society in which the problems of the future are more clearly exhibited than anywhere." [1]

The new politics rejects a great many things associated with older, traditional politics. This is not an out-of-hand rejection but one based on the following reasoning. According to the advocates of the new politics, the old political styles and issues are dead. These styles and issues are no longer useful; in fact, they are likely to obscure unresolved and critical problems. It is certainly true that many of the traditional activities associated with old-line politicians seem so antiquated today that their mere recitation sounds like something out of another century, certainly another generation: machine organization, boss rule, padded registration lists, fraudulent balloting, the bloc voting of "hyphenated Americans" (for example, Irish-Americans), Depression politics and New Deal solutions. Hence, spokesmen for the new politics contend that as long as the old guard is in charge of things the political system will not be organized to meet and solve the new and pressing problems.

These individuals, the "new politicians," argue that we are facing almost overwhelming problems, perhaps even a crisis in American society, and politics as usual will not do the job. Traditional politics and traditional politicians do not have the sense of urgency nor the will and the drive to solve contemporary problems. As a consequence, there is need for a new approach that will involve large numbers of people, will appeal to groups not presently a part of the power structure, and will confront the problems that prevent American society from realizing its true greatness.

Moreover, unprecedented forces are whiplashing American society. The first of these is an explosion of new knowledge, particularly scientific knowledge and its handmaiden, technology. This has resulted in the most rapid rate of social change man has ever experienced. It has also had disruptive effects on traditional values and patterns of behavior. There has always been a gap between generations. However, when large numbers of young people reject the traditional way of doing things, or feel alienated by it, the gap becomes wider. Konrad Lorenz notes, "The continuity of our western culture is being threatened. There is an alarming break of traditional continuity between the generation born at about 1900 and the next. This fact is incontestable . . ." It is also a truism that our political and social institutions have not kept pace with the technological advance.

Because efficiency, the assembly-line system, and large-scale enterprise are hallmarks of the industrial order, a number of social critics indict technology for contributing to the alienation of the individual, the destruction of the environment, and, in fact, the obsoleteness of man. Much technological progress has been purchased at the cost of environmental deterioration. The revolution in weaponry

[1] Carey McWilliams, "Time for a New Politics," *The Nation*, CXCIV, 21 (May 26, 1962), 466.

has made man's survival an unanswered question. Finally, the inability of technology to eradicate social ills has created disillusionment and, in some cases, rejection of technology itself.

The new politics seeks to bring about a closer relationship between people and government, as well as a quicker response to popular demands. It attempts to bring into the mainstream of political life such disadvantaged groups as the young, the poor, the Blacks, the Indians, and the majority that feels like a minority group—women. Its object is to align our political, social, and economic institutions with the industrial system in such a way as to permit the fullest development of the unique potentialities of every person. Finally, the new politics is issue- and action-oriented. Proponents insist that we identify our national priorities and make these concerns the goals of our politics. They also insist that we act without delay to implement those goals.

The political and historical threads running through the new politics have their sources in many movements and many philosophies. There is the democratic faith and the liberal heritage countered by a touch of authoritarianism, a hint of anarchy, and sometimes even a rejection of the liberal tradition. There is a romantic, idealistic base and more than a hint of populism. There is Locke's optimistic faith in man and Rousseau's antirationalism; utopian notions of progress and a mounting urge for radical reform; a sincerity bordering upon sentimentality and the sickening awareness of life's absurdity—all these currents spiral into a crescendo of forces, stirrings, moods, and movements that characterize the "new politics."

The future of the "new politics" is as snarled as its roots. Is it a fad or fancy, a mood, a brief interlude in the constant interplay of power politics? Will the new politics have a permanent impact upon the two major parties? Will the movement restructure American government and American society along more realistic and relevant lines? Can the new politics stay within the democratic tradition or will the inertia and obstructionism of the vested interests force the movement to move more and more toward the radical left? These are some of the questions posed in *The New Politics: Mood or Movement?*

1

THE THEORY AND PRACTICE
OF AMERICAN POLITICS:

IS THE "OLD POLITICS" OBSOLETE?

American politics has long been considered in such terms as balance, compromise, moderation, and coalition. Political scientists have recently come to use more sophisticated terms like group process, consensus, balance of interests, or value system, to describe how American politics works. But regardless of the terminology, it has been a commonly accepted theory that the American system is responsible and open enough to accommodate most of the demands made upon it by "legitimate" interest groups. Since the United States is such a prosperous country, there is virtually enough to go around for all who choose to share in the consensus, or belief system ("rules of the game"). Only those groups committed to violence or radical change of the system itself are excluded. If one has a grievance, he need only form a group of like-minded persons to lobby at any of the many points of access to the system, and patiently await the redress that will come in the form of public policy. The main condition of success is the group's patient faith in the system's ultimate ability to meet legitimate demands—demands made through established, and peaceful, procedures.

Basic to American politics is the two-party system, which usually seeks to build the kind of interest group coalitions necessary to win both nominations and elections, and to govern effectively after election. The convention, to which delegates are selected by a variety of complex and vague methods among the states, facilitates this process by bringing together representatives of the dominant interests. These group advocates are expected to compromise their differences and nominate "available" candidates for public office. In the highly pluralistic American society, the candidate and the political party that seek to win must of necessity be moderate and compromising in their stated views. At the same time, however, political parties cannot afford to be deaf to the most important issues and group demands of their time.

Between elections, interest groups will generally attempt to have their demands met through lobbying before all branches of government at all levels of the American political system. Because of its relative openness and decentralization of power, most groups are afforded numerous points of access to, and influence in, the system.[1] Thus, the American citizen is not required or expected to wait until election time to try to influence the decision-making processes of government. In fact, he can probably be more effective as a citizen through his membership in influential interest groups.

In this highly complex system of checks and balances, the public interest is theoretically served by the natural tendency of the political process to respond to the most pressing (and allegedly also the most significant) interests in the country at any given time. Hence the system also implies the existence of a kind of self-adjusting, balancing process by which enough needed social change is produced to make most people reasonably content. Violence or radical change have no place in the process, and the advocates of such tactics are usually automatically excluded. In other words, only those who do not share in the consensus are denied some minimal amount of representation. As Clinton Rossiter enthusiastically explained in his *Parties and Politics in America,*

> It . . . strikes me as admirable, which is to say that the durability of the politics of American democracy should be a cause of modest rejoicing rather than of gnawing frustration. It may be such a politics will have no place in the fanciful world of 2060 . . . but for the time being it can serve the peculiar needs of American democracy better than can any other politics we have been pressed to adopt.[2]

But even such a strong proponent of the group process theory as David B. Truman has warned that "confidence in gradual adaptation assumes that the system will not operate to produce domestic or international disasters that will result in its being completely discredited."[3] It may well be that recent protest, in some cases, violent protest, has served to challenge the validity of the group and consensus theories, by demonstrating that theory does not necessarily measure up to reality.

As a few contemporary critics have recently pointed out, one of the great limitations of the traditional system of American politics is that

> It allows injustices to be inflicted upon those who cannot readily introduce their interests into the political system. Since it depends upon the interaction

---

[1] Morton Grodzins has called this feature the "multiple crack" attribute of American government, which results from having undisciplined, decentralized political parties.

[2] Clinton Rossiter, *Parties and Politics in America* (Ithaca, N.Y.: Cornell University Press, 1961), pp. 186–87.

[3] David B. Truman, *The Governmental Process* (New York: Alfred A. Knopf, 1958), p. 535.

of "groups with different interests," those people who do not recognize the interests they share with others, who cannot act as a group, and who have little power to make conflicting groups compromise—those people are subject to, rather than participants in, the political order.[4]

Since the American system of group politics depends to a very great extent upon both compromise, and the willingness to compromise, among the diverse interests, it is essential that those interests also possess sufficient political or economic power to compel other groups to compromise with them.

Another limiting characteristic of American politics is that our political parties are not strongly issue oriented. Compromise among many diverse groups naturally requires either an avoidance of the most divisive issues, or a willingness to settle for less than complete solutions of all problems. But it is also apparent that compromise is often purchased at the price of minimizing consideration of many of the most pressing issues in American life. Numerous political leaders tend to regard their roles as disinterested brokers and mainly seek to avoid political conflict of any kind. As a consequence, political parties and politicians often deserve the contempt which is felt by those voters who regard them as evasive, double-dealing, and interested only in perpetuating their monopoly of political power. The avoidance of issues also means that election campaigns at all levels more often than not become mere personality contests between candidates and political parties that represent few or no meaningful choices to the voters.

It follows that if any large group begins to realize that it is being denied access to public decision making, or that its demands are being ignored by the coalition that may at any time dominate American politics, then the group may threaten to undermine the coalition, or it may demand a change in the system's operation. According to the traditional view of American politics, such a group can attempt to form a third party, or it can lobby, or it can attempt to work within one of the existing, major parties until its outstanding demands are met. Because these tactics have often brought success to groups representing such large segments of American society as business, labor, and agriculture (interests that are also very well-represented within the system), the theory is that the same peaceful methods will work for other legitimate groups as well. But what if the affected group lacks power, or the initiative to use it, or is so effectively excluded from political decision making as to be unable to realize its potential? To cite one group, for example, neither political party and no leading economic interest group has ever made more than token efforts to speak for the interests of black citizens, rich or poor, northern or southern. Thus the allegedly self-adjusting, naturally balancing system of group politics has actually overlooked a great deal of injustice in American life.

The following selections offer several points of view concerning the opera-

---

[4] James Finn, *Protest, Pacifism, and Politics* (New York: Random House, Inc., 1967), p. 506

tion of the American political system. I. F. Stone bemoans the "loss of confidence" that pervades all sectors of society, but he can offer no solution to the situation, except to call for new leadership in the White House. Richard Rubinstein describes the "myth of peaceful progress," which, although very much a part of American political theory, overlooks the role that violence has repeatedly played in social change. At the other end of the scale, Edward Banfield extols the virtues of the American party system and points out the dangers in attempting to reform it. Finally, Carey McWilliams describes some of the most pressing political problems now facing American politics, but also calls upon the protestors to begin concentrating on the real political issues. All the authors thus consider, directly or indirectly, the question of whether the "old politics" is obsolete.

THE TRADITIONAL SYSTEM—PRO AND OTHERWISE

The Danger of Meddling

EDWARD C. BANFIELD

A political system is an accident. It is an accumulation of habits, customs, prejudices, and principles that have survived a long process of trial and error and of ceaseless response to changing circumstance. If the system works well on the whole, it is a lucky accident—the luckiest, indeed, that can befall a society, for all of the institutions of the society, and thus its entire character and that of the human types formed within it, depend ultimately upon the government and the political order.

To meddle with the structure and operation of a successful political system is therefore the greatest foolishness that men are capable of. Because the system is intricate beyond comprehension, the chance of improving it in the ways intended is slight, whereas the danger of disturbing its working and of setting off a succession of unwanted effects that will extend throughout the whole society is great.

Democracy must always meddle, however. An immanent logic impels it to self-reform, and if other forces do not prevent, it must sooner or later reform itself out of existence.[1]

The logic of this is as follows. The ideal of democracy legitimates only such power as arises out of reasonable discussion about the common good in which all participate. Power that comes into being in any other way (for example, by corruption, logrolling, appeals to sentiment or prejudice, the exercise of charm or charisma, "hasty generalization," terror, and so forth) is radically undemocratic, and people inspired by the democratic ideal will therefore endeavor to eliminate it by destroying, or reforming, whatever practices or institutions give rise to it.

No society, however, can be governed *solely* by reasonable discussion about the common good; even in a society of angels there might be disagree-

Reprinted from Edward C. Banfield, "In Defense of the American Party System," in Robert A. Goldwin, ed., Political Parties, U.S.A. (Chicago: Rand McNally and Company, 1964), pp. 37–39. Copyright 1961, 1964 by The Public Affairs Conference Center, Kenyon College, Gambier, Ohio.

[1] For data and analysis pertinent to the discussion that follows, see James Q. Wilson, *The Amateur Democrat* (Chicago: University of Chicago Press, 1962).

ment about what the common good requires in the concrete case.[2] In most societies, far more power is needed to maintain civil discipline and protect the society from its enemies than can be got simply by reasonable discussion about the common good. Therefore the logical culmination of democratic reform, viz., the elimination of all undemocratic sources of power, would render government—and therefore the preservation of the society—impossible. Democratic reform can never reach this point, of course, because, before reaching it, democracy itself would be destroyed and the impetus to further reform removed.

So far as it does succeed, however, the tendency of democratic reform is to reduce the power available for government. Such loss of power as occurs from the elimination of undemocratic sources of it will seldom be offset by increases in power of the kind that arises from reasonable discussion about the common good. Since there is a point beyond which no increase in democratic power is possible (the capacity of a society to engage in reasonable discussion about the common good being limited), reform, if carried far enough, must finally reduce the quantity of power.

There is, then, a danger that reform will chip away the foundations of power upon which the society rests. But this is not the only danger. A greater one, probably, is that in making some forms of undemocratic power less plentiful, reform may make others more plentiful, and by so doing set off changes that will ramify throughout the

political system, changing its character completely. If, for example, politicians cannot get power by the methods of the machine (corruption, favor-giving, and patronage), they may get it by other methods, such as charm, salesmanship, and "hasty generalization." The new methods may be better than the old by most standards (they cannot, of course, be better by the standard of democracy, according to which *all* power not arising from reasonable discussion about the common good is absolutely illegitimate); but even if they are better, the new methods may not serve as well as the old, or may not serve at all, in maintaining an effective political system and a good society.

Reform is, of course, far from being the only force at work. Compared to the other forces, some of which tend to produce competing changes and others of which tend to check all change, reform may be of slight effect. This is certainly true in general of such reform as is sought through formal organizations by people called "reformers." It is much less true of reform in the broader sense of the general view and disposition of "the great body of right-thinking people." This kind of reform is likely to be of pervasive importance in the long run, although its effects are seldom what anyone intended.

Jefferson may have been right in saying that democracy cannot exist without a wide diffusion of knowledge throughout the society. But it may be right also to say that it cannot exist *with* it. For as we become a better and more democratic society, our very goodness and democracy may lead us to destroy goodness and democracy in the effort to increase and perfect them.

---

[2] See Yves R. Simon, *The Philosophy of Democratic Government* (Chicago: University of Chicago Press, 1951), Chap. 1.

Our Double Standard Morality

I. F. STONE

As a young newspaperman during the world depression I never felt the despair I am beginning to feel now about the future of our country. When I try to analyze the difference I think one reason is that then even the revolutionaries had rational goals, not just a blind frustrated urge to destroy. And, of course, the election of 1932 soon provided a fresh, electric and responsive leadership. It was as if in 1968 McCarthy or Bobby Kennedy had won the election and transformed despair into hope overnight.

Today there is a loss of confidence that extends into every sector of society, even those which usually find it reassuring to have a Republican president. The banks are carrying on their books many businesses which are overripe for the bankruptcy courts, lest a general collapse engulf the banks with them. The social landscape does not encourage long-range investment. Black and chicano minorities are in revolt, and an urban guerrilla movement confronts us in the cities and on the campuses. Another Kent State could set off a tidal wave of violence on the nation's campuses. The police have become a target for snipers, as have firemen. Guns are ready everywhere. A tiny

I. F. Stone, "Our Double Standard Morality," I. F. Stone Weekly (Sept. 21, 1970).

minority of firebrand youngsters is making good on its threat to "bring the war home."

It begins to look as if it may be easy to break down the fabric of American society. To rebuild it will be very hard. Anarchy and barbarity, race war and gang rule, not utopia, lie at the end of the road on which our instant revolutionaries would put us. The power of the guerrillas is that they can start a widening chain reaction it is almost impossible to prevent. The inescapable counter-measures necessitated by a rash of bombings threaten to precipitate wider clashes in the ghettoes and on the campuses, mobilizing whole communities in war with the police and the National Guard. One looks on, helpless to avoid the collision one sees coming.

The panic, hysteria, and hate which may soon be set loose can hardly provide the crucible in which to create that New Man of whom Mao and Che dreamed. The reforms society needs all require—no matter under what "system"—an increase in every man's concern for his fellows, a greater readiness to understand, to forgive and to share. Without these qualities, Communism has already failed. You cannot beat men into angels, nor make them better by calling them "pigs."

But how do you preach to youth

the sanctity of human life when established society, in its institutionalized violence and exploitation, treats it so lightly? How often have we heard it said in Washington, in cold-blooded defense of bombing North Vietnam that "hurting them" would force them to make peace? Now our country is hurting.

There is no moral arithmetic to cancel out the crime of murder. But how do you answer those who say coolly of the young man who died in that Army Mathematics building at Wisconsin, "What if he had been drafted and died in Vietnam?" How do you restore the moral bearings of the young when we now learn from the private papers in the John F. Kennedy Library that he and former Senator Smathers of Florida on many occasions discussed the feasibility of arranging the assassination of Fidel Castro? The craziest of our mixed-up kids are no crazier than the end-justifies-the-means morality of American imperialism.

Human society, as it grows more complex, grows more vulnerable. Hijackings, bombings, snipers, and political kidnappings; Fedayeen, Tupamaros, and Weathermen, all reflect the power this gives a desperate few. But technology is not the essence of their power. At its inner core is a sustaining moral indignation which gives these few the strength to live and die as outlaws.

They will not be stopped until this inner sense of righteousness is undermined, and this can be done only by society's willingness to take a fresh look at the morality of its own behavior, and to begin to right the wrongs which provoke the resistance.

Society's moral weakness is its double standard. The sufferings of the

hijacked in the desert aroused worldwide sympathy and their release worldwide relief. But how many stopped to think that several hundred thousand of the Arab refugees from Palestine have been living for two decades in a similar stinking horror in desert camps, stifling by day, freezing by night, on a beggar's pittance? The papers are full of proposals to deal with the hijackers but little about the need to deal with the grievances behind them.

Men are moral beings, and to take from the terrorists their moral justification is the only way to strike at the heart of the terror spreading around the globe. A society operates by habit and consent, and if these begin to break down, it is helpless. Police are effective only if they confront occasional and peripheral disorder. If even a sizable minority declines to obey the rules, the task of law and order becomes insuperable. This is especially true when the authorities confront dedicated, scattered terrorists so loosely organized that they are hard to infiltrate and cannot be crushed by striking at their head, for they have no centralized direction.

If by some miracle we could acquire new leadership in the White House, if that leadership recognized the evils of our society and mobilized to deal with them, we could not only separate the mass of the youth, the blacks, the chicanos and the other discontented from the desperadoes but deprive the desperadoes themselves of the self-righteousness that sustains them.

I imagine an America with a new Roosevelt, with a president who said— and made us feel he meant it—"We are embarking on a 10-year crusade to wipe out racism, illiteracy, pollution, urban blight and war. To do so we are withdrawing from Vietnam and cutting our military down to bare-bones size. Come and help us build a new and shining America." Think of what we could do with the zeal that now moves some of our best youth to destruction.

Rebels in Eden: The Myth of Peaceful Progress

RICHARD E. RUBENSTEIN

The fact is that the present state of domestic disorder in the United States is not the product of some destructive quality mysteriously ingrained in the substance of American life. It is a product of a long sequence of particular events whose interconnections our received categories of self-understanding are not only inadequate to reveal but are designed to conceal. We do not know very well what kind of society we live in, what kind of history we have had, what kind of people we are. We are just now beginning to find out, the hard way. . . .[1]

Ironically, as Geertz suggests, despite the fact that we are a nation of amateur historians, we do not know "what kind of history we have had." But this is not surprising. Societies troubled by internal conflict and moral doubt often explore the past more for justification than enlightenment. . . .

Reprinted from Richard E. Rubenstein, Rebels in Eden: Mass Political Violence in the United States *(Boston: Little, Brown and Company, 1970), pp. 1–10, 18–20. Copyright © 1970 by Richard E. Rubenstein. Reprinted by permission of the publisher.*

[1] Clifford Geertz, in "Is America by Nature a Violent Society?" *New York Times Magazine,* April 28, 1968, p. 25.

The United States, consensus scholars believed, was the one nation in which extremely diverse groups had learned to compromise their differences peaceably. American society, they held, was blessed by a blurring of divisions between a multiplicity of economic, social, political and ethnic groups. For one reason or another (either because the land was fertile or the people hardworking, or because no true aristocracy or proletariat ever developed on American soil, or because the two-party system worked so well) any sizable domestic group could gain its proper share of power, prosperity and respectability merely by playing the game according to the rules. In the process, the group itself would tend to lose coherence and to be incorporated into the great middle class. The result, it was said, was something unique in world history—real progress without violent group conflict. In such an America there was no need— there never had been a need—for political violence. Rising domestic groups had not been compelled to be revolutionary, nor had the "ins" generally resorted to force to keep them out. America had mastered the art of peaceful power transference, a feat which established both her uniqueness as a nation and her fitness to lead the world.

This is the myth of peaceful progress, which since the racial uprisings beginning in 1964 has spawned a corollary—the myth of Negro uniqueness. For clearly, the only way to explain what happened in Watts, Newark and Detroit without challenging the prevailing belief in the norm of peaceful progress is to assume that black people are historically aberrant—the exception to the rule. Adherence to the myth cuts across party lines, with conservatives emphasizing black laziness, loose morality and disrespect for law, and liberals discussing the weakness of Negro family structure, the prevalence of racial discrimination and the culture of poverty. Either way, it is assumed that the existing political and economic system can make good on its promise to blacks without radical institutional change. The situation can be salvaged, faith in America confirmed, and violence ended without any great national political upheaval, so long as the government spends enough money on both reform programs and law enforcement.

"This then is the mood of America's absolutism," wrote Louis Hartz, "the sober faith that its norms are self-evident." [2] But what if the black community is not unique at all, but merely the latest of a long line of domestic groups motivated to resort to violence? What if the institutions designed to make economic and political advancement possible have broken down frequently in the past, compelling other large groups to embrace the politics of violence? What if political violence on

a massive scale is, as H. Rap Brown has stated, "as American as cherry pie"? Then, clearly, the myth of peaceful progress collapses and the immunity of hallowed domestic institutions from criticism is at an end.

Particularly if prior outbreaks of violent revolt in America are found to be patterned, the suspicion may arise that not just violence-prone or "exceptional" groups are responsible, but American institutions themselves—or at least the relationship between certain groups and certain institutions. In such event, modern Americans may be compelled to stop worrying exclusively about black skin and white prejudice, and start wondering whether something more fundamental is wrong—something not merely psychological and temporary, but structural and (so far) permanent. That this has not happened testifies not only to the severity of the trauma but to the remarkable staying power of the myth of peaceful progress. Indeed, the myth continues even now to shape our attitudes towards political violence.

Whether in the White House, Congress or the street, reactions to recent riots and demonstrations reveal a widely held belief that such episodes are "un-American"—rare occurrences in American life bearing little relationship to the way other domestic groups succeeded in advancing themselves. As we shall see, this is a false assumption. For more than two hundred years, from the Indian wars and farmer uprisings of the eighteenth century to the labor-management and racial disturbances of the twentieth, the United States has experienced regular episodes of serious mass violence related to the social, political and economic objectives of insurgent groups. Nevertheless, the

---

[2] Louis Hartz, *The Liberal Tradition in America*, 1955, p. 58.

shocked question "How can this be happening here?" implies that mass violence in America is anomalous. More important, the question implies its own answer: mass violence is the product of group characteristics (disrespect for law, mob hysteria, or sheer impatience) rather than characteristics of the social system (elitism, exclusion of political minorities or economic exploitation). In order to preserve intact the myth of peaceful progress we generate a steady stream of racist stereotypes (the "Indian savage," "wild Irishman" or "unassimilable Negro") which are intended to explain group violence without implicating the existing social or political system. In other words, the assumption that *violence* is un-American forces the conclusion that *the violent* are un-American—alien, racially inferior perhaps, or under foreign domination. The result of such reasoning, as will be seen, has sometimes been to involve Americans in suppression of minorities on a genocidal scale.

Closely associated with the belief in the abnormality of domestic political violence is the idea that riots or insurrections in the United States have always been both unnecessary and useless. Given the assumption of the adequacy of existing institutions to advance the interests of oppressed minorities, how could one reason otherwise? The proposition, however, is fallacious no matter how one interprets it. For example, it is false if it means that the established political machinery has permitted all major "out-groups" to move nonviolently up the ladder of power. On the contrary, our individualistic institutions seem better designed to facilitate the advancement of talented individuals than oppressed groups. Most groups which have engaged in

mass violence have done so only after a long period of fruitless, relatively nonviolent struggle in which established procedures have been tried and found wanting. Similarly, the proposition is false if it means that the established order is self-transforming, or that groups in positions of power will always share that power with outsiders without being threatened by actual or potential violence. The eighteenth-century farmer revolts, as well as tumultuous urban demonstrations in sympathy with the French Revolution, were used by Jeffersonians to create a new two-party system over the horrified protests of the Federalists. Northern violence ended the southern slave kingdom and southern terrorism ended Racial Reconstruction. The transformation of labor-management relations was achieved during a wave of bloody strikes in the midst of a depression and amid widespread fear of revolution. And black people in urban ghettos made their greatest political gains, both in Congress and in the cities, during the racial strife of the 1960's.

We may assert, therefore, that domestic political violence is neither un-American nor, in every case, unnecessary and useless. To this we must add: outbreaks of mass violence in America are not always, or even usually, the products of outside agitation, incitement to riot, foreign influence or conspiracy by a small minority. Although those engaging in violent action are almost always a minority of any given group (just as the United States Army constitutes a minority of American citizens), most major uprisings have expressed the felt desires and perceived interests of large domestic groups. Of course, it is traditional for those in power to deny that mass violence is representative, for to admit this would be to confess that the political system is failing. Thus, the ghetto uprisings of the 1960's were attributed to a few "mean and willful men" (President Johnson after the Detroit riot of 1967), the lawless and the unemployed (California Governor's Commission reporting on the Watts riot of 1965—the McCone Commission), and Communist agitators (George Wallace during the presidential campaign of 1968). The National Advisory Commission on Civil Disorders (Kerner Commission), on the other hand, found "no evidence that all or any of the disorders [of 1967] or the incidents that led to them were planned or directed by any organization or group, international, national or local"; and similar findings have been made with respect to virtually every major racial outbreak of the 1960's.[3] Moreover, the Kerner Report demonstrated conclusively that the typical rioter was *not* a member of a criminal, unemployed or migrant "underclass," while other studies have documented the positive responses of black nonrioters towards the uprisings.[4] In April 1968 one could not find a black political leader of consequence ready to condemn the disorders following Dr. King's assassination.

The strategy of attributing violent eruptions to small, unrepresentative minorities in order to vindicate the existing political structure is as old as America. Indian revolts of the late eighteenth and early nineteenth centuries were said to be the work of British agents, slave revolts were attributed by southerners to abolitionist spies, and unnamed Confederate plotters were accused of fomenting the New York draft riot of 1863. Employers consistently blamed violent strikes on "foreign agitators" or "anarchist conspirators," while anarchists of a more modern variety were said to have provoked antiwar disturbances at the 1968 national Democratic convention and elsewhere. In each of these cases (as well as in others discussed later) those in power have understated the militancy of a large group in order to justify suppression of the violent vanguard. Where the violent actors constitute a group too large to be considered a "tiny minority," however, this dodge will not work, and a new description is trotted out. Now mass violence becomes "mob hysteria" and is dismissed as irrational.

This characterization, like the the-

[3] *Report of the National Advisory Commission on Civil Disorders* (Kerner Report), 1968, Bantam edition, pp. 201–202. See also Fred C. Shapiro and James W. Sullivan, *Race Riots New York, 1964*, 1964; Lenora E. Berson, *Case Study of a Riot: The Philadelphia Story*, 1966; University of California at Los Angeles, Institute of Government and Public Affairs, *Los Angeles Riot Study*, 1967; Robert Conot, *Rivers of Blood, Years of Darkness: The Unforgettable Classic Account of the Watts Riot*, 1967; Thomas Hayden, *Rebellion in Newark: Official Violence and Ghetto Response*, 1967; Ronald Goldfarb, *Report on the Washington Riot*, 1969.

[4] Kerner Report (see note 3), pp. 128–35. See also P. Meyer, "A Survey of Attitudes of Detroit Negroes after the Riots of 1967," The Urban League of Detroit, 1967; William McCord and John Howard, "Negro Opinions in Three Riot Cities," *American Behavioral Scientist,*

March-April 1968; T. M. Tomlinson and David Sears, "Negro Attitudes Toward the Riots," *Los Angeles Riot Study*, 1967 (see note 3); Nathan Caplan, "The New Ghetto Man: A Review of Recent Empirical Studies," scheduled to appear in the *Journal of Social Issues*, 1969; Jay Schulman, "Ghetto Residence, Political Alienation and Riot Orientation," in *Urban Disorders, Violence and Urban Victimization*, L. Masotti, ed., 1968; Jerome H. Skolnick, *The Politics of Protest*, 1969, Ballantine ed., pp. 145–48.

ories of outside agitation and minority incitement, is intended to deprive violent uprisings of political content by characterizing them as a form of evil or madness. . . . Discarding the myth of peaceful progress, however, one sees that mass violence may be both irrational *and* political, or, more accurately, that the academic distinction between "expressive" and "instrumental" violence is often irrelevant in practice. . . .

It is important, . . . , not to misuse history by asserting that violence always works, or is always necessary. Clearly, this would be to create a new myth—a myth of violent progress—which could be disposed of easily by citing examples of violence with no group advancement (like the American Indian revolts) and advancement with comparatively little violence (as among American Jews). The point, really, is that political and economic power is not as easily shared, or turned over to powerless outsiders, as has been thought. Because of their size, degree of absolute or relative deprivation, and relationship to more powerful forces, the demands of some domestic groups for equality and power have been impossible to meet within the context of *existing* political and economic arrangements. To admit Indian tribes, or members of labor unions, or the mass of oppressed black people to full membership in American society meant that existing systems would have to be transformed, at least in part, to make room for the previously excluded; and that in the transformation, land-hungry settlers, large corporations, and urban political machines and commercial interests, respectively, would have to give ground. Transformation and concomitant power realignments were refused

in the first case, granted (only partially and after great social disorder) in the second, and are in doubt in the third. The moral is not that America is a "sick society" (what a curiously prideful claim that is!) but that, like all other societies, it has failed to solve the oldest problem of politics—the problem of nonviolent power transference.

One further bit of comparative history may make this clearer. President Rutherford B. Hayes, a Republican, helped to break the railroad strikes of 1877. President Grover Cleveland, a Democrat, almost singlehandedly broke the railroad strike of 1894. As a result, union leaders like Eugene V. Debs realized that, from their point of view, it did not matter which party was in power. The transference of formal political power from Republicans to Democrats was a mere ritual, disguising the fact that the same interests effectively controlled both parties. The plight of American blacks in modern times, faced by conservative business opposition among Republicans and conservative union opposition among Democrats, with both parties bidding for southern support, is comparable. Third party politics, to be sure, was one method by which large excluded groups sometimes attempted to force a system transformation, but the technique was rarely effective, given the strength of the American Center and its systematic discrimination against minority parties. It was when such desperation tactics proved useless that the probability of mass political violence was highest, for no large American group, to my knowledge, gave up the struggle for admission to power without a fight. Nor have the holders of power, from George III of Britain to Mayor Richard Daley of Chicago, meekly stood by while upstarts challenged their hard-won pre-eminence.

Many Americans recognize inwardly that the dream of peaceful system transformation and nonviolent power sharing *is* a dream—a utopia yet unachieved—and this recognition helps to explain why we have not machine-gunned black rioters or student demonstrators. For if mass violence were always un-American, unnecessary and useless, as official rhetoric claims, the correct response would be to crush it, immediately and brutally. Instead, half realizing that riots and insurrections imply a failure of the dream, our initial reaction is that of George Washington, upon hearing of the Shays Rebellion: "If they have *real* grievances, redress them, if possible; or acknowledge the justice of them and your inability to do so at the moment. If they have not, employ the force of Government against them at once . . . "[5] The difficulty arises, however, when well-intended reforms do not lead to a redress of grievances, and violence continues. The result may be the escalation of both rebellion and suppression to the level of open warfare.

[5] Orville J. Victor, *History of American Conspiracies*, 1863, p. 426.

two

THE NEW POLITICS

Protest, Power, and the Future of Politics

CAREY McWILLIAMS

A preoccupation with power—black power, student power, flower power, poor power, "the power structure"—is

Reprinted from The Nation (January 15, 1968), pp. 71–77. Copyright 1968 by The Nation Associates Inc. Reprinted by permission of the publisher.

the most striking aspect of the American political scene at the moment. Oddly enough, obsession with power goes hand in hand with a fear of power. Some of the New Left groups that talk the toughest about power are extremely reluctant to see power operate in institutional form; within their own organizations, they shun "hierarchies" and formally structured relations of authority. What the preoccupation with power reflects, essentially, is a deep-seated, pervasive feeling of powerlessness. The feeling is not restricted to particular groups; most citizens, a majority perhaps, are bedeviled by it. "A feeling of having no choice," Mary McCarthy has noticed, "is becoming more and more widespread in American life."

So intense is the feeling of powerlessness that it has given rise to "anti-movements" and "anti-politics." Instead of building new, strong, viable organizations through which to exercise political power, the tendency—at least on the Left—has been to move in the reverse direction, that is, to reject the instruments of politics. Discussion has been superseded by "uproar," debate by demonstrations, dialogue by confrontation, civil disobedience by overt resistance. Often in the past, young voters have bade "farewell to reform" and then turned to radical politics; this time they have swung toward no politics at all. The idea of government by and through elected representatives is seriously questioned by some and indignantly rejected by others. The very process of politics has come under direct attack from young and old alike.

Apart from increasing evidence of this active disaffection, there is among those who have by no means despaired of politics a widespread anxiety about what Walter Lippmann has called "the rot of the American political system." On November 10, N.B.C. presented an analysis of voter attitudes on the 1968 election, and found that most voters had little faith that any major candidate for the Presidency could master either of the two major problems we face (war and race), and worse, seemed to feel that the electorate was being denied live options on most issues. The survey indicated "a stunning lack of confidence in the President and in his political opponents." A mountain of supporting evidence might be cited. Yet despite the active disaffection and the mounting general concern, little attention has been focused on what it is that accounts basically for the malfunctioning of the political system. The problem has two aspects. Power has been concentrated in our society in such a way, and to such a degree, that normal political processes are perhaps no longer able to cope with it. But one can't be sure of that because if certain specific weaknesses in the political system not directly related to the concentration of power, were remedied (at the moment they are not widely recognized, much less discussed) the reform might go far to remove the "rot" from the system. . . .

The concentration of power became much tighter after we entered World War II. Under the stress of rapid mobilization, a remarkable fusion of economic and political power took place; more accurately, perhaps, a fusion of economic and administrative or Executive power. This had been true also in World War I, but unlike the procedure after 1918, the war-making machine of World War II was never fully dismantled. The swift onset of the cold war, then the fighting in Korea and Vietnam, set the pattern for a permanent war economy. The rapid pace of military technology, which began to diverge sharply from civilian advances, created a political rationale for continuous research and improvement in weapons systems and the like. Nuclear weapons and virtually instantaneous delivery systems authorized an ever-larger permanent military establishment; in any future war, it was said, there would be "no time to mobilize." In the past, industries had "converted" to war production and then "reconverted" to peacetime production. After 1945 new defense industries came into being specifically to manufacture military hardware. At the same time the magnitude of the military budget revolutionized government finance. Defense-related expenditures will this year probably exceed $100 billion. In a recent survey, the AP referred to the Pentagon as wielding "the mightiest concentration of economic power in the world today." . . . For this reason, the defense complex has not been challenged by either party; in fact both have been about equally responsible for it. But it is doubtful that the growth of the complex could have been arrested even if one of the major parties had been willing to incur the risk of such a stand. And it is doubtful today that the Republican Party can bring itself to challenge the disastrous course of present policies, not because it is blind to the dangers or fails to appreciate the political possibilities in capitalizing on the existing discontent, but because power is now so bipartisan in structure that the opposition party cannot, apparently, muster the resources or the will to make the effort. . . .

As the militarization of the society has proceeded, the power of the Congress relative to the Presidency has steadily declined. The recent report of the Senate Foreign Relations Committee on "National Commitments" November 20) points out that the last twenty years have seen a nearly complete reversal of the positions of the Executive and legislative branches in the area of foreign affairs. Dr. Ruhl Bartlett, of the Fletcher School of Law and Diplomacy, told the committee that "the greatest danger to democracy in the United States and to the freedom of its people and to their welfare—as far as foreign affairs are concerned—is the erosion of legislative authority and oversight and the growth of a vast pyramid of centralized power in the Executive branch of the government." Dr. Edgar Eugene Robinson of Stanford suggested in a recent speech that the acquisition by the President of immense power over foreign affairs during the last twenty years means that the Constitution is outdated. "There is no possibility," he says, "of real change in the President's foreign policy except by removal . . . by death, resignation, impeachment or defeat at the polls." What in his view makes this development particularly dangerous is the dexterity with which the President can fuse two constitutional functions: his role as commander in chief and his responsibility for the conduct of foreign affairs. Once war has become an instrument of national policy, it is hard to tell which role a President is playing. If his foreign policy is challenged, he can always assert his powers as commander in chief, and these powers are almost unlimited. (See, also, Senator Frank Church's speech, October 29, on "President and Congress in Foreign Policy: The Threat to Constitutional Government.")

The process by which political and economic power have been concentrated through expansion of the war-making machine has been hastened by a series of postwar "revolutions": the organizational revolution, the scientific and technological revolution, the cybernetic revolution and, most notably, the communications revolution. As Dr. Robinson also pointed out, the communications revolution has made it possible for a new Presidential order, decision or proclamation to be carried instantaneously by radio and television. "Consequently, the effectiveness of that action is amplified millions of times by the miracle of swift communication." . . .

Any erosion of the power of Congress is an erosion of the power of the people. Given a society in which for a period of twenty years—almost the span of a generation—the real power of decision has been increasingly ceded to the President, it is not hard to account for the prevalent sense of "powerlessness." Just as the ghetto dweller feels that he lives in "occupied territory," so many people come to feel that they have been "displaced" from their role as electors. A force which they cannot control or directly influence has taken charge of their lives and destinies. "There are many signs," writes A. H. Halsey (*New Society*, October 26), "from love-ins in the Haight-Ashbury district of San Francisco to the 'privitization' of affluent workers . . . that a theory of the impotence of politics is being accepted." If the country has in fact been "occupied" by a power not sanctioned by the Constitution, then it must be "liberated." But given the degree to which power has been concentrated, can the direction of policy be reversed by conventional political means? In such a situation, public protests become increasingly

directed against the symbols of power, and that has the effect of diverting energies from the political process and, at the same time, discrediting it.

In the nature of things, it is difficult for "anti-movements" to cooperate with movements—of any kind. The objectives, the sense of tactics, the style of action, are different or divergent. That some of the "anti-movements" share with the infinitely larger movement of "concerned" and "dissatisfied" citizens the short-term objective of stopping the war does not mean that they see the war in the same terms or that they agree on other objectives. The "anti-movement" of Negro nationalists does not even share the short-term objective of stopping the war (at least, it is not for them a priority objective). And, to complicate matters, the larger movement is itself not well organized and lacks sufficient program.

By and large, "anti-movements" are not elated when a dove defeats a hawk; they have lost confidence in the political process as it now exists—not without reason—and they want to discredit it, the better, no doubt, to fill the political vacuum with a new politics. If the "anti-movements" openly espoused revolutionary objectives, then a measure of "parallel" politics might be possible (it may still be, depending on developments). But as of now, the Black Nationalists and the New Activists, as William Appleman Williams has observed, "have no vision of a Socialist commonwealth, let alone even the beginnings of serious proposals to create and govern such a society." They seem less concerned with the concentration of power, and the growing political vacuum which could set the stage for an American fascism, than with the hateful discrepancy between liberal ideals and liberal practice. They give little thought to the possibility that something about the functioning of a capitalist economy may lead to the concentration of power. The heroes of the "anti-movements" are Debray and Che Guevara, not Gramsci who thought that the proper place to find those who aspired to lead revolutionary movements was in the reading rooms of public libraries. Because they are not really concerned with the *political* consequences of particular protests and demonstrations, they discount polls which show that certain recent demonstrations have stimulated a reaction and strengthened the President's hand. This, of course, is a logical attitude for those who have lost confidence in the political process. But it carries a distressing echo of the "social fascism" line that the Communist Party pursued in the early 1930s.

However, the "anti-movements" have had some highly desirable political consequences. The stress on personal commitment, on values, on life styles, the exposure of liberal pretense, have released new energies, focused attention on particular issues, and pointed up the relation between morality and politics. One of the only means whereby individuals can make what they think and feel relevant in a society in which power is highly concentrated is to stress the morality—or immorality—of public policies. But it is precisely in such a period that as Iris Murdoch has noted, "political moralizing comes to be thought of as an idle idealism, a sort of utopianizing which is just a relief from looking at unpleasant facts." This was the position into which many cold-war liberals were driven, or into which they retreated, when they decided that there was little point in at-

tempting to bring moral judgments to bear in the field of foreign policy. Today many of these same individuals have recoiled in horror from the consequences of the "crackpot realism" of Dulles and Acheson and Rusk. For this shift in attitude, the "anti-movements" are entitled to some credit. But if we are to answer the cynic in ourselves, moral judgments, as Miss Murdoch stresses, must be *realistic enough* to be political judgments as well. For the ultimate cynicism is to conclude that politics is a futile game. Such a conclusion severs the relation between morality and politics. To stress the immorality of the war in Vietnam, while rejecting the possibility of stopping it *by political means,* is self-defeating. Before anyone declared politics obsolete, he should at least try to identify the rot which has brought such discredit upon the institution. . . .

　　　• • • • •

The collapse of the Left is an essential key to explaining the rot because the absence of ideological differences has been the historic weakness of American politics. Not only has the American Left contributed to this weakness; the lack of a consistent ideological drive explains the feebleness of the Left itself. "The American Left," as Michael Davie points out, "has always been more eccentric than effective. In Europe, men have had to battle for the establishment of their basic rights, and have needed a theory of drastic social change to go to war with." But not here. As Tom Hayden, one of the leaders of the New Left observes: "How *do* you act as a revolutionary against a nation-state that celebrates your values while betraying their substance?" Even in the fiercest American struggles, everyone of major political importance has believed in the same basic things. . . . Al Capone once said to Claud Cockburn that "this American system of ours . . . gives to each and every one of us a great opportunity if we only seize it with both hands and make the most of it." Capone's view is still shared by most Americans. That it was never really true Indians and Negroes and others can testify, but it seemed to be true until fairly recent times. In the past, a debilitated American Left tried to mount a critique of the prevailing ideology, but the collapse of the Left in the postwar period silenced this type of criticism precisely when it was most needed.

The abdication of the Left in the postwar period, and the failure of the New Left thus far to fill the vacuum, have meant that the idea of a radical politics and the function it can serve in our kind of political system has been forgotten. Radical political pressures played a role in bringing the Republican Party into being. Radical political pressures also helped to shape the New Deal. Radical politics revivified the labor movement in the 1930s. . . . A radical politics, whether organized as a party or as a movement, is needed today—as it has always been needed— to goad the two major parties, to offer a general critique of the society, and to give *political* expression to the discontents that can gain a hearing in neither major party. The New Left may meet this need; it has not done so to date.

A secondary but relevant explanation of the rot is that the major parties are hopelessly old-fashioned. On essential matters they have changed little in the last century. At the *national* level they are loosely organized. They spend a pittance on research and planning, and even less on education. They rally briefly during national elections but for the rest of the time are "demobilized" and lethargic. This slackness of organization mirrors the attitude of most voters, who are content to limit their political enterprise to the ritual act of voting every two years— when they bother to vote. The professionals who run the parties do not encourage any greater activity. The parties engage the active support of perhaps not more than 3 to 5 per cent of the membership. There was a time when various organizations and interest groups participated directly in political decision-making, but this pluralistic pattern has almost vanished, and today most of the interest groups are long since "integrated" into the power structure, that is, they are more dependent on the party in power than it is on them. The New Left groups, therefore, quite properly attempt to build new bases of local power which may eventually acquire enough votes or enough "disruptive" power to engage the major parties and particular state and local administrations in meaningful bargaining. Even if this were to occur, however, national political decisions would still need to be made, national priorities established, and for that purpose well-organized national parties are indispensable.

At the national level, both major parties are still loosely organized coalitions formed for the purpose of conducting campaigns. The Republican coalition, established at the time of the Civil War, was ascendant until the successful New Deal coalition was put together in 1932. Since then, the Republicans have been unable or unwilling to form a new coalition and the New Deal coalition is now disintegrating. At the moment it would be difficult to say which party is the more sharply divided internally. Neither seems able to confront the new issues (too risky) or appeal to the new constituencies which have emerged since 1932 (to do so, just now, would endanger what is left of the old coalition). Yet recent polls show that a large—perhaps a third or more—and steadily increasing percentage of the electorate is dissatisfied with the candidates and programs and styles of both parties and therefore disinclined to participate actively in politics.

Instead of addressing themselves to the new issues and the new constituencies, both parties evade their responsibilities by resort to excessive "personality politics," TV-style (with the result that rising campaign costs threaten to make the Senate once more the "millionaire's club" that it was in the 1890s). The effect of all this is to encourage the feeling of "powerlessness" and enforce the conviction that political action is futile. It needs to be stressed that whereas at one time national coalition parties functioned reasonably well, today's problems are much more complex, the resistances to be overcome are much greater and the concentration of power is formidable. To make politics alive once more, national parties must be coherently and purposefully organized, and they must command enough energy, not merely to secure adoption of new programs but to make certain that they are properly administered. Neither party today is so qualified. . . .

The party system has been further weakened by a new situation. A combination of factors, with heavy emphasis on the mass media, has made a measure of "direct democracy" possible. Representative government is at best slow, cumbersome, exasperating. Nowadays many decisions must be made quickly if they are to be effective. Let's say that the mayor announces the immediate closing of a city hospital. There isn't time to distribute leaflets, interview officials, petition the parties, organize a campaign. So those opposing the closure chain themselves to the office furniture, after first giving the TV news rooms notice of time and place. A vast audience is immediately alerted, with little effort, at minimal expense.

In a sense, *the new media become a substitute for the party.* Often official reaction is swift and responsive; whereas when petitioners go through channels, elected officials can stall, appoint commissions, order investigations, and so forth. A pamphlet by John Morris on "Direct Democracy," published recently in London, explains the theory. The universal defect of representative democracy, so the argument goes, is the formation of controlling elites. Such government lets the people vote periodically for politicians or for parties, but seldom for policies. This, of course, merely echoes Michels' cynical comment: "The one right which the people reserve is the ridiculous privilege of choosing from time to time a new set of masters." Representative government was once a necessity; people had to *send* representatives to the capital. But modern communications have made a degree of direct democracy possible and people are beginning to like it. Polls have somewhat replaced primaries as a means of registering voter preference. Experiments are being made to test the possibility of "instant" opinion polls by the use of computer techniques. Up to a point, there is much to be said for direct democracy and we shall see more of it; but it cannot substitute for partisan debate on significant issues, much less for representative government which extends and clarifies the partisan debate and, in the end, should resolve it. Direct democracy can stimulate and supplement representative government; it can never replace it.

. . . . .

Given the extent of the rot that currently besets the American political system—and given the degree to which power is concentrated—it is not surprising that many people feel powerless, or that they have lost confidence in politics or are voicing doubts about representative government and liberal political institutions. Nor is it surprising that many young people have turned to "anti-movements" of one kind or another and taken to the streets to air their grievances and express their frustrations. What *is* surprising, given these factors, is the way in which "concerned" and "dissatisfied" citizens have tried to find new but democratic ways of expressing their judgments and preferences, with no aid and little encouragement from either party. . . . It may be impossible, in the end, to cope with the concentration of power that exists today by normal political processes, but we shall never know until we give the system a chance to function. It is not a question of either/or but of both, a great deal more of both. Action protests can be combined with radical politics; action protests can also be combined with conventional politics. But action protests without politics will not stop the war, much less reverse the direction of American policy, much less open the structural changes needed by American society. The task of those who are concerned with these objectives, then, is to concentrate, for a change, on the political problems.

2

IDEAS AND ACTION:

REVOLUTION OR REFORMATION

The new politics is many things to many people. It may be, in fact, more of a reaction to existing conditions, procedures, institutions, or ideas than a consistent, structured ideology. Basic to the new politics is a demand for change, which is a result of dissatisfaction with the world as it is now. Beyond this basic demand, the new politics branches out into an aggregation of ideas and actions which are at least as numerous as the persons or groups that currently demand change. Out of this seeming chaos, however, emerge several ideas or patterns of action common to most of the "new politicians." These include populism, romanticism, a critique of liberalism, a rejection of the "establishment," and an appeal to direct action.

Populism, a word derived from the Populist revolt of the 1890's, simply means a demand for the popular control of government. Then, as now, the cure for the defects of democracy was considered to be more democracy. As John D. Hicks explained the views of the nineteenth century reformers:

> Once permit the people really to rule, once insure that the men in office would not or could not betray the popular will, and such regulative measures as would right the wrongs from which people suffered would quickly follow.[1]

In the populism of the 1960's and 1970's, we see a similar line of thought. To the groups involved, the new politics means a purification of democracy, a transfer of power from the political bosses to the people, a rejection of control by the "power elite," and consideration of the "real" issues by the political parties and educational institutions. In other words, if the American political system

---

[1] John D. Hicks, *The Populist Revolt* (Minneapolis: The University of Minnesota Press, 1931), p. 406.

could somehow be made more democratic and responsive to the popular will, it would be better able to respond to the demands of the disaffected groups.

This new populism can be said to be moving in two general directions: one direction is within the existing political system, and has as its end the improvement of conditions to permit the increased participation of new groups in the system; the other direction is toward a denial of the value of working within the system, and has as its end the development of something new. An example of populism within the existing system is provided by Senator Eugene McCarthy, who in 1968 called for a "purified and revitalized" political system, as well as a new politics "with a new constituency—not a constituency of special interests or of separate groups put together like a jigsaw puzzle, but a constituency of conscience, of common concern, and of common commitment." [2]

The populist strain in the new politics is voiced most stridently by the young people and the Blacks. In regard to black citizens, the fact that there are yet only some 1500 elected black public officials (or about .3 per cent of the total of over 500,000 elected officials) in the United States indicates that any move for more representation tends to be populist in nature because Blacks have been denied political power within the white-dominated system for so long.

Frustration over lack of achievements leads from this type of populism to one that seeks to rebuild American society into something entirely new. A relatively positive concept of a new society has been espoused by the New Left and called "participatory democracy." This is a kind of Rousseauist "general will" idea, which in practice means that every individual must somehow share in all decision-making. It is based on an idealistic and romantic view of the nature of man as a basically rational, free, and good creature who has somehow become subjected to domination by power elites, military-industrial complexes, university administrations, and white colonialists.

Other groups do not reject the system so completely, but they commonly share an implicit threat that if justice is not achieved, or that if legitimate demands for recognition and representation are not realized, then frustration will inevitably lead to radicalism. As Stokely Carmichael has warned, "As long as people in the ghettoes . . . feel that they are victims of the misuse of white power without any way to have their needs represented . . . these communities will exist in a constant state of insurrection." [3] But, so far at least, the weight of black militancy is committed to trying to realize in practice the dominant values of the "American dream" while working largely outside the established system (whose channels are usually closed to Blacks anyway) to achieve the desired goals of more independence and power.

[2] Senator Eugene J. McCarthy, *First Things First: New Priorities for America* (New York: The New American Library, 1968), p. 9.

[3] Quoted in Vincent Harding, "Black Radicalism: The Road From Montgomery," in Alfred F. Young, *Dissent* (DeKalb, Ill.: Northern Illinois University Press, 1968), pp. 343–44.

American liberalism is either criticized for its failings or rejected outright by most of the leading spokesmen for the new politics. The reason for this criticism or rejection is the wide gap that exists between the rhetoric and the practice of contemporary American political thought. Carl Oglesby, of the Students for a Democratic Society, for example, criticizes our "anti-Communist corporate liberalism," which serves a function like that of the Church in feudal times, "that is, to protect the state from change." [4] Nathan Wright attacks "post-Victorian liberalism," which involves the "viewing of reality through tinted glasses" while ignoring "the effective indolence and abject hopelessness of black people, occasioned in large part by the centuries long experience of giving one's best efforts for unjustly meager rewards." [5] But, nowhere, perhaps, does the rejection of American liberalism appear so eloquently as in the works of Herbert Marcuse, who condemns the entire system of "corporate liberalism" that dominates American life and denies real freedom to the people. We live, as he says, in a one-dimensional state, which does not liberate but demands the total submission of the individual to an affluent, pseudo-democratic system.

Along with the criticism of liberalism for its hypocrisy goes a rejection of the so-called "establishment" or "power elite," which generally is seen to consist of those persons, groups, or institutions that make the important political decisions in America. As we said above, this modern antiestablishmentarianism often appears in the form of a conspiratorial view of American life, that pictures our society as run by powerful groups that structure the system in order to maintain their domination of powerless groups. For example, the 1966 S.N.C.C. position paper on Black Power stated, "More and more we see Black people in this country being used as a tool of the White Liberal establishment." [6] A similar form of exploitation is felt by students, Indians, Chicanos, the poor, and women —in other words, all those who do not share equally in the benefits of American citizenship.

Finally, the new politics offers an appeal for immediate and direct action to bring about the desired changes in society. This action may consist of legal acts taken entirely within the system, or it may take the form of civil disobedience, or violence, depending on the situation and the degree of militancy of the group involved. The legal approach was exemplified most dramatically by the "children's crusade" on behalf of Senators McCarthy and Robert Kennedy in their campaigns for the presidency in 1968.

Civil disobedience has been defined as a politically motivated self-help tactic

[4] Carl Oglesby, "Let Us Shape the Future," in Mitchell Cohen and Dennis Hale, eds., *The New Student Left: An Anthology* (Boston: Beacon Press, 1967), p. 320.

[5] Nathan Wright, *Ready to Riot* (New York: Holt, Rinehart and Winston, Inc., 1968), pp. 100–101.

[6] "Who is the Real Villain—Uncle Tom or Simon Legree?"; SNCC position paper on Black Power, in Thomas Wagstaff, *Black Power: The Radical Response to White America* (New York: The Free Press, 1969), p. 115.

characterized by open, but nonviolent, lawbreaking. It has been manifested in such forms as disruptive university confrontations, lunch counter demonstrations, protest marches, sit-ins, or picketing, all of which are designed, as one authority explained, "to make the cost—political, economic, and emotional—of not adopting the change that is pressed . . . greater than society is willing to pay." [7]

The President's Commission on the Causes and Prevention of Violence reported recently that the United States is one of the world leaders in civil strife and violence. Frustration in the achievement of goals by legal or nonviolent methods has led in recent years to a resurgence of violence in this country. A method frequently used in American history, political violence has now become an important means of direct action for the more radical of the "new politicians." The late Algerian rebel, Frantz Fanon, advocated violence as the only way for the masses to achieve national identity and "decolonization." Thus, the moral end will justify the immoral means, no matter what the cost. If a better world should actually emerge as a result of the urban riots, the convention confrontations, and the university "takeovers," then one might eventually be tempted to conclude that these actions were justified after all. As Carl Oglesby has said, "Revolutions do not take place in velvet boxes." [8]

From the above consideration, it would appear that the new politics, though not offering a precise, well-ordered ideology to answer the great questions of our era, is not at the same time devoid of conceptual content. Briefly, it calls for broadened representation and new forms of governance to realize the democratic ideals of popular sovereignty and equal justice in America, while providing a selection of several methods to achieve the desired goals. It is also, to a great extent, a reaction against what is regarded as an unyielding, hopelessly dominated political system that in interested only in self-perpetuation. The nucleus of the new politics, then, may lie somewhere between revolution on the one side, and reformation, on the other.

The articles and essays in this section are concerned in varying ways with the role of ideas and action in politics. Populism is considered as a nineteenth century phenomenon by Richard Hofstadter, and as a feature of the "new politics" by Paul Goodman. Tom Hayden describes the concept of participatory democracy in the S.D.S. convention manifesto of 1962, and Jack Newfield explains the existentialist facet of the "new politics." Michael Harrington criticizes the "liberalism" of the last three decades, and calls for a move to the "democratic left," while Harry Ashmore also criticizes liberalism, but contrasts it favorably with the radicalism of the 1960's. Herbert Marcuse, the Marxist, attacks the establishment and calls for the "Great Refusal," while Edmund Burke points out the dangers inherent in radical change. Four types of action to effect change in

---

[7] Sanford J. Rosen, "Civil Disobedience and Other Such Techniques: Law Making Through Law Breaking," *The George Washington Law Review*, XXXVII, 3 (March, 1969), 449.

[8] Carl Oglesby, "Let Us Shape the Future," in Cohen and Hale, *The New Student Left*, p. 314.

American politics are offered by Senator Eugene McCarthy, who discusses "working within the system," Stephen Saltonstall, who calls for a "strategy of disruption" on college campuses, Eldridge Cleaver, who bemoans the failures of the nonviolent approach, and Sidney Hyman, who discusses the theory of civil disobedience. The wide range of views presented by these authors only serves to demonstrate the difficulty of assigning specific limits to the new politics.

POPULISM: THE PEOPLE YES, NO, OR MAYBE?

The Folklore of Populism

RICHARD HOFSTADTER

For a generation after the Civil War, a time of great economic exploitation and waste, grave social corruption and ugliness, the dominant note in American political life was complacency. Although dissenting minorities were always present, they were submerged by the overwhelming realities of industrial growth and continental settlement. The agitation of the Populists, which brought back to American public life a capacity for effective political indignation, marks the beginning of the end of this epoch. In the short run the Populists did not get what they wanted, but they released the flow of protest and criticism that swept through American political affairs from the 1890's to the beginning of the first World War.

Where contemporary intellectuals gave the Populists a perfunctory and disdainful hearing, later historians have freely recognized their achievements and frequently overlooked their limitations. Modern liberals, finding the Populists' grievances valid, their programs suggestive, their motives creditable, have usually spoken of the Populist epi-

From The Age of Reform by Richard Hofstadter, pp. 60–67, 93. Copyright 1955 by Richard Hofstadter. Reprinted by permission of Alfred A. Knopf, Inc.

sode in the spirit of Vachel Lindsay's bombastic rhetoric:

Prairie avenger, mountain lion,
Bryan, Bryan, Bryan, Bryan,
Gigantic troubadour, speaking like a siege gun,
Smashing Plymouth Rock with his boulders from the West.

There is indeed much that is good and usable in our Populist past. While the Populist tradition had defects that have been too much neglected, it does not follow that the virtues claimed for it are all fictitious. Populism was the first modern political movement of practical importance in the United States to insist that the federal government has some responsibility for the common weal; indeed, it was the first such movement to attack seriously the problems created by industrialism. The complaints and demands and prophetic denunciations of the Populists stirred the latent liberalism in many Americans and startled many conservatives into a new flexibility. Most of the "radical" reforms in the Populist program proved in later years to be either harmless or useful. In at least one important area of American life a few Populist leaders in the South attempted something profoundly radical and humane—to build a popular movement that would cut across the old barriers of race—until persistent use of the Negro bogy distracted their following. To discuss the broad ideology of the Populist does them some injustice, for it was in their concrete programs that they added most constructively to our political life, and in their more general picture of the world that they were most credulous and vulnerable. Moreover, any account of the fallibility of Populist thinking that does not acknowledge the stress and suffering out of which that thinking emerged will be seriously remiss. But anyone who enlarges our portrait of the Populist tradition is likely to bring out some unseen blemishes. In the books that have been written about the Populist movement, only passing mention has been made of its significant provincialism; little has been said of its relations with nativism and nationalism; nothing has been said of its tincture of anti-Semitism.

The Populist impulse expressed itself in a set of notions that represent what I have called the "soft" side of agrarianism. These notions, which appeared with regularity in the political literature, must be examined if we are to re-create for ourselves the Populist spirit. To extract them from the full context of the polemical writings in which they apeared is undoubtedly to oversimplify them; even to name them in any language that comes readily to the historian of ideas is perhaps to suggest that they had a formality and coherence that in reality they clearly lacked. But since it is less feasible to have no labels than to have somewhat too facile ones, we may enumerate the dominant themes in Populist ideology as these: the idea of a golden age; the

concept of natural harmonies; the dualistic version of social struggles; the conspiracy theory of history; and the doctrine of the primacy of money. The last of these I will touch upon in connection with the free-silver issue. Here I propose to analyze the others, and to show how they were nurtured by the traditions of the agrarian myth.

The utopia of the Populists was in the past, not the future. According to the agrarian myth, the health of the state was proportionate to the degree to which it was dominated by the agricultural class, and this assumption pointed to the superiority of an earlier age. The Populists looked backward with longing to the lost agrarian Eden, to the republican America of the early years of the nineteenth century in which there were few millionaires and, as they saw it, no beggars, when the laborer had excellent prospects and the farmer had abundance, when statesmen still responded to the mood of the people and there was no such thing as the money power.[1] What they meant— though they did not express themselves in such terms—was that they would like to restore the conditions prevailing before the development of industrialism and the commercialization of agriculture. It should not be surprising that they inherited the traditions of Jacksonian democracy, that they revived the old Jacksonian cry: "Equal Rights for

[1] Thomas E. Watson: *The Life and Times of Andrew Jackson* (Thomson, Ga., 1912), p. 325: "All the histories and all the statesmen agree that during the first half-century of our national existence, we had no poor. A pauper class was unthought of: a beggar, or a tramp never seen." Cf. Mrs. S. E. V. Emery: *Seven Financial Conspiracies Which Have Enslaved the American People* (Lansing, ed. 1896), pp. 10–11.

All, Special Privileges for None," or that most of the slogans of 1896 echoed the battle cries of 1836.[2] General James B. Weaver, the Populist candidate for the presidency in 1892, was an old Democrat and Free-Soiler, born during the days of Jackson's battle with the United States Bank, who drifted into the Greenback movement after a short spell as a Republican, and from there to Populism. His book, *A Call to Action*, published in 1892, drew up an indictment of the business corporation which reads like a Jacksonian polemic. Even in those hopeful early days of the People's Party, Weaver projected no grandiose plans for the future, but lamented the course of recent history, the growth of economic oppression, and the emergence of great contrasts of wealth and poverty, and called upon his readers to do "All in [their] power to arrest the alarming tendencies of our times."[3]

Nature, as the agrarian tradition had it, was beneficent. The United States was abundantly endowed with rich land and rich resources, and the "natural" consequence of such an endowment should be the prosperity of the people. If the people failed to enjoy prosperity, it must be because of a harsh and arbitrary intrusion of human greed and error. "Hard times, then," said one popular writer, "as well as the bankruptcies, enforced idleness, starvation, and the crime, misery, and moral degradation growing out of conditions like the present, being unnatural, not in accordance with, or the result of any natural law, must be attributed to that kind of unwise and pernicious legislation' which history proves to have produced similar results in all ages of the world. It is the mission of the age to correct these errors in human legislation, to adopt and establish policies and systems, in accord with, rather than in opposition to divine law."[4] In assuming a lush natural order whose workings were being deranged by human laws, Populist writers were again drawing on the Jacksonian tradition, whose spokesmen also had pleaded for a proper obedience to "natural" laws as a prerequisite of social justice.[5]

Somewhat akin to the notion of the beneficence of nature was the idea of a natural harmony of interests among the productive classes. To the Populist mind there was no fundamental conflict between the farmer and the worker, between the toiling people and the small businessman. While there might be corrupt individuals in any group, the underlying interests of the productive majority were the same; predatory behavior existed only because it was initiated and underwritten by a small parasitic minority in the highest places of power. As opposed to the idea that society consists of a number of different and frequently clashing interests—the social pluralism expressed, for instance, by Madison in the *Federalist*—the Populists adhered, less formally to be sure, but quite persistently, to a kind of social dualism: although they knew perfectly well that society was composed of a number of classes, for all practical purposes only one simple division need be

[2] Note for instance the affectionate treatment of Jacksonian ideas in Watson, op. cit. pp. 343–44.

[3] James B. Weaver: *A Call to Action* (Des Moines, 1892), pp. 377–78.

[4] B. S. Heath: *Labor and Finance Revolution* (Chicago, 1892), p. 5.

[5] For this strain in Jacksonian thought, see Richard Hofstadter: "William Leggett, Spokesman of Jacksonian Democracy," *Political Science Quarterly*, XLVIII (December 1943), pp. 581–94, and *The American Political Tradition*, pp. 60–61.

considered. There were two nations. "It is a struggle," said Sockless Jerry Simpson, "between the robbers and the robbed." [6] There are but two sides in the conflict that is being waged in this country today," declared a Populist manifesto. "On the one side are the allied hosts of monopolies, the money power, great trusts and railroad corporations, who seek the enactment of laws to benefit them and impoverish the people. On the other are the farmers, laborers, merchants, and all other people who produce wealth and bear the burdens of taxation. . . . Between these two there is no middle ground." [7] "On the one side," said Bryan in his famous speech against the repeal of the Sherman Silver Purchase Act, "stand the corporate interests of the United States, the moneyed interests, aggregated wealth and capital, imperious, arrogant, compassionless. . . . On the other side stand an unnumbered throng, those who gave to the Democratic party a name and for whom it has assumed to speak." [8] The people versus the interests, the public versus the plutocrats, the toiling multitude versus the money power—in various phrases this central antagonism was expressed. From this simple social classification it seemed to follow that once the techniques of misleading the people were exposed, victory over the money power ought to be easily accomplished, for in sheer numbers the people were overwhelming. "There is no power on earth that can defeat us," said General Weaver during the optimistic days of the campaign of 1892. "It is a fight between labor and capital, and labor is in the vast majority." [9]

The problems that faced the Populists assumed a delusive simplicity: the victory over injustice, the solution for all social ills, was concentrated in the crusade against a single, relatively small but immensely strong interest, the money power. "With the destruction of the money power," said Senator Peffer, "the death knell of gambling in grain and other commodities will be sounded; for the business of the worst men on earth will have been broken up, and the mainstay of the gamblers removed. It will be an easy matter, after the greater spoilsmen have been shorn of their power, to clip the wings of the little ones. Once get rid of the men who hold the country by the throat, the parasites can be easily removed." [10] Since the old political parties were the primary means by which the people were kept wandering in the wilderness, the People's Party advocates insisted, only a new and independent political party could do this essential job. [11] As the silver question became more promi-

[6] Elizabeth N. Barr: "The Populist Uprising," in William E. Connelley, ed.: A Standard History of Kansas and Kansans, vol. II, p. 1170.

[7] Ray Allen Billington: Westward Expansion (New York, 1949), p. 741.

[8] Allan Nevins: Grover Cleveland (New York, 1933), p. 540; Heath, Labor and Finance Revolution, p. 27: "The world has always contained two classes of people, one that lived by honest labor and the other that lived off of honest labor." Cf. Governor Lewelling of Kansas: "Two great forces are forming in battle line: the same under different form and guise that have long been in deadly antagonism, represented in master and slave, lord and vassal, king and peasant, despot and serf, landlord and tenant, lender and borrower, organized avarice and the necessities of the divided and helpless poor." James A. Barnes: John G. Carlisle (New York, 1931), pp. 254–55.

[9] George H. Knoles: The Presidential Campaign and Election of 1892 (Stanford, 1942), p. 179.

[10] William A. Peffer: The Farmer's Side (New York, 1891), p. 273.

[11] Ibid, pp. 148–50.

nent and the idea of a third party faded, the need for a monolithic solution became transmuted into another form: there was only one *issue* upon which the money power could really be beaten and this was the money issue. "When we have restored the money of the Constitution," said Bryan in his Cross of Gold speech, "all other necessary reforms will be possible; but . . . until this is done there is no other reform that can be accomplished."

While the conditions of victory were thus made to appear simple, they did not always appear easy, and it would be misleading to imply that the tone of Populistic thinking was uniformly optimistic. Often, indeed, a deep-lying vein of anxiety showed through. The very sharpness of the struggle, as the Populists experienced it, the alleged absence of compromise solutions and of intermediate groups in the body politic, the brutality and desperation that were imputed to the plutocracy—all these suggested that failure of the people to win the final contest peacefully could result only in a total victory for the plutocrats and total extinction of democratic institutions, possibly after a period of bloodshed and anarchy. "We are nearing a serious crisis," declared Weaver. "If the present strained relations between wealth owners and wealth producers continue much longer they will ripen into frightful disaster. This universal discontent must be quickly interpreted and its causes removed." [12] "We meet," said the Populist platform of 1892, "in the midst of a nation brought to the verge of moral, political, and material ruin. Corruption dominates the ballot-box, the Legislatures, the Congress, and touches even the ermine

[12] Weaver, *A Call to Action*, p. 5.

of the bench. The people are demoralized. . . . The newspapers are largely subsidized or muzzled, public opinion silenced, business prostrated, homes covered with mortgages, labor impoverished, and the land concentrating in the hands of the capitalists. The urban workmen are denied the right to organize for self-protection, imported pauperized labor beats down their wages, a hireling standing army, unrecognized by our laws, is established to shoot them down, and they are rapidly degenerating into European conditions. The fruits of the toil of millions are boldly stolen to build up colossal fortunes for a few, unprecedented in the history of mankind; and the possessors of these, in turn, despise the Republic and endanger liberty." Such conditions foreboded "the destruction of civilization, or the establishment of an absolute despotism." . . .

Not only were the gentlemen of this imperialist elite better read and better fed than the Populists, but they despised them. This strange convergence of unlike social elements on similar ideas has its explanation, I believe, in this: both the imperialist elite and the Populists had been bypassed and humiliated by the advance of industrialism, and both were rebelling against the domination of the country by industrial and financial capitalists. The gentlemen wanted the power and status they felt due them, which had been taken away from their class and type by the *arriviste* manufacturers and railroaders and the all-too-potent banking houses. The Populists wanted a restoration of agrarian profits and popular government. Both elements found themselves impotent and deprived in an industrial culture and balked by a common enemy. On innumerable matters they disagreed, but both were strongly nationalistic, and amid the despairs and anxieties of the nineties both became ready for war if that would unseat or even embarrass the moneyed powers, or better still if it would topple the established political structure and open new opportunities for the leaders of disinherited farmers or for ambitious gentlemen. But if there seems to be in this situation any suggestion of a forerunner or analogue of modern authoritarian movements, it should by no means be exaggerated. The age was more innocent and more fortunate than ours, and by comparison with the grimmer realities of the twentieth century many of the events of the nineties take on a comic-opera quality. What came in the end was only a small war and a quick victory; when the farmers and the gentlemen finally did coalesce in politics, they produced only the genial reforms of Progressivism; and the man on the white horse turned out to be just a graduate of the Harvard boxing squad, equipped with an immense bag of platitudes, and quite willing to play the democratic game.

In Praise of Populism

PAUL GOODMAN

The world is increasingly confronted with half a dozen social-political horrors, more or less related, that might doom mankind or at least civilization. The stockpiling of nuclear and biochemical weapons. Ecological catastrophes deriving from the abuse of technology. Excessive urbanization on all continents. The deepening poverty of two-thirds of mankind, aggravated by the "help" of the affluent powers. Perhaps overpopulation, though I am dubious about this until more obvious social and political abuses are remedied.

Nevertheless, in recent years there is one horror, the degeneration of the advanced countries toward the condition described in *1984*, that has everywhere begun to diminish; and conceivably this might alleviate the other disastrous policies and tendencies. There has been a worldwide resurgence of grass-roots populism, which defies central authority, bureaucracy, social engineering, technocracy, mandarinism, and imperialism. It is occurring in Fascist, corporate liberal, and Communist countries, and has transcended ideological, class, or racial definition. It is pervasive among the young, whether students, ghetto-dwellers, guerrilla fighters, or Red Guards; but it extends also to intellectuals and professionals, solid citizens and housewives. Like any grass-roots movement it has local and

Reprinted from Commentary, *by permission. Copyright © 1968 by the American Jewish Committee. June, 1968, pp. 25, 26, 30.*

particular demands: against censorship, administrative tyranny in universities, high-handed physical planning, fixed prices of consumers' goods, military draft, overcentralized economic planning, bureaucratic social services, etc., etc. The occasions for protest may be grand or trivial, but what is striking, and constitutes a movement, is the epidemic conviction that effective action is possible, where it had seemed that nothing could be done. And as in any populism, there are experiments at running things in a different way on a more human scale.

Once it has started, such a movement may lose every campaign but it is irreversible and must grow, since people gain initiative by exercising it and thus become more confident. It develops its own culture, and begins to find itself as an international. It can be crushed only by overwhelming repressive force, and this is not in the offing, for the central powers are in fact morally bankrupt. Indeed, the essential idea of this resurgent populism, in my opinion, is that the powers-that-be in the world are incompetent, their authority is irrational, they cannot cope with modern conditions, and they are producting ultimate horrors. It does not follow, of course, that populist actions are themselves wise, undemagogic, or peaceful; but at least they weaken the concentration of power and cannot do as much widespread damage.

Present-day populism is a developing worldwide social revolution that will, if it has a chance, take a couple of decades to mature. One way it can be interrupted is by a panic reflex of the central powers, especially nuclear war. Another way, unfortunately characteristic of populist movements, is by counter-revolution spawned by the movement itself (this is called "taking power"), as Leninism interrupted the Russian social revolution in 1917. Counter-revolutions of this kind are likely to occur if the reactionary powers are stupidly intransigent to change, if they crack down, invade, and so forth. A steady development of populism would consist in *piecemeal* campaigns, extending initiative and decision-making in various overcentralized areas and functions, and correcting intolerable background conditions till they become tolerable. In my view, freedom and decency are sufficient goals for politics; and the piecemeal approach is the only safe and relevant way to transform our vastly complicated societies. Besides, an aggressive populism, that exerts its power and makes decisions, including mistakes, on problems where it is directly concerned, is the only means of educating vigilant citizens. . . .

It is in this context of reviving worldwide populism that I regard the already satisfactory American campaign of '68. If now the nominations and election themselves move us further toward freedom and decency, it is up to us to continue popular pressure on the new officials to change the deep structural defects in our society and economy. If the formal democratic process fails us, so much the worse for the formal democratic process; the populists will continue otherwise. Too many people, and especially the white and black young, are too much in motion to be sold out or "co-opted" by electoral machinery and campaign promises. Too much has happened on campuses and streets and in courts and jails for us to repeat the treacherous campaign of 1964, and the illegitimacy, as I see it, of the past four years. Also, the abiding underlying tyranny has been named

—the military-industrial, the hidden government of CIA and FBI, the perverted universities, the rubber-stamp Congress, the brutal police, etc.—and there have developed a myriad of techniques, and of technicians, to challenge all this if government does not come across.

Meanwhile, it is touching to see the wistful and cagey hope of Americans that perhaps the American democratic process still has some life in it, as it has shown life in crises of the past. This process, in its extreme definition from Jefferson to William James, is a kind of slowed-down populist revolution without *too* much violence. Usually, in the nature of the case, the massive general will accepts the official government as sovereign; but in critical periods, sovereignty reverts to the people. First are heard a few voices in the wilderness crying out a new truth. If protected by civil liberties—so Spinoza and Milton assured us—feeble truth grows in power, for evidence cumulatively sustains it. Then there are other thoughtful people who take up the unpopular cause, and there are very many citizens "humbly petitioning"—we do it by ads in the *Times,* and find one another. These numbers swell to become an impressive and demanding crowd. Emboldened, many begin to deny the legitimacy of the official position, pointing out that it does not represent the "general will"; they are willing to defy the law and go to jail to prove they are in earnest. Usually there are fringes and flare-ups of violence, mutinies of despair at being disregarded. Then suddenly, through the courts, or by forming a new party, or by a change in the constituency of an old party, the new truth bids for the government by constitutional means and takes over. Actions that were called "illegal" prove to

be legal after all, and former mutineers are honored as courageous and foresighted citizens.

This idyllic scenario is not a bad description of actual critical periods in American history, for example, abolitionism, the agrarian-progressive movement, the suffragette movement, the labor movement, the recent civil-rights movement. Of course, ossification soon sets in. As soon as the victory is won, the aroused public goes back to sleep and the surviving forces of reaction importantly nullify the advances. But there *has* been a revival of freedom and conditions *are* more tolerable. Other methods do not guarantee as much. . . .

In conclusion, let me mention some other populist attitudes toward the campaign of '68. The most self-conscious and vociferous wing of American populism is the Movement, an alliance of white students and ex-students and black students and non-students, concentrating mainly on "gut" issues of anti-militarism, draft resistance, Negro rights, Student Power, and Black Power. Whether the Movement engages in the election this year, or tries to disrupt it, or disregards it, is sometimes a matter of theory and sometimes a matter of empirical judgment of resources, costs, and possible benefits. Maoists and other insurrectionists naturally regard the election as bourgeois fakery, like other "bourgeois civil liberties." Some in the Movement, for instance the majority in Students for a Democratic Society, who are interested in community development and "politicizing" the poor and the professionals, judge that it is not worth the cost to field or support candidates. To a large group, the campaign offers an occasion for dramatic disruption, especially at the August convention in Chicago. In California, the Peace and Freedom Party, allied with the Black Panthers, is fielding its own candidates for State offices, for example, Robert Scheer and Paul Jacobs; the national candidate might be Dick Gregory—though people in P & F have said they would run "anybody over 35" if he believes in the cardinal tenets of immediate withdrawal from Vietnam and Black Power, for they want precisely to avoid personalities and to emphasize the gut issues. Some draft-resisters would support McCarthy if they felt sure that he would stop the Vietnam war.

I do not think there is anything in the usual criticism that para-electoral politics is futile, does not affect policy, throws away votes, and so forth. Recent political history has shown that ads, teach-ins, demonstrations, community organizing, direct action, and going to jail do powerfully affect policy. Peace and Freedom conceives of itself as educational (being on the ballot, it will get TV time), and as being a gadfly to force candidates of the major parties to answer pointed questions and to drive them to more radical positions. Historically, this strategy has certainly worked in American politics, as is shown by the fact that most of the planks of the Socialist party in 1912 eventually became the law of the land. Besides, if, as is usual, an election really poses no issues or if elected officials are institutionally powerless to make meaningful changes, then to vote for major candidates, or perhaps to vote at all, is evil in itself, because it legitimizes the status quo. Non-voting, however, should be aggressive, with picketing, and, if possible, massive.

But I object to the politics of most of the Movement on a different ground.

To concentrate exclusively on "gut" issues is to be finally irrelevant and, paradoxically, merely symbolic. Gut issues like the draft, police brutality, or rent gouging are, of course, *prima facie* and must be met; they create hot commitment and solidarity; they might have some immediate tangible payoff. But they do not address the tremendous questions of our times which will determine our fate including the fate of the gut issues—How to prevent nuclear war? How to avert ecological catastrophe? How to use modern technology? What to automate and what not to automate? What and how to decentralize? What should Research and Development policy be? What is a possible structure of mass education that will not process and brainwash? What kind of help ought to be given to underdeveloped regions? How to cope with galloping urbanization? How to weaken the nation states? These are issues of high politics that require patient inquiry, debate, and professional knowledge. Hot commitment will not take us far. The global answer of the insurrectionists that all these puzzles will be quickly or gradually solved when we "build socialism" is not serious. The issues are more pressing than that; and in these matters, actual "socialist" societies have either not yet really come to the crisis of modern times or they are as stupid as we are. (I do not mean by this that corporate capitalism does not have its *specific* ways of preventing solutions.) It is understandable that poor blacks are hung up on gut issues; they cannot afford to worry about atom bombs, and so forth, though of course they should. But it is disgusting that Peace and Freedom, Students for a Democratic Society, and the rest of the bright and lively youth of the affluent majority cannot look further. The only issue of high politics that they have persistently explored is how to recapture democratic participation, that is, populism itself. No doubt the fault belongs with my own generation, which sold out in various ways, taught nothing, has provided no relevant program. What a pity it would be if this most promising political opening throughout the world should come to nothing because of ignorance!

two

ROMANTICISM AND EXISTENTIALISM: IS MAN A PLASTER SAINT?

Manifesto Notes: Problems of Democracy

TOM HAYDEN

One of our central problems is: What does it mean, in theory and practice, to be "for a democratic society"? I don't hope to answer such a question fully, nor even exhaust the approaches to an answer, in these pages. I begin, however, with the insistence that our traditional democratic images are the subject of genuinely serious criticism, and if we are to view ourselves as responsible members of a community of discourse, then we better work out defenses, accommodations, or other capitulations to the critics, else we surrender by default.

This paper intends to (1) offer a definition of "participatory democracy," (2) enumerate several of the problems posed by its critics or by persons who, though sympathetic, cannot share democratic faith any longer.

THE PARTICIPATORY DEMOCRACY

In this society, man is seen as both creator and creature; that is, while in a sense, her personality is no more than the buffeted consequence of all the social, physical, and historical forces which have shaped him, he is also an individual with felt identity, a sense of purpose, and independence. "Human nature" is not an evil or corrosive substance to be feared or contained; rather, it represents a potential for material and spiritual development which, no matter how lengthily or rapidly unfolded, can never be dissipated. The liberation of this individual potential is the just end of society; the directing of the same potential, through voluntary participation, to the benefit of society, is the just end of the individual. For a participatory democracy, freedom is present since man needs the opportunity to become. But freedom is more than the absence of arbitrary restrictions on personal development. For the democratic man, freedom must be a condition of the inner self as well, achieved by reflection confronting dogma, and humility overcoming pride. "Participation" means both *personal initiative*—that men feel obliged to help resolve social problems—and *social opportunity*—that society feel obliged to maximize the possibility for personal initiative to find creative outlets.

In the democracy of participation, government and politics are not negative phenomena isolated from the highest experiences of life, nor are they mere tools with which man prevents himself from destroying his fellows, nor are they monstrosities that inexorably come to dominate and subvert the individual capacity for initiative. On the contrary, government and politics represent a desirable, necessary (though not sufficient) part of the experience through which man discovers and develops himself; they are among the instruments by which man becomes the measure and maker of all things. The institutional form of this process involves the organizing of representative polit-

ical parties or other associations to advance or change public policies, to link the individual to the state decisions-making structure, to channel private problems to public issue and make public issues relevant to private problems, to guarantee peaceful transitions, and to clarify at all times the meaning of the issues.

Like the political experience, the economic one is of decisive and positive character for the individual. It is a means by which man comes to understand his capacities, unleash his creative potential in a useful manner, and gain influence over the direction of his life. Therefore the individual should not be isolated from the control and ownership of his work, and the society should not be divided into economic groups who own and are owned, or who manage and are managed. The individual should have responsibility for his own occupational development, and the society should be organized in a way that allows the greatest opportunity for the exercise of this responsibility.

Participation is especially needed in a large, fragmented society, since it can integrate the many sentiments and roles of the individual into the function of "citizenship," whereby identity is found in relation to the general society, not to a limited, isolated or fragmented part. Participation in the full life of society is the process by which man comes to a consciousness of his dignity and a respect for the same fundamental quality in his striving fellows. Participation animates the abstract ideas of freedom and responsibility, and ensures that morality has meaning in the practical life of men.

. . . . .

Accept, if you can, the above as an adequate etching of the ideal that democrats seek to realize in society. If it is inadequate as ideal, then continue to etch until contours become acceptable. This done, I think our task is to examine, or better, find a way to examine in some detail the real meaning of these seductive moral statements: what values remain implicit and unexplored, what parts of the ideal are less clear than others, what values should be exported from or imported into the structure, etc. etc. As this examination proceeds, we will naturally be drawn into empirical findings in political behavior, in comparative political and cultural systems, and so on.

Some of the quite relevant problems, presumably, are the following (these obviously do not exhaust the list):

(1) Some arguments against democracy rest on a view of "human nature" that precludes participation of the kind suggested. One such view holds that democracy depends on the "rationality" of man: his ability to comprehend his true self-interest, and devise methods of obtaining that interest. However, man is seen as decidedly not rational: he is a package of confusion, irrationality and anxiety not competent to consistently, if at all, judge the "best course." From this judgment usually follows a statement of the need for a rational elite that will look on the inferior majority with compassion, and necessarily an elite which submits itself to examination via checks-and-balances, rigorous constitutionalism and periodic elections.

It is usually added as a reinforcing point that man *by nature* is selfish, or aggressive, or power-lusting, or cursed by original sin, or combinations of these. Or it is insisted that all men

really do not desire freedom (Mencken: "The average man does not want to be free; he wants to be safe"). Again, the next step is the construction of an elite principle of some kind.

In all of this it is clear that the aim of political organization, as Sheldon Wolin wrote of the early American political theorists, is "not to educate men, but to deploy them; not to alter their moral character, but to arrange institutions in such a manner that human drives would cancel each other or, without conscious intent, be deflected toward the common good." A similar distrust of men leads writers to concur with Andrew Scott, author of a contemporary political theory anthology, in this curious form of hopefulness: "The existence of a dark side of man's nature does not vitiate a belief in democracy. If man is irrational, he has been that way a long time; yet democratic regimes have persisted through it all. Man is not always rational, but he is sufficiently so for democratic government to work passively well."

In this view, it seems, the idea of a fully participatory democracy is not only impossible to achieve, but misguided—since it is based on a false estimate of man's "nature."

(2) Other thinkers have remained agnostic toward the issue of "human nature" and, instead, claimed that the problem of popular democracy derives from a mistaken idea of human "capacity" or "ability" for public participation—in other words, all metaphysical questions about "nature" aside, the facts of history demonstrate conclusively that people never have—and therefore can't—govern themselves. People, it is insisted, are never "informed" enough to permit their full participation in the

major events of history. Not only are they mal-informed, they are apathetic as well. Furthermore, they have not the proper training to inherit central positions in real government. The traditional glorification of the "sovereign public" is nonsense propounded by utopian liberals, or worse, it is mythmaking by the manipulative men of power.

In this formulation is included a statement about the growing complexity of modern society: complexity of information, of administration in the large and organized society, of the more general trends expressed in science, industrialization, geographic and demographic change and interconnected institutions of the other fields of knowledge.

In this confused situation, modern man is in need of leadership—an elite, preferably, of experts equipped with the training, knowledge and maturity to make proper decisions about public matters. Special guidance becomes increasingly required as the functions of life undergo division and subdivision. Man is "incapable" in the sense that he is without the time, the breadth of understanding, the preparation, and the interest to undertake the direction of society. Democracy is now conceived not as the free participation of people in their common affairs but as the free competition of elites for the periodic consent of electors (whose business is finished after voting). The criterion is not: Does the individual have the opportunity to develop his consciousness and potential? but rather: Is there a way to guarantee equality of opportunity for anyone who wants to seek political office? The realization of the second statement is not seen as conditional on acceptance of the first; that is,

there can be a free competition and circulation of elites without participation by the mass of men.

The needs for technical expertise and specialized skill are usually seen in conjunction with such social phenomena as apathy, reliance on habit, enforced remoteness of the individual from the centers of power, the psychological urge for authority, and so on; the final vision is for permanent although perhaps beneficent, oligarchy or oligarchies. When Robert Michels said sadly that socialists might win, but socialism never, he was predicting the impossibility of dismantling the structure of oligarchy and the tendencies that sustain it. Once an incoming leadership stabilizes itself, no matter how revolutionary its goals when it *sought* power, it creates new interests in conflict with those of the movement it originally represented. A "tragicomic" process is set off, in which "the masses are content to devote all their energies to effecting a change of masters." Social change is simply a progression of elites, each promising to its followers a dream that is tarnished by the first brush with power. True or false?

(3) How much democracy does an organized, rational bureaucratic society need? Curiously, as Wolin points out, it seems "that there still exists in the West an impressive capacity for political participation and interest which is not, however, being diverted towards the traditional forms of political life." This kind of "participation," he indicates, is diverted toward the institutions commonly thought "private" at one time: chief among these is the large corporation, which is probably the most important institution in contemporary society. The goal of the corporation, or

any similarly imposing institution, is not *simply* profit or other forms of aggrandizement. The goals now prominently include providing a sense of personal warmth and fraternity for the worker. In the language of A. A. Berle, the corporation is "the collective soul" and "conscience carrier" of modern life. What does all this mean for a theory which gives the decisive place in public decision-making to government and the political, but not such to economic institutions? Is there a way to understand the corporation as a "public" institution subject to the control of the political representatives of the people? And is organizational "togetherness" the perversion or perfection of "participation"?

(4) The idea (or ideas) of "mass society" is obviously related to the problem of participatory democracy.

"When the normal inhibitions enforced by tradition and social structure are loosened . . . the *undifferentiated mass* emerges," writes Philip Selznick. While men are forced into greater and more complicated interdependence, they also are estranged from each other radically, in the absence of unifying values. Their tastes are shaped by institutions geared to the lowest common human denominator. Their activity is divided into a number of roles, often without coherent or even anticipated pattern. Herbert Blumer analogizes mass society to the audience at a movie theatre, each person "separate, detached, and anonymous," with "no social organization, no organized group of sentiments, no structure of status roles and no established leadership." Liberals and conservatives alike seem uneasy, and often terrified, of the "mass"—it invokes images of anarchy, the mob, violence, corruption.

This apparent consensus among writers of different political affiliations is a happening worth consideration, since traditionally the "left" has hallowed the masses (the popular will, the proletariat, the brotherhood of man, and so forth) while the "right" has reviled them as the most dangerous of threats to civilization. Today the conservative has not changed his mind about the mass, but the liberal has done so more and more—is this a sign of disenchantment among men whose expectations were never realized? Should younger radicals heed it?

From the generally accepted notion of the mass, participatory democracy is criticized thoroughly. It opens the possibility for mass man to dominate society, bringing about the feared "sovereignty of the unqualified." If the masses imprint their concerns everywhere in society, then incompetence permeates the decisive institutions, and the potential of great men is constrained for the benefit of the sluggish progress of lesser men. Perhaps even revolution will result, since the masses are susceptible to charisma, new symbols, and sudden outlets. The democrats, it is claimed, don't recognize the importance of a creative elitist minority which nurtures and preserves the essence of culture, the values of civilization, the stability of traditional institutions. As Selznick outlines the aristocratic view, the democrat wants "a levelling process in education, literature, and politics (which) substitutes the standardless appetites of the mass market for the canons of refinement and social restraint." The democrat advocates implicitly the breakup of standards and moral direction for society since his form of democracy: 1) expands the number of elite groups so greatly that none can decisively influence the whole society, and 2) ends the insulation of elites from the mundane burdens of life, thus making it more difficult for them to pursue their role of renewing and preserving culture.

(5) What is involved in an ideal "totalitarian" form of participation? How is it different from "democratic participation"? Surely there is considerable evidence that dictatorships exist not only through total control of the means of violence or through the enforcement of whatever conditions make rebellion impossible, but also often through sincerely expressed popular support. People in such a society can be mobilized by a sense of mission, an identity with some transcendent cause that appears to be attainable. For this goal they will sacrifice their freedom willingly, and continue to make the sacrifice so long as their movement seems to be progressing. Such people might find genuine pleasure in their work, be it on a collective farm or in a factory, in a bureaucratic political post or in a university professorship. They sense a solidarity with their fellows. They are swept up not only in a vision of their goal but also usually in a reinforcing image of their enemies. They are happy, integrated into a group, purposeful, dedicated, sacrificing. Yet they truly are separated from the means of decision-making. They are manipulated from "above" by an open, controlling elite. They have only tangential influence over the tactics and direction of their group and their society. They are not "free" in any liberal or democratic sense.

Numerous questions immediately come to mind. What are the moral issues involved in claiming that an exuberant, creative man is not living "the good life"? Is there anything innate in man that yearns for attachment to a consuming cause or a transcendent form of being? If so, how does the non-totalitarian society deal with that human yearning? Can a non-totalitarian society generate the same elan, mission, purposefulness? If totalitarianism involves an attack on privacy, what place do we give to privacy in our participatory society? And if privacy really has no place, if the really democratic political order is universal, how is it different from totalitarianism?

(6) How are we to apply the idea of participation to a country engaged in the colonial revolution? Where industrialization is just beginning, where educated and competent leadership is scarce and poverty, illiteracy and disease are prevalent? Where tribal patterns are as important as Cold War politicking? Where counterrevolution and complete anarchy are twin menaces? Are our democratic notions applicable only to the industrialized nations? If not, by what values do we judge the *development* of these new nations?

In evaluating a form of development, is centralized economic planning our primary concern, or the establishment of democratic institutions, or the existence of political parties or the form of the national government, or cold war policies? These questions indicate the real inadequacy of our ideal theory and demand that we develop at least two instruments: 1) a theory of social change, and 2) a scale of greater and lesser values. The former will allow us to grasp what is absolutely necessary for a country's development, what is peripheral, what is flexible and what is not: the prerequisites of evaluation, in other words. The latter will give us a formula for judging the quality of various institutions or nations. For example, Erich Fromm in *May Man Prevail?* seems to argue that noncorrupt government, economic planning, individual hope, technical skill and capital are needed before democracy can exist. And explicitly, he asks that we "look at the problem of democracy in *several dimensions*," then lists the four "most important" qualities of democracy as: 1) *political democracy* in the Western sense: a multiparty system and free elections (provided they are real, and not a sham)"; 2) "an atmosphere of *personal freedom*" in which the individual can "feel free to voice any opinion (including one critical of the government), without fear of any reprisals"; 3) "If one wants to judge the role of the individual in any given country, one cannot do so without *examining for whose benefit the economic system works.* If a system works mainly for the benefit of a small upper class, what is the use of free elections for the majority? Or rather, how can there be any authentically free election in a country which has such an economic system? Democracy is only possible in *an economic system that works for the vast majority of the population*"; 4) ". . . there is a *social criterion of democracy, namely the role of the individual in his work situation, and in the concrete decisions of his daily life.* Does a system tend to turn people into conforming automatons, or does it tend to increase their individual activity and responsibility?" Fromm's criteria are perhaps inadequate, but his *style* of evaluating democracies is perhaps the kind that

must be developed in relation especially to underdeveloped nations.

A special consideration for SDS, of course, is that of importing democratic ideas into the university experience. Briefly, it might be said our primary interest must be: what are the decisive elements in the structure and activity of the university, and who regulates them? These surely include: content of curriculum; academic requirements, opportunity for free inquiry, nonacademic living and working conditions. Generally these decisions are governed undemocratically: by authoritarian fiat of administration, and occasionally with faculty participation. The various rationalizations for this procedure are similar to the attitude toward democracy already mentioned: "Students are not capable of exercising rights responsibly"; "The university is too delicate an enterprise to risk student influence"; "Even if students were capable, they are apathetic"; "If you give rights away indiscriminately, you are inviting license, perhaps of a catastrophic kind"; "Why not hire trained specialists to do the complicated work of governing?" Supplementing these are several new themes: "Educational institutions are like business establishments, not societies"; "Parents expect us to keep a fatherly eye on their kids, especially those who are away from home the first time"; "Students are transient, the administration staff is permanent"; and so forth.

How are we to respond to these theses? Presumably the answer itself might carry the thinker into the more general problems of democratic social structure and pattern of life.

The Movement

JACK NEWFIELD

We want to create a world in which love is more possible.
　　　　　　　—Carl Oglesby, *SDS President*

There is a time when the operation of the machine becomes so odious, makes you so sick at heart that you can't take part; you can't even tacitly take part, and you've got to put your bodies upon the levers, upon all the apparatus, and you've got to make it stop. And you've got to indicate to the people who run it, to the people who own it, that unless you're free, the machine will be prevented from working at all.
　　　　　　　—Mario Savio, *leader of the FSM*

I can't get no satisfaction.
　　　　　　　—The Rolling Stones

I've got nothin', Ma, to live up to.
　　　　　　　—Bob Dylan

A new generation of radicals has been spawned from the chrome womb of affluent America. The last lingering doubts that the Silent Generation had found its voice vanished forever on April 17, 1965, when more than 20,000 of this new breed converged on the nation's capital to protest against the war in Vietnam. It was the largest anti-war

Reprinted by permission of The World Publishing Company from A Prophetic Minority by Jack Newfield. An NAL book. Copyright © 1966 by Jack Newfield, pp. 19–24.

demonstration in the history of Washington, D.C.—and it had been organized and sponsored by a student organization—SDS.

Assembled in the warm afternoon sunshine that Saturday were the boys and girls who had "freedom rode" to Jackson, Mississippi; who had joined the Peace Corps and returned disillusioned; tutored Negro teen-agers in the slums of the great cities; vigiled against the Bomb; rioted against the House Un-American Activities Committee; risked their lives to register voters in the Black Belt; and sat-in for free speech at the University of California at Berkeley.

There were the new generation of American radicals, nourished not by the alien cobwebbed dogmas of Marx, Lenin, and Trotsky, but by the existential humanism of Albert Camus, the Anti-colonialism of Frantz Fanon; the communitarian anarchism of Paul Goodman; the poetic alienation of Bob Dylan; and the grass-roots radicalism of that "prophetic shock minority" called SNCC. They were there not to protest anything so simple as war or capitalism. They came to cry out against the hypocrisy called Brotherhood Week, assembly lines called colleges, manipulative hierarchies called corporations, conformity called status, lives of quiet desperation called success.

They heard Joan Baez sing Dylan's sardonic poem, "With God on Our Side," and cheered spontaneously when she sang, "Although they murdered six million, in the ovens they fried/Now they too have God on their side."

They sang "Do What the Spirit Say Do," the latest freedom hit to come out of the jails and churches of the South, an indication perhaps of their deepest concern—human freedom and expression. Thus, Freedom now, "Oh Freedom," freedom ride, free university, freedom school, Free Speech Movement, and the Freedom Democratic Party.

And the 20,000 listened to the visionary voices of the New Radicalism.

Staughton Lynd, a romantic, a Quaker, and a revolutionary told them:

> We are here today in behalf of Jean-Paul Sartre . . . we are here to keep the faith with those of all countries and all ages who have sought to beat swords into plough-shares and to war no more.

They heard Bob Parris, SNCC's humble visionary, who told them:

> Listen and think. Don't clap, please. . . . Don't use Mississippi as a moral lightning rod. Use it as a looking glass. Look into it and see what it tells you about all of America.

An they listened to Paul Potter, the tense, brilliant, twenty-four-year-old former president of SDS, who said:

> There is no simple plan, no scheme or gimmick that can be proposed here. There is no simple way to attack something that is deeply rooted in the society. If the people of this country are to end the war in Vietnam, and to change the in- stitutions which create it, then the people of this country must create a massive social movement—and if that can be built around the issue of Vietnam, then that is what we must do.
>
> By a social movement I mean more than petitions and letters of protest, or tacit support of dissident Congressmen; I mean people who are willing to change their lives, who are willing to challenge the system, to take the problem of change seri- ously. By a social movement I mean an effort that is powerful enough to make the country understand that our problems are not in Vietnam, or China or Brazil or outer space or at the bottom of the ocean, but here in the United States. What we must be- gin to do is build a democratic and humane society in which Vietnams are unthinkable. . . .

Then, after three hours of speeches and freedom singing, the 20,000 stood in the lengthening shadow of the Washington Monument, linked arms, and, swaying back and forth, sang the anthem of their movement. Reaching out to clasp strange hands were button-down intellectuals from Harvard and broken-down Village hippies; freshmen from small Jesuit schools and the over-alled kamikazes of SNCC; curious faculty members and high-school girls; angry ghetto Negroes and middle-aged parents, wondering what motivates their rebellious children; all together, sing-ing and feeling the words, "Deep in my heart/I do believe/We shall over-come someday."

The SDS march, which had drawn twice the participation everyone, in-cluding its sponsors, had expected, sud-denly illuminated a phenomenon that had been growing underground, in campus dorms, in the Missisippi delta, in bohemian subcultures, for more than five years. It was the phenomenon of students rejecting the dominant values of their parents and their country; becoming alienated, becoming political, becoming active, becoming radical; protesting against racism, poverty, war, Orwell's 1984, Camus executioner, Mill's Power Elite, Mailer's Cancerous Totalitarianism; protesting against irrational anti-Communism, nuclear weaponry, the lies of statesmen, the hypocrisy of laws against narcotics and abortion; protesting against loyalty oaths, speaker bans, HUAC, *in loco parentis—* and finally, at Berkeley, protesting against the computer, symbol of man's dehumanization by the machine; in sum, protesting against all those obscenities that form the cryptic composite called the System.

In the weeks immediately following the SDS march the mass media suddenly discovered that the Brainwashed Generation, as poet Karl Shapiro had tagged the campus catatonics of the 1950's, had become a protest generation, that a cultural and sociological revolution had taken place while they had been preoccupied with the Bogart cult, J. D. Salinger, and baseball bonus babies. Within an eight-week period, *Time, Newsweek, The Saturday Evening Post, The New York Times Magazine, Life,* and two television networks all popularized the New Left. They smeared it, they psychoanalyzed it, they exaggerated it, they cartooned it, they made it look like a mélange of beatniks, potheads, and agents of international Communism; *they did everything but explain the failures in the society that called it into being.*

The New Radicalism is pluralistic,

amorphous, and multilayered. Its three political strands—anarchism, pacifism, and socialism—mingle in different proportions in different places. It's different in every city, on every campus. In Berkeley there is a strong sex-drug-literary orientation. In New York there is a politically sophisticated component. In the South there is extra emphasis on the nonviolent religious element.

At its surface, *political* level, the New Radicalism is an anti-Establishment protest against all the obvious inequities of American life. It says that Negroes should vote, that America should follow a peaceful, noninterventionist foreign policy, that anti-Communism at home has become paranoid and destructive, that the poverty of forty million should be abolished. It is a series of individual criticism many liberals can agree with.

At its second, more complex level, this new government is a *moral* revulsion against a society that is becoming increasingly corrupt. The New Radicals were coming to maturity as McCarthy built a movement based on deceit and bullying, as Dulles lied about the CIA's role in the 1954 Guatemala *coup,* as Eisenhower lied to the world about the U-2 flight over the Soviet Union, as Adlai Stevenson lied to the UN about America's support of the Bay of Pigs invasion, as Charles Van Doren participated in fixed quiz shows on television, as congressmen and judges were convicted for bribery. They saw the organs of masscult lie about their movement, the clergy exile priests for practicing brotherhood, older men redbait their organizations. Feeling this ethical vacuum in the country, the New Radicals have made morality and truth the touchstones of their movement. Like Gandhi, they try to "speak truth to power." Their politics are not particularly concerned with power or success, but rather with absolute moral alternatives like love, justice, equality, and freedom. Practical, programmatic goals are of little interest. They want to pose an alternate vision, not just demand "more" or "better" of what exists. They don't say welfare programs should be better subsidized; they say they should be administered in a wholly different, more dignifying way. They don't say Negroes need leaders with better judgment; they say Negroes should develop spokesmen from their own ranks.

At its third, subterranean level, the New Radicalism is an *existential* revolt against remote, impersonal machines that are not responsive to human needs. The New Radicals feel sharply the growing totalitarianization of life in this technological, urban decade. They feel powerless and unreal beneath the unfeeling instruments that control their lives. They comprehend the essentially undemocratic nature of the military-industrial complex; the Power Elite; the multiversity with its IBM course cards; urban renewal by technocrats; canned television laughter; wire taps; automation; computer marriages and artificial insemination; and, finally the mysterious button somewhere that can trigger the nuclear holocaust.

The New Radicals are the first products of liberal affluence. They have grown up in sterile suburbs, urban complexes bereft of community, in impersonal universities. They are the children of economic surplus and spiritual starvation. They agree with C. Wright Mills when he writes, "Organized irresponsibility, in this impersonal sense, is a leading characteristic of modern industrial societies everywhere. On every hand the individual is confronted with seemingly remote organizations; he feels dwarfed and helpless before the managerial cadres and their manipulated and manipulating minions."

And they can only chant "amen" to Lewis Mumford, who observed in *The Transformations of Man*, modern man has already depersonalized "himself so effectively that he is no longer man enough to stand up to his machines."

From their fury at arbitrary power wielded by impersonal machines (governments, college administrations, welfare bureaucracies, draft boards, television networks) come some of the New Radicals' most innovative ideas. Participatory democracy—the notion that ordinary people should be able to affect all the decisions that control their lives. The idea that social reformation comes from organizing the dispossessed into their own insurgent movements rather than from forming top-down alliances between liberal bureaucratic organizations. The insistence on fraternity and community inside the movement. The passion against manipulation and centralized decision-making. The reluctance to make the New Left itself a machine tooled and fueled to win political power in the traditional battle pits. The concept of creating new democratic forms like the Missisippi Freedom Democratic Party, the Newark Community Union Project, and the *Southern Courier*, a newspaper designed to represent the Negroes of the Black Belt rather than the white power structure or the civil-rights organizations. It is its brilliant insight into the creeping authoritarianism of modern technology and bureaucracy that gives the New Radicalism its definitive qualities of decentralism, communitarianism, and existential humanism.

Historically, the New Radicals' forebearers are the Whitman-Emerson-Thoreau transcendentalists, and the Joe Hill-Bill Hayward Wobblies. Like the IWW mill strikers at Lawrence, Massachusetts, in 1912, the New Left wants "bread and roses too."

three

LIBERALISM: REASSESSMENT OR RESURGENCE?

Utopian Pragmatism

MICHAEL HARRINGTON

The American system doesn't seem to work any more. The nation's statesmen proclaim that they seek only to abolish war, hunger and ignorance in the world and then follow policies which make the rich richer, the poor poorer and incite the globe to violence. The Government says that it will conduct an unconditional war on poverty and three years later announces that life in the slums has become worse. And supposedly practical people propose that the country make a social revolution but without the inconvenience of changing any basic institutions. . . .

Given these intolerable contrasts of American pretense and practice both at home and abroad, we have good reason to suspect the new utopias urged by men who will not even carry out the old reforms. This is particularly true when President Johnson suggests that fundamental transitions in the nation's life and values are to be achieved almost effortlessly. The corporations and the unions, the racial majority and the minorities, the religious believers and the atheists, the political machines and the reformers are all supposed to unite in making a gentle upheaval. And

Reprinted with permission of The Macmillan Company from Toward a Democratic Left: A Radical Program for a New Majority, *pp. 3, 6, 7–8, 14–16, 20–21, 25, 30–32. Copyright © by Michael Harrington, 1968.*

in a society where making money has traditionally been the most respected activity, spiritual considerations are suddenly going to come first.

Yet it would be wrong to dismiss all these unfulfilled promises as mere dishonesty. These pathetic utopias of the practical men are an admission—and a reflection—of the fact that the United States must take some first steps toward utopia in the best sense of that word. It is of some moment that tough-minded manipulators have been driven to visions even if they do little about them. Then there are now the rudiments of a public awareness of the national plight, and the case for radical change can therefore be made with the help of official figures. Finally, our documented inadequacies make a precise statement of what needs to be done, and the program for reform can thus be more specific than ever before. . . .

To take America's urgent goals seriously and to make the system work again will demand vigorous democratic conflict and a vivid social imagination. Such an undertaking, which is the work of the democratic Left, challenges an orthodoxy which prevails both in the groves of Academe and in the smoke-filled rooms.

America believes in utopian pragmatism.

The pragmatism of this formula is familiar enough. All of the politicians and most of the professors hold that this country is a blessedly unideological land where elections are naturally won at the Center rather than on the Right or Left. The utopianism of this no-nonsense creed is not so obvious, since it is either shamefaced or unconscious. It is found in the assumption that the world has been so benevolently created that the solutions to problems of revolution-

ary technological, economic and social change are invariably to be discovered in the middle of the road. Not since Adam Smith's invisible hand was thought to vector a myriad of private greeds into a common good has there been such a touching faith in secular providence.

Utopian pragmatism became fashionable after World War II, in part as a reaction to the rigid intellectual categories popular during the Depression. In that era Marxism was regularly vulgarized so as to project a United States which was the mere reflex of oversimplified class antagonisms. This attitude produced more than its share of crudities and, as befits a dialectical method, therefore provoked its own negation. In the postwar years semi-affluence intensified the revulsion from this theory, and many thinkers proceeded to ignore the crisis of the Fifties, Sixties and Seventies on the grounds that the breadlines of the Thirties had not returned. So it was said on all sides that America is a pluralist nation in which power is shared, statesmen are quite properly the brokers of interest groups and endless progress is possible as long as no one gets too principled.

The notion that America is a unique place exempt from the polarizations of the class struggle is hardly new. At the beginning of the century Werner Sombart was already claiming that the abundance of roast beef and apple pie explained the absence of a mass socialist movement in this country. But the current belief in utopian pragmatism goes far beyond this simple sociology. Everything in American life—its geography, its constitutional institutions and even its latest technology—are seen as conspiring to deliver this society from the European curse of ideology. And these happy accidents are, often enough, supposed to have converged in the best of all possible worlds. . . .

So it is necessary to speak of major social changes as the Sixties come to an end, even though the forces of reform and renewal are everywhere on the defensive. For the history I have just sketched makes it clear that the democratic Left cannot wait for political victory and only then begin to work out a program. When Franklin Roosevelt began to improvise the New Deal after his electoral triumph in 1932, his audacious pragmatism accomplished many things—but it did not end the Depression. Now the problems before the nation are infinitely more complex than the gross catastrophe which confronted the Thirties, and the Johnson Administration proves that they are not susceptible to jerry-built solutions. Therefore it is precisely in the dark days when the horrible war in Vietnam has put an end to innovation that we must prepare for an advance that cannot even be foreseen. For the next time the nation decides to start moving again, there must be a democratic Left with some idea of where it is going.

Last generation's reforms will not solve this generation's crises. For all the official figures prove that it is now necessary to go far beyond Franklin Roosevelt. And this, as Washington has so magnificently documented, cannot be done by trusting in the incremental zigs and zags of utopian pragmatism somehow to come out right. The country has no choice but to have some larger ideas and to take them seriously.

Liberalism, as it has been known for three decades, cannot respond to this challenge unless it moves sharply to the democratic Left.

One consequence of that extraor-dinary consensus which Barry Goldwater organized among his enemies was to make the traditional liberal domestic program the official, national ideology of the United States. Everyone except the Neanderthals agreed on Federal management of the economy, the goal of full employment, Medicare, formal legal equality for Negroes and, above all, economic growth. There was even a vague unanimity about a misty future called the Great Society. So liberalism was no longer a subversive, prophetic force. It had arrived at the very center of the society.

To be sure, the liberal demands were adopted more on principle then in practice. Harry Truman's call for universal national medical insurance was turned into a Medicare program which covered some of the needs of people over sixty-five and some of the poor. In this area, and in many others, a struggle is still demanded to get the nation to honor its own commitments. But that is a matter, however important, of quantitative change. And liberalism, which is as far Left as this country has ever gone, must propose qualitatively new innovations if it is to be true to its own traditions. . . .

In the Third World the economic necessities as they have been artificially defined by the West provide a strong argument for anti-democratic rule. In such circumstances to think that the work of human liberation is accomplished simply by dismantling the old order is often to make way for a new tyranny. In the advanced nations the application of science to production collectivizes intelligence and creates huge, impersonal organizations. Thus there are tendencies toward an inhuman, manipulative society in the poverty of the ex-colonies and the affluence of the big powers. So in addition to ex-coriating the past and present, one must propose the future.

The old liberalism does not offer an adequate response to these massive historic trends and can even be used as a screen for corporate collectivism. And so long as the new Leftism is only an opposition it may help people to change their masters but not to free themselves. To deal with the crises it has officially certified at home and abroad, the United States will have to be quite concrete. It must, among other things, redefine economics, recover its passion for equality and, in the doing, reduce the profit motive to fourth-rate importance and raise the non-profit motive to the first rank.

According to the prevailing, but not universal, notion of economics in the Western world, it is uneconomical:

for advanced countries to trade with impoverished nations so as to improve the relative position of the latter and help close the global gap between the rich and the poor;
for private capital to be invested in balanced economic development in the Third World;
for the corporations to abolish the slums of America;
for urban space to be "wasted" on beauty, history or civility;
to subsidize the humanities and not just the physical and social sciences.

These are only a few examples. They express the fact that there is much more money to be made by investing in the misshapen development of the world economy and in the distortion of affluence than in human decency. Decisions to act in this way are not necessarily made by malevolent men and

are, often enough, the work of sincere people. It is just that these choices are economical and justice is not. . . .

In saying these things I am not advocating charity. For, as later chapters will show, the power of the American state has been used to reinforce the maldistribution of wealth in the society, and the rich and the middle class have received more handouts than the poor. In these circumstances it would be justice, not *noblesse oblige*, to channel public funds to those who most desperately need them. In the process, the nation might even resurrect one of its hallowed, and forgotten, ideals: equality.

The current rediscovery of the problems of the American underclass is not, by far and large, a response to an egalitarian movement. It came as a result of mass pressure only in the sense that the country would never have noticed its own poverty were it not for the Negro movement. In their struggle for equality before the law, black Americans also laid bare the inequalities of the economy and probably did more for their white fellow citizens than for themselves. Beyond that, the War on Poverty derived from reformist conscience at the top of the society rather than from revolutionary consciousness at the bottom. The Cold War slackened and social criticism became less suspect, the intelligentsia less complacent; John Kennedy awakened the idealism of the youth and middle class; and in the wake of the ghetto riots of the mid-Sixties there was a fearful advocacy of amelioration. When, for instance, Henry Ford came out in support of the anti-poverty effort in 1966, he did so out of the explicit worry that, if these miseries were not attended to, they might menace the *status quo*. The De-

troit riots of 1967 proved him prescient. . . .

I am not proposing another exercise in futurism, an attempt to guess
the inventions that will take place in the
next twenty or so years. There are already distinguished study commissions
engaged in that undertaking. Throughout this book I simply assume that unprecedented change will be a commonplace, as in the recent past. If the pace
of the next twenty years is only as
headlong as that of the last twenty,
that will provide imperative enough for
the kinds of political, social and economic reform urged here. If, as is quite
possible, there is some unforeseen scientific breakthrough, then a transformation of our minds and institutions becomes even more urgent. In either case,
America desperately needs a democratic Left.

I do not here pretend to have
made an exhaustive description of that
Left. I have identified some of the
most important evils in the society and
tried to see them not as isolated out-
rages but as part of a system in motion. They are typical instances of what
is grievously wrong with America rather
than a comprehensive inventory. And
the solutions are put forth to illustrate
new ways of thinking, to initiate, rather
than to close, the discussion.

And yet in saying that there must
be first steps toward a new civilization
I do not mean to effect a vague rhetoric.
Along with the social tragedies, the
Government has also catalogued the
awesome possibilities that are already
present among us. It is quite clear that
this nation, and the world, are in for
profound, qualitative change; that we
are heading, willy-nilly, for a new epoch
in man's history.

The National Commission on Tech-

nology, Automation and Economic
Progress reported that, if America were
to take all of its productivity gains from
1965 to 1985 in the form of increased
leisure, it would then be able to choose
between a twenty-two-hour week, a
twenty-seven-week year and retirement
at thirty-eight.

There are now around sixty million
housing units in the United States. By
the year 2000 it will be necessary to
build an *additional* seventy million, or
more than now exist. This means, in the
Johnson Administration's phrase, the
construction of a "second America." On
what principles and according to what
design?

By 1975, according to the special
Counsel to the Senate Subcommittee
on Anti-Trust, three hundred corporations will own 75 percent of the industrial assets of the world.

George Ball, formerly of the State
Department and now chairman of the
foreign-operations branch of Lehman
Brothers, predicted in 1967, "Before
many years we may see supernational
corporations incorporated under treaty
arrangements without a domicile in any
particular nation state." Such entities,
one might add, could well turn out to
be more powerful than the United Nations.

There are thus fundamental choices
to be made, choices which will affect
the relation of man to himself, his fellow
citizen and the entire world. And yet
all that America has really done is to
take note of this tremendous fact and
then file it in the Library of Congress.
As a result, the system no longer seems
to work, for it cannot keep its own
promises.

That is why there must be a democratic Left.

Where Have All the Liberals Gone?

HARRY S. ASHMORE

Encyclopaedia Britannica defines liberalism as "the creed, philosophy, and movement which is committed to freedom as a method and policy in government, as an organizing principle in society, and as a way of life for the individual and community." So it was, in its seventeenth-century beginnings, in its eighteenth-century revolutionary triumphs, and in its nineteenth-century consolidation as the dominant political order of the West. But by the turn of our own century it was clear that Adam Smith's invisible hand, which was presumed to set human affairs aright if all were guaranteed freedom of thought and economic action, had disappeared in the smoke of the urbanizing Industrial Revolution. In an increasingly complex society free men could starve, and properly endowed democrats could founder in political impotence. In 1911 one of the high priests of the order, L. T. Hobhouse, of Oxford, wrote: "Liberty without equality is a name of noble sound and squalid meaning." Summarizing the condition of liberalism in the second half of the twentieth century, Britannica notes: "It might certainly be said that the classical and largely negative

Reprinted, by permission, from the July 1969 issue of The Center Magazine, Vol. II, #4, a publication of the Center for the Study of Democratic Institutions in Santa Barbara, California.

phases of liberalism had gone with the winds of history. What was not clear was whether this applied also to the democratic and welfare phases of the affirmative liberal state."

The surviving liberalism can best be described as a cast of mind and a code of personal conduct. The commitment is to the maintenance of an open society which accords all its members social justice. The liberal recognizes that, in his own time at least, the ideal is impossible to attain, and that his primary task may be to see that the necessary compromises are not fatal. While his own history has made him skeptical of the short-range results of democracy, he sees no substitute for self-government as the only feasible check on the managerial and scientific/technological elites required for the functioning of an advanced society. He acknowledges the existence of power, and distrusts it; he accepts the use of force only when it is allied with constituted authority and the rule of law; he puts his ultimate trust in the capacity of men to reconcile their differences without coercion if society can be made to approximate Thomas Jefferson's free marketplace of ideas. There can be no community without consensus, he holds, and an enduring consensus can only grow out of dialogue. Hence tolerance is the liberal's cardinal virtue, and he cherishes civility as the literal and essential derivation of civilization.

The stance, of course, is not satisfactory to moralists. In his concern with the parts of society, and his acceptance of imperfection, the liberal offends classical philosophers, who condemn him as a pragmatist addicted to an untidy pluralism. Holding that if there is ever to be a new man he will be no less the product of evolution than the current model, he cuts himself off from the radical utopians. The vision of the apocalypse is alien to the liberal not only because of the gratuitous cruelty of its mass indictment but because he can find no rational basis for locating all of mankind's moral guilt among those who do not profess the innocence of self-alienation. He would agree with Stringfellow Barr that "it's very hard to think when you are top dog," but he would insist that coherent thought is hardly easier for the underdog, beset as he is by real and fancied persecutions and the debilitating necessities of survival. Thinking, in his view, requires a degree of detachment, or self-doubt, even of self-irony, all of which are conspicuous elements in the liberal style and are conspicuously absent in that of the radical.

The liberal's habit of skepticism, and his concession that his own human limitations embody the possibility of error, apply even in the most weighty considerations of life and death. Thus in the great days of religious influence, and now in its period of decline, he might find himself inside the institutional church criticizing its professions and practices, or outside attacking the whole system of theological thought. In either position he respects the other. Conceding that he was incapable of sharing the moment of truth of a Tolstoy or a Simone Weil, Sir Herbert Read wrote: "To those who have not received it, the grace of God seems an arbitrary gift, and I resent the suggestion of the initiates that we who live in outer darkness do so because of our intellectual pride. I am completely humble in my attitude toward the mystery of life, and accept gratefully such intuitions as come to me from the writings of the mystics, and from works of art."

The liberal is properly accused of having difficulty in deciding what to do in the face of crisis. However, he knows what not to do—what, indeed, he cannot do without abandoning the values he lives by. When Marxist theory emerged in the last century to challenge the economic and social precepts of Western liberal democracy, he could find merit in its scathing analysis and in some of its prescriptions. He could become a socialist, and many liberals did. But he could not become a Communist, or at least could not remain one after he faced up to the inhuman physical and spiritual repressions the Marxist revolution would require on the road to utopia. Irving Howe, in a more or less autobiographical essay in *Commentary*, has recounted the shattering experience of the group of influential New York intellectuals who lived through the unmasking of Joseph Stalin: "During the nineteen-thirties and -forties their radicalism was anxious, problematic, and beginning to decay at the very moment it was adopted. They had no choice: the crisis of socialism was worldwide, profound, with no end in sight, and the only way to avoid that crisis was to bury oneself, as a few did, in the left-wing sects. Some of the New York writers had gone through the 'political school' of Stalinism, a training in coarseness from which not all recovered; some even spent a short time in the organizational coils of the Communist Party . . . [but] no version of orthodox Marxism could retain a hold on intellectuals who had gone through the trauma of abandoning the Leninist *Weltanschauung* and had experienced the depth to which the politics of this century, most notably the rise of totalitarianism, called into question the once-sacred Marxist categories. From now on, the comforts of the system would have to be relinquished."

In what Seymour Krim has described as "the overcerebral, Europeanish, sterilely citified, pretentiously alienated" world of New York's radical intellectuals, where endless polemics provide much of the mental exercise, the old anguish of the nineteen-thirties has continued, in one way or another, down to the present day. Here is Professor Howe's reflection on the inevitable aftermath of the great Stalinist cleavage: "Like anti-capitalism, anti-Communism was a tricky politics, all too open to easy distortion. Like anti-capitalism, anti-Communism could be put to the service of ideological racketeering and reaction. Just as ideologues of the fanatic Right insisted that by some ineluctable logic anti-capitalism led to a Stalinist terror, so ideologues of the authoritarian Left, commandeering the same logic, declared that anti-Communism led to the politics of Dulles and Rusk. There is, of course, no 'anti-capitalism' or 'anti-Communism' in the abstract; these take on political flesh only when linked with a larger body of programs and values, so that it becomes clear what *kind* of 'anti-capitalism' or 'anti-Communism' we are dealing with.

To young revolutionaries who consider all history ancient, the foregoing is also consigned to the wonderfully capacious category of irrelevance. Yet two of the most durable gurus of the movement, the two who have earned acceptance across the age barrier by attempting to endow the revolution with some coherent theoretical structure, are conspicuous products of the period. Professor Howe places Paul Goodman in the political spectrum by describing him as "a very courageous writer, who stuck to his anarchist beliefs through years in which he was mocked and all but excluded from the New York journals." The elusive doctrine of Herbert Marcuse, he finds, is based on "contempt for tolerance on the ground that it is a veil for subjection, a rationale for maintaining the status quo, and his consequent readiness to suppress 'regressive' elements in the population lest they impede social 'liberation.' About these theories, which succeed in salvaging the worst of Leninism, Henry David Aiken has neatly remarked: 'Whether garden-variety liberties can survive the ministrations of such "liberating tolerance" is not a question that greatly interests Marcuse.' "

The question does, of course, greatly interest liberals, who find the most striking contradiction of the new movement in its nihilistic devotion to the personal desires of its members and its calculated dismissal of the rights of others. If for no other reason, the legitimacy of the revolution would be questioned by conventional Marxists because of its rejection of the stern, puritan self-discipline the master demanded of all his followers, high and low. If even the mild dissidence of the Czechs proced anathema to the mellowing Soviet commissars, it is easy to imagine what would happen to a cadre of pot-smoking, free-loving, gut-communicating rebels in Mao's China, where the real, 100-proof doctrine is still in vogue.

It is evident that Marx, and all the other radical philosophers who approached their analytic and dialectic task with the tools of scholarship and the standards of science, have given way to Freud as the godhead of liberation. A new sensibility has been proclaimed, in which the rational, insofar as it is admitted at all, is subordinate to the sensory. Professor Howe describes its basis as the psychology of unobstructed need: "Men should satisfy those needs which are theirs, organic to their bodies and psyches, and to do this they now must learn to discard or destroy all those obstructions, mostly the result of cultural neurosis, which keep them from satisfying their needs. This does not mean that the moral life is denied; it only means that in the moral economy costs need not be entered as a significant item. In the current vocabulary, it becomes a matter of everyone doing 'his own thing,' and once all of us are allowed to do 'his own thing' a prospect of easing harmony unfolds. Sexuality is the ground of being, and vital sexuality the assurance of the moral life."

It follows that the manifestation of the revolution must be consciously irrational and profoundly antiintellectual. Viewing it from without, it also appears in its public aspect to be uncompromisingly self-centered, trivial, and, if one can be pardoned the expression, irrelevant to the purposes of what professes to be, among other things, a cult of love. The dully repetitive obscenity of the early days has developed into an exhibitionist sexuality that causes the uninitiate to wonder whether it is not,

in fact, a substitute for the real thing.

As we grope for the inner meaning of the movement we are warned by an insider, Susan Sontag, that it must be viewed as a broadly cultural rather than a narrowly political phenomenon. "Our task is seen as not one of forming but of *dismantling* a consciousness," Miss Sontag wrote in *Ramparts*, "becoming simpler, discharging dead weight. Hence the anti-intellectualism of the brightest kids; their distrust of books, school; their attraction to nonverbalizable experiences like rock and to states, such as that under drugs, which confound verbalizing; their belief in instinct, in vibrations." . . .

The liberal has an inevitable concern with this institutional collapse. The fallen university is his spiritual and often his actual home. As Professor Barzun said, if the university is to be restored it will have to be endowed once again with the traditional liberal values, "the way of discussion, civility, and decent behavior." The monumental task is possible only to those who spurn the punitive, reject the conspiracy theory of history, and understand that nobody is guilty because everybody is. And certainly restoration will demand full exercise of the liberal habit scorned by radicals as an outmoded manifestation of the Protestant ethic: hard, concentrated, self-sacrificing work.

The liberal also may be indispensable to melioration of the black man's agony in his transition into the larger white society. In any case he can't escape involvement, since this is the final stage of the task liberals set for themselves in the earliest days of Abolition, when they insisted that slavery must end not as a matter of charity but of human right. Termination of chattel ownership of one man by an-

umph humanists can claim in the entire sweep of recorded history, and its full promise will not be fulfilled as long as the American society excludes any man on the basis of race or color.

The long political and legal struggle for institutional desegregation has advanced in this generation to the point where it is becoming possible to get on with the even more difficult job of social integration. For all the reasons he could not support the youth revolution, the liberal is bound to reject as expedient and destructive the demand that the terminal effort be abandoned in favor of a return to segregation in the name of Black Power and racial therapy. He stands on Harry Golden's premise: "To say that the Negroes cannot catch up is to use the results of racial segregation as a means to perpetuate it."

If the shouting ever dies down, the brief list of liberal verities may again become comprehensible to the young and the black, and perhaps even to the middle class as it swings between complacency and panic. The lessons to be drawn from the raucous action and reaction of the nineteen-sixties seem to me to confirm the traditional liberal view that innocence arbitrarily prolonged is ignorance; entry into the world of ideas requires apprenticeship; the senses are important but not ultimate; feeling is a part of learning but only an auxiliary to wisdom; the past is prelude and no man can move forward without first looking back.

In this perspective it is possible to see that, while anger and frustration come easily to the young, so should laughter, the healthy, gay, unashamed laughter that can cure a sick society when it once again sounds on campus to mark the pleasures of discovery. When they can laugh again the young will observe that in the receding ranks of their elders fools are far more numerous than scoundrels, and they may be comforted to find that even a fool is capable of loving his children.

four

THE ESTABLISHMENT: REPRESSIVE OR STRUCTURED SOCIETY?

Introduction to *An Essay on Liberation*

HERBERT MARCUSE

Up to now, it has been one of the principal tenets of the critical theory of society (and particularly Marxian theory) to refrain from what might be reasonably called utopian speculation. Social theory is supposed to analyze existing societies in the light of their own functions and capabilities and to identify demonstrable tendencies (if any) which might lead beyond the existing state of affairs. By logical inference from the prevailing conditions and institutions, critical theory may also be able to determine the basic institutional changes which are the prerequisites for the transition to a higher stage of development: "higher" in the sense of a more rational and equitable use of resources, minimization of destructive conflicts, and enlargement of the realm of freedom. But beyond these limits, critical theory did not venture for fear of losing its scientific character.

I believe that this restrictive conception must be revised, and that the revision is suggested, and even necessitated, by the actual evolution of contemporary societies. The dynamic of their productivity deprives "utopia" of its traditional unreal content: what is denounced as "utopian" is no longer that which has "no place" and cannot have any place in the historical universe, but rather that which is blocked from coming about by the power of the established societies.

Utopian possibilities are inherent in the technical and technological forces of advanced capitalism and socialism: the rational utilization of these forces on a global scale would terminate poverty and scarcity within a very foreseeable future. But we know now that neither their rational use nor—and this is decisive—their collective control by the "immediate producers" (the workers) would by itself eliminate domination

An Essay on Liberation (Boston: Beacon Press, 1969), pp. 3–6. Copyright © 1969 by Herbert Marcuse. Reprinted by permission of Beacon Press.

and exploitation: a bureaucratic welfare state would still be a state of repression which would continue even into the "second phase of socialism," when each is to receive "according to his needs."

What is now at stake are the needs themselves. At this stage, the question is no longer: how can the individual satisfy his own needs without hurting others, but rather: how can he satisfy his needs without hurting himself, without reproducing, through his aspirations and satisfactions, his dependence on an exploitative apparatus which, in satisfying his needs, perpetuates his servitude? The advent of a free society would be characterized by the fact that the growth of well-being turns into an essentially new quality of life. This qualitative change must occur in the needs, in the infrastructure of man (itself a dimension of the infrastructure of society): the new direction, the new institutions and relationships of production, must express the ascent of needs and satisfactions very different from and even antagonistic to those prevalent in the exploitative societies. Such a change would constitute the instinctual basis for freedom which the long history of class society has blocked. Freedom would become the environment of an organism which is no longer capable of adapting to the competitive performances required for well-being under domination, no longer capable of tolerating the aggressiveness, brutality, and ugliness of the established way of life. The rebellion would then have taken root in the very nature, the "biology" of the individual; and on these new grounds, the rebels would redefine the objectives and the strategy of the political struggle, in which alone the concrete goals of liberation can be determined.

Is such a change in the "nature" of man conceivable? I believe so, because technical progress has reached a stage in which reality no longer need be defined by the debilitating competition for social survival and advancement. The more these technical capacities outgrow the framework of exploitation within which they continue to be confined and abused, the more they propel the drives and aspirations of men to a point at which the necessities of life cease to demand the aggressive performances of "earning a living," and the "non-necessary" becomes a vital need. This proposition, which is central in Marxian theory, is familiar enough, and the managers and publicists of corporate capitalism are well aware of its meaning; they are prepared to "contain" its dangerous consequences. The radical opposition also is aware of these prospects, but the critical theory which is to guide political practice still lags behind. Marx and Engels refrained from developing concrete concepts of the possible forms of freedom in a socialist society; today, such restraint no longer seems justified. The growth of the productive forces suggests possibilities of human liberty very different from, and beyond those envisaged at the earlier stage. Moreover, these real possibilities suggest that the gap which separates a free society from the existing societies would be wider and deeper precisely to the degree to which the repressive power and productivity of the latter shape man and his environment in their image and interest.

For the world of human freedom cannot be built by the established societies, no matter how much they may streamline and rationalize their dominion. Their class structure, and the perfected controls required to sustain it, generate needs, satisfactions, and values which reproduce the servitude of the human existence. This "voluntary" servitude (voluntary inasmuch as it is introjected into the individuals), which justifies the benevolent masters, can be broken only through a political practice which reaches the roots of containment and contentment in the infrastructure of man, a political practice of methodical disengagement from and refusal of the Establishment, aiming at a radical transvaluation of values. Such a practice involves a break with the familiar, the routine ways of seeing, hearing, feeling, understanding things so that

the organism may become receptive to the potential forms of a nonaggressive, nonexploitative world.

No matter how remote from these notions the rebellion may be, no matter how destructive and self-destructive it may appear, no matter how great the distance between the middle-class revolt in the metropoles and the life-and-death struggle of the wretched of the earth—common to them is the depth of the Refusal. It makes them reject the rules of the game that is rigged against them, the ancient strategy of patience and persuasion, the reliance on the Good Will in the Establishment, its false and immoral comforts, its cruel affluence.

Reflection on Change, Continuity, and Stability

EDMUND BURKE

If civil society be the offspring of convention, that convention must be its law. That convention must limit and modify all the descriptions of constitution which are formed under it. Every sort of legislative, judicial, or executory power are its creatures. They can have no being in any other state of things; and how can any man claim, under the conventions of civil society, rights which

From the book Reflections on the Revolution in France by Edmund Burke. Intro. and Notes by A. J. Grieve. Everyman's Library edition. Published by E. P. Dutton & Co., Inc. and reprinted with their permission and the permission of J. M. Dent & Sons Ltd: Publishers.

do not so much as suppose its existence? Rights which are absolutely repugnant to it? One of the first motives to civil society, and which becomes one of its fundamental rules, is, *that no man should be judge in his own cause.* By this each person has at once divested himself of the first fundamental right of uncovenanted man, that is, to judge for himself, and to assert his own cause. He abdicates all right to be his own governor. He inclusively, in a great measure, abandons the right of self-defence, the first law of nature. Men cannot enjoy the rights of an uncivil and of a civil state together. That he may obtain justice he gives up his right of determining what it is in points the most essential to him. That he may secure some liberty, he makes a surrender in trust of the whole of it.

Government is not made in virtue of natural rights, which may and do exist in total independence of it; and exist in much greater clearness, and in a much greater degree of abstract perfection: but their abstract perfection is their practical defect. By having a right to every thing they want every thing. Government is a contrivance of human wisdom to provide for human *wants*. Men have a right that these wants should be provided for by this wisdom. Among these wants is to be reckoned the want, out of civil society, of a sufficient restraint upon their passions. Society requires not only that the passions of individuals should be subjected, but that even in the mass and body as well as in the individuals, the inclinations of men should frequently be thwarted, their will controlled, and their passions brought into subjection. This can only be done *by a power out of themselves;* and not, in the exercise of its function, subject to that will and to those passions which it is its office to bridle and subdue. In this sense the restraints on men, as well as their liberties, are to be reckoned among their rights. But as the liberties and the restrictions vary with times and circumstances, and admit of infinite modifications, they cannot be settled upon any abstract rule; and nothing is so foolish as to discuss them upon that principle.

The moment you abate anything from the full rights of men, each to govern himself, and suffer any artificial, positive limitation upon those rights, from that moment the whole organization of government becomes a consid-eration of convenience. This it is which makes the constitution of a state, and the due distribution of its powers, a matter of the most delicate and complicated skill. It requires a deep knowledge of human nature and human necessities, and of the things which facilitate or obstruct the various ends, which are to be pursued by the mechanism of civil institutions. The state is to have recruits to its strength, and remedies to its distempers. What is the use of discussing a man's abstract right to food or medicine? The question is upon the method of procuring and administering them. In that deliberation I shall always advise to call in the aid of the farmer and the physician, rather than the professor of metaphysics.

The science of constructing a commonwealth, or renovating it, or reforming it, is, like every other experimental science, not to be taught *à priori*. Nor is it a short experience that can instruct us in that practical science; because the real effects of moral causes are not always immediate; but that which in the first instance is prejudicial may be excellent in its remoter operation; and its excellence may arise even from the ill effects it produces in the beginning. The reverse also happens: and very plausible schemes, with very pleasing commencements, have often shameful and lamentable conclusions. In states there are often some obscure and almost latent causes, things which appear at first view of little moment, on which a very great part of its prosperity or adversity may most essentially depend. The science of government being therefore so practical in itself, and intended for such practical purposes, a matter which requires experience, and even more experience than any person can gain in his whole life, however sagacious and observing he may be, it is with infinite caution that any man ought to venture upon pulling down an edifice, which has answered in any tolerable degree for ages the common purposes of society, or on building it up again, without having models and patterns of approved utility before his eyes.

These metaphysic rights entering into common life, like rays of light which pierce into a dense medium, are, by the laws of nature, refracted from their straight line. Indeed in the gross and complicated mass of human passions and concerns, the primitive rights of men undergo such a variety of refractions and reflections, that it becomes absurd to talk of them as if they continued in the simplicity of their original direction. The nature of man is intricate; the objects of society are of the greatest possible complexity: and therefore no simple disposition or direction of power can be suitable either to man's nature, or to the quality of his affairs. When I hear the simplicity of contrivance aimed at and boasted of in any new political constitutions, I am at no loss to decide that the artificers are grossly ignorant of their trade, or totally negligent of their duty. The simple governments are fundamentally defective, to say no worse of them. If you were to contemplate society in but one point of view, all these simple modes of polity are infinitely captivating. In effect each would answer its single end much more perfectly than the more complex is able to attain all its complex purposes. But it is better that the whole should be imperfectly and anomalously answered, than that, while some parts are provided for with great exactness, others might be totally neglected, or

perhaps materially injured, by the overcare of a favourite member.

The pretended rights of these theorists are all extremes: and in proportion as they are metaphysically true, they are morally and politically false. The rights of men are in a sort of *middle*, incapable of definition, but not impossible to be discerned. The rights of men in governments are their advantages; and these are often in balances between differences of good; in compromises sometimes between good and evil, and sometimes between evil and evil. Political reason is a computing principle; adding, subtracting, multiplying, and dividing, morally and not metaphysically, or mathematically, true moral denominations.

By these theorists the right of the people is almost always sophistically confounded with their power. The body of the community, whenever it can come to act, can meet with no effectual resistance; but till power and right are the same, the whole body of them has no right inconsistent with virtue, and the first of all virtues, prudence. Men have no right to what is not reasonable, and to what is not for their benefit; . . .

. . . Sir, I never liked this continual talk of resistance, and revolution, or the practice of making the extreme medicine of the constitution its daily bread. It renders the habit of society dangerously valetudinary; it is taking periodical doses of mercury sublimate, and swallowing down repeated provocatives of cantharides to our love of liberty.

This distemper of remedy, grown habitual, relaxes and wears out, by a vulgar and prostituted use, the spring of that spirit which is to be exerted on great occasions. . . . Hypocrisy, of course, delights in the most sublime speculations; for, never intending to go beyond speculation, it costs nothing to have it magnificent. But even in cases where rather levity than fraud was to be suspected in these ranting speculations, the issue has been much the same. These professors, finding their extreme principles not applicable to cases which call only for a qualified, or, as I may say, civil and legal resistance, in such cases employ no resistance at all. It is with them a war or a revolution, or it is nothing. Finding their schemes of politics not adapted to the state of the world in which they live, they often come to think lightly of all public principle; and are ready, on their part, to abandon for a very trivial interest what they find of very trivial value. Some indeed are of more steady and persevering natures; but these are eager politicians out of parliament, who have little to tempt them to abandon their favourite projects. They have some change in the church or state, or both, constantly in their view. When that is the case, they are always bad citizens, and perfectly unsure connexions. For, considering their speculative designs as of infinite value, and the actual arrangement of the state as of no estimation, they are at best indifferent about it. They see no merit in the good, and no fault in the vicious, management of public affairs; they rather rejoice in the latter, as more propitious to revolution. They see no merit or demerit in any man, or any action, or any political principle, any further than as they may

forward or retard their design of change: they therefore take up, one day, the most violent and stretched prerogative, and another time the wildest democratic ideas of freedom, and pass from the one to the other without any sort of regard to cause, to person, or to party. . . .

The worst of these politics of revolution is this: they temper and harden the breast, in order to prepare it for the desperate strokes which are sometimes used in extreme occasions. But as these occasions may never arrive, the mind receives a gratuitous taint; and the moral sentiments suffer not a little, when no political purpose is served by the deprivation. This sort of people are so taken up with their theories about the rights of man, that they have totally forgotten his nature. Without opening one new avenue to the understanding, they have succeeded in stopping up those that lead to the heart. They have perverted in themselves, and in those that attend to them, all the well-placed sympathies of the human breast.

. . . Plots, massacres, assassinations, seem to some people a trivial price for obtaining a revolution. A cheap, bloodless reformation, a guiltless liberty, appear flat and vapid to their taste. There must be a great change of scene; there must be a magnificent stage effect; there must be a grand spectacle to rouse the imagination, grown torpid with the lazy enjoyment of sixty years' security, and the still unanimating repose of public prosperity. . . .

five

APPEAL TO ACTION: "THE PERPETUAL SENSE OF OUTRAGE"

America is Hard to See

EUGENE McCARTHY

The campaign was quite properly labeled "new politics." It was not just the politics of the outs trying to get in, or of the independents wresting control from the machine. It was new politics in every aspect: the new kind of people who were involved; the new ways that were opened for raising a challenge; and new in the substance of the challenge itself.

One cannot overrate the contribution of the new people. There has not been a campaign in the history of this country in which persons below the voting age were as extensively and directly and effectively involved as they were in the campaign of 1968. There were more of them involved than ever, they were given more responsibility, and they were truly, because of their mobility, a national force. In conse-

Reprinted from The Year of the People (Garden City, N. Y.: Doubleday and Company, Inc., 1969), pp. 256–62, 268–69. Copyright 1969 by Eugene J. McCarthy. Reprinted by permission of the publisher.

quence of the campaign, there are thousands of young people who will never again be indifferent to politics.

There were risks involved in using young people as we did. Few of them had had any political experience, and yet they were quite ready to challenge the position of older, practiced people. Although our procedures for screening those who were admitted to official and active roles in the campaign were careful and thorough, there was always the fear that agitators might attach themselves, not only to the detriment of the campaign but also to the reputation of the whole student movement. There was also a continuing fear of accidents to the busses and cars in which the young people traveled. From the beginning in New Hampshire in January through the primaries and the summer, there was not a serious incident until the attack on our student group by the Chicago police at the August Democratic convention.

Many adults, who had previously

been indifferent or not actively involved, joined the students in what came to be known as "participatory politics"—a rather awkward term that encompasses acceptance of civic responsibility and, following that, political action. Included among them and deserving special attention were members of the academic community, a large number of nuns, a great many educated young women—professional women as well as wives and mothers, especially in the suburban areas. There were also business and professional men who traditionally have shied away from politics, especially liberal politics, who committed themselves openly in my campaign.

Except for the nomination of Senator Goldwater by the Republicans in 1964, the contests within the major political parties in recent presidential years have centered more on personalities than on issues. Because the position on issues taken by Senator Goldwater was not shared by many Republicans, they were left in 1964 without a candidate who came close to what they felt they had a right to expect from their own party. The electorate was really not challenged to make a serious choice because of the extreme position taken by Senator Goldwater, and so victory went to President Johnson, a victory almost by default, misinterpreted as a mandate.

By 1968, however, the division within the Democratic party was not one of personality, but at root a difference on an issue and on an approach to government and politics. The party, acting through a majority of the delegates at the Democratic convention, refused to adjust the official party position to what a strong minority at the convention was advocating. Instead, the Democratic party went to the elec-

torate with a foreign policy which was practically indistinguishable from that of the Republicans. Consequently, a large section of American voters was denied a chance in the general election to make the kind of choice which the voters had clearly demonstrated in Democratic primaries across the land they wanted to make. When, in fact, there was a deep difference of opinion in the general public's mind about the war, the two parties acted as if there was no contest. The technique of the Humphrey and Nixon campaigns was like freezing in professional basketball. When a game is tight, or in the case of a tie—the team in possession will hold onto the ball in the closing moments, hoping to shoot at the last second and score when there is not enough time left for the opposition to take the ball and make any offensive move.

Those who were frozen out of the electoral process in 1968 want reform —particularly in the Democratic party. Though party leaders in the past have taken account of what a strong minority wanted, they have done so often through undemocratic procedures. Now, I believe, the demand is for a perfection of procedures so that the position of a strong minority is sure to be reflected in the party platform and the position of its candidates and not left to chance. When the party deals with an issue like the war in Vietnam it will not be enough to say that a majority of the party at a convention has prevailed. The moral and emotional weight of such an issue raises it to a level of importance beyond what can be measured by a simple percentage of delegate votes. Without procedural reform, I doubt very much whether anyone could persuade the young people or the relatively independent practitioners of politics to test the processes within the Democratic party again in 1972.

The establishing of the Commission on Party Reform and Delegate Selection indicates that progress of this kind may take place within the Democratic party, although the preliminary announcement in April 1969 of extensive hearings was not particularly encouraging. Enough was already known about undemocratic procedures within the party to establish a basis for reform without the delay or distraction of hearings across the country.

If party procedures are not reformed, both in the Democratic party and the Republican party, I anticipate that a third party or a fourth party will develop on the liberal side with the same strength and thrust that the George Wallace party had on the conservative side in 1968. There was growing evidence in 1968 that those who had been content to be considered independents, hoping to influence parties and candidates by this means, are more and more coming to the view that it is not effective to exercise such a second-class or residual citizenship in presidential years, passing judgment only after the two parties have developed platforms and chosen presidential candidates. They are beginning to see that it is necessary to be active in decisions both as to platform and as to candidates. The Wallace decision not to go the primary route in 1968 was a politically sound decision on his part.[1]

The concept of one man-one vote, which has now been clearly defined by the Supreme Court in setting up legislative districts, must be established not only in the practices of the political parties, but in many other areas of American life: on college campuses for both faculty and students who want to have something more to say about their life on campus and their education; at stockholders' meetings at which participant stockholders accept that they have an intellectual and moral responsibility for the operation of the corporation; in movements like the National Farmers Organization in agriculture.

More important than politics and power was the substance of the challenge of 1968 and the response of the people of the country. Some time during the period of the primaries before California, a judgment was passed by the

---

[1] Mark Acuff, the writer, who directed our campaign in Nebraska, said of the McCarthy movement: "I am certain that it is far more important than any of the issues raised in the campaign to date—more important than early settlement of the war, more important than relief for the ghettos, and far more important than the solution of the balance of payments problem. For in a way, the problem of the ghettos and the poor is linked closely with McCarthy's middle-class movement, though perhaps only a few Blacks see it that way. And the exasperation and helplessness so painful to the youth of the prosperous middle class, though we call the problem 'alienation,' is not, at base, much different from the disfranchisement of the black man and the urban poor.

"Assorted Swedes and Frenchmen have been warning us for years that our inherently most difficult problem will be the adaptation of democracy to a technological culture with a population of hundreds of millions. Today, however, it is not only the Black and the poor and the young who feel powerless to affect the machinations of the system. In the last half of the 20th century, the smog-bound, tax-hounded, and radar-trapped suburbanite also feels cast adrift in a sea of technocracy where no one cares and, worse, no one listens.

"To my way of thinking, the failure of the system to provide a mechanism for the people to involve themselves in the ordering of government and society is more to blame for riots, arson and crime waves than any immediate economic and social deprivation. And George Wallace is every bit as much the benefactor of this upwelling of frustration as is McCarthy."

people of this country against the war. In a subtle way this judgment affected the politics after the primaries and also affected the action at the convention. When they were still giving it intellectual and moral support, the people of the country generally were more concerned about the war and about casualty reports. Following their judgment against the war, however, I sensed that they felt a release from responsibility—as though the war was no longer theirs but belonged to the administration in power.

This attitude still persists. Ever since President Johnson withdrew from the presidential race, the war has been an official or administration or politicians' war rather than a "popular," or people's, war. The change in attitude might have taken place without a primary challenge, but I doubt it. The primaries gave the people a chance to pass a judgment on the war, and in Democratic primary after primary they indicated their opposition. In part because of that opposition, President Nixon is now free to act—with little practical danger—to bring the war in Vietnam to an end and also free to adopt much more open policies toward Russia and mainland China if he is willing. This would also have been true, I believe, of Hubert Humphrey if he had been elected.

The campaign also helped to strengthen the challenge to the militarization of American life and American foreign policy—the challenge that was being raised especially by the Foreign Relations Committee of the Senate before my campaign, which was pursued by it during the campaign, and which is still being pushed with courage and vigor. . . .

The American people were tested in 1968, and they were not found wanting. A general constituency of conscience was shown to exist in America. And there was a return of the spirit that moved this country in 1776 and 1789—a spirit of "public happiness" described by John Adams as a delight in public office, in participating in public activities and in the government. John Adams said that the men of colonial America went to town meetings and participated in assemblies because they delighted in the dialogue, because they delighted in discussion—not because they had any special interest which they wished to advance, but because they were concerned with advancing the public good.

The campaign demonstrated clearly that the political system of America is really much more open than people believe it to be. If a group has an issue and a reasonably good candidate, neither the lack of funds nor the lack of organization nor the power of party opposition need deter it from making a challenge. Finances are less important than they have been in the past if proper use of public media is made.

Despite all that happened in 1968, the year revealed that there is within the people of this country a great reservoir of good will as well as ability and energy. We have always done best for our country and for the world when we were prepared to make mistakes, if we had to make them, on the side of an excess of trust rather than on the side of mistrust or suspicion; when we were willing to make mistakes because of an excess of liberality or generosity, rather than an excess of self-seeking and self-concern; when we were prepared to make mistakes because of an excess of hope rather than an excess of fear. These have been the marks of America in its best times and the marks of America at its best in politics: reason and trust and generosity and hope. These were the marks that distinguished our new politics of 1968.

"America is hard to see," as Robert Frost has written, but if one looks hard and long one will see much that is good.

Toward a Strategy of Disruption

STEPHEN SALTONSTALL

The "silent generation" has been a thing of the past for nearly seven years now. Since about 1960, when the nuclear disarmament and sit-in movements got underway, student activism has been gathering momentum steadily, in militance and in numbers of those involved. The last academic year saw Berkeley shut down by a student strike, and Hubert Humphrey roughed up in Ann Arbor and Palo Alto. It witnessed the downfall of reactionary administrators at Howard University and Boston University; it saw former Harvard professor Robert McNamara mobbed in Cambridge. One-half of America's state universities will this fall have New Left student body presidents.

But simultaneous with the success of the new politics on the campuses has come the triumph of reaction outside them. The government continues its systematic annihilation of Vietnamese peasants. Billions of dollars are spent by Congress to send sterilized nose-

Reprinted by permission from the Center Occasional Paper, "Students and Society," I, 1, (1967). A publication of the Center for the Study of Democratic Institutions in Santa Barbara, California.

cones to the moon, but not one cent to curb New York's eight million rats. Gag-rule is the byword as the administration scuttles in search of ways to silence Jim Garrison one day, or Rap Brown the next.

A plausible reason for the failure of our students' program, I suggest, is the anomaly of our conservative tactics in the light of our radical goals. In particular, we have failed up to now to question two myths which the American establishment has always used to keep radical reformers in line.

The first of these myths is mouthed by house-leftists like Michael Harrington as well as by imposingly-titled corporate defenders of the *status quo* like Freedom House. The only acceptable means of bringing about reform, we are told, are those consistent with the "democratic process"—whatever that is. Persuasion, education, and the exercise of franchise is "responsible protest." Coercion is "irresponsible" and "undemocratic." This cliché of the liberal center is historically naive. Nearly all of our radical reforms have been brought about (or thwarted) by coercion. Without men like Denmark Vesey or Nat Turner, indeed without the Civil War, slavery might not have ended—and without the Clansmen and their vicious Mississippi plan it might not have been reinstituted. Without the Boston Riot of 1903, the challenge to Booker Washington's power by black radicals like W. E. B. DuBois and Monroe Trotter would never have gotten off the ground. Without the Homestead and Pullman strikes, without Coeur D'Alene and Cripple Creek, trade unionism would never have flourished.

Moreover, if coercion were to be discarded from the reformer's inventory, there would be very little left on the shelf; for nearly all tactics are coercive, at bottom. Martin Luther King has conceded that the difference in coerciveness between non-violent and violent tactics is often only a matter of degree. Furthermore, those who employ coercive tactics usually do so in the face of more brutal and pervasive forms of coercion on the part of those against whom their protests are directed.

The second often-heard argument against radical action is that civil disobedience and disruption alienates more people than it converts. We are supposed to infer that it is necessary to change minds before changing institutions. One is reminded of the so-called Southern moderates who insist that racial justice must be accomplished not by governmental or organizational coercion but through a "change of heart."

Thus liberals caution us, win over your adversaries; change the laws. Now, everyday politics not only presupposes the franchise (which most of us lack), but it presupposes dialogue. Dialogue, especially as practiced at the Center for the Study of Democratic Institutions, is a fine ideal; it is also an impractical means of effecting radical reform. It takes two to dialogue, and our goals are too inimical to the interest of the dominant classes in our society for dialogue to add up to anything but political suicide.

It is obvious, for example, that President Johnson is not interested in entering into a dialogue on Vietnam. This would mean his defeat; for his position is irrational. So he sends his representatives to the universities not to talk with us about the war, but to lie to us. For the administration, dialogue may be possible within, say, the framework of State Department policy, but not outside it. As for the students, they talk, they petition, they picket; their effect is negligible.

What the student movement needs, then, is a viable coercive strategy. I do not advocate desultory civil disobedience, which gives pleasure to those performing their "witness," but which cannot change the course of history. Nor do I believe that arming ourselves is the answer—not that this would be a morally unjustifiable tactic; it would be impractical. No matter how much force we could muster, the government could muster more. Blacks, not police, died in large numbers in Newark and Detroit. But students are capable of sabotaging the society with disruption.

Our contemporaries in the ghettos are way ahead of us. They have demonstrated this summer that a small, concentrated minority group can significantly disrupt American society. (It is important to note here that most of those involved in the rebellions, according to Daniel Moynihan, were between seventeen and twenty-two.) The universities, populated by a large, exploited, powerless mass, are the middle-class ghettos. With a little effort, they too can be made to explode.

Clark Kerr has unwittingly pointed the way. For the meta-message of his writings is that the federal government cannot survive without the university's help. I propose, then, that we seek to destroy the university's capacity to prop up our political institutions. By stalemating America's intellectual establishment, we may be able to paralyze the political establishment as well.

First, we have the capability to immobilize the R.O.T.C. on the campuses. This would seriously affect the army's capacity to wage war, as more officers are turned out by the colleges than by the service academies, and there is already a critical shortage of second lieutenants in Vietnam. A small, disciplined group of "shock-troops" could pack classes, break up drills, and harass army "professors."

Second, we can stop the defense research being carried on under university auspices. The Kissingers and Rostows could be blocked from entering their offices, and harried at their homes. Students could infiltrate the office staffs of the electronic accelerators and foreign policy institutes, and hamper their efficiency. The introduction of a small quantity of LSD in only five or six government department coffee-urns might be a highly effective tactic. Students should prevent their universities from being used as forums for government apologists. Public figures like Humphrey and McNamara, when they appear, should be subject to intimidation and humiliation.

Finally, college administrations can be slowed to a near-standstill if students overuse the bureaucracy.

Floods of petitions can be filed with deans and registrars. Appointments by the score can be made with their assistants just for the hell of it. An inordinate number of library books can be checked out. IBM cards can be bent so they will be rejected by computers.

The economy seems as vulnerable a target for disruption as the university. Our generation has already inadvertently alarmed corporations with our lack of enthusiasm for business careers; even a partially successful boycott of corporate employers might prove disastrous. The clothing industry would probably collapse if all students, say, suddenly decided not to wear button-down collars. Mass-refusal to purchase American automobiles would do great damage. Small bits of sabotage by individuals—the sending of business reply cards through the mails, or overpaying one's phone bill by a penny—would have a decided cumulative effect.

This strategy of creative disruption is directed mostly, of course, at ending the Vietnam war. But I believe it is entirely possible that, if effective, the technique would have wide ramifications for the furthering of student power on the polity as a whole. If students demonstrate to the politicians that they can mobilize themselves to exert the coercive power inherent in their numbers, they will have to be reckoned with as a political force. Students will have to be consulted—and heeded—on the issues that concern them.

Many of us have lost hope. But this need not be so. We have the power to bring the American Juggernaut to a halt. Let us paralyze the university; let us ball up the economy. One day soon, Congressmen and Presidents may petition us, not we them. Let us therefore disrupt. We have nothing to lose.

Requiem for Nonviolence

ELDRIDGE CLEAVER

The murder of Dr. Martin Luther King came as a surprise—and surprisingly it also came as a shock. Many people, particularly those in the black community who long ago abandoned nonviolence and opted to implement the slogan of Malcolm X—"black liberation by any means necessary"—have been expecting to hear of Dr. King's death for a long time. Many even became tired of waiting. But that Dr. King would have to die was a certainty. For here was a man who refused to abandon the philosophy and the principle of nonviolence in face of a hostile and racist nation which has made it indisputably clear that it has no intention and no desire to grant a redress of the grievances of the black colonial subjects who are held in bondage.

To black militants, Dr. King represented a stubborn and persistent stumbling block in the path of the methods that had to be implemented to bring about a revolution in the present situation. And so, therefore, much hatred, much venom and much criticism was focused upon Dr. King by the black militants. And the contradiction in which

Reprinted from Robert Scheer, ed., Eldridge Cleaver: Post-Prison Writings and Speeches (New York: Random House, Inc., 1969), pp. 73–79. Copyright 1967, 1968, 1969 by Ramparts Magazine, Inc. Reprinted by permission.

he was caught up cast him in the role of one who was hated and held in contempt, both by the whites in America who did not want to free black people, and by black people who recognized the attitude of white America and who wanted to be rid of the self-deceiving doctrine of nonviolence. Still, black militants were willing to sit back and watch, and allow Dr. King to play out his role. And his role has now been played out.

The assassin's bullet not only killed Dr. King, it killed a period of history. It killed a hope, and it killed a dream.

That white America could produce the assassin of Dr. Martin Luther King is looked upon by black people—and not just those identified as black militants—as a final repudiation by white America of any hope of reconciliation, of any hope of change by peaceful and nonviolent means. So that it becomes clear that the only way for black people in this country to get the things that they want—and the things that they have a right to and that they deserve—is to meet fire with fire.

In the last few months, while Dr. King was trying to build support for his projected poor people's march on Washington, he already resembled something of a dead man. Of a dead symbol, one might say more correctly.

Hated on both sides, denounced on both sides—yet he persisted. And now his blood has been spilled. The death of Dr. King signals the end of an era and the beginning of a terrible and bloody chapter that may remain unwritten, because there may be no scribe left to capture on paper the holocaust to come.

That there is a holocaust coming I have no doubt at all. I have been talking to people around the country by telephone—people intimately involved in the black liberation struggle —and their reaction to Dr. King's murder has been unanimous: the war has begun. The violent phase of the black liberation struggle is here, and it will spread. From that shot, from that blood, America will be painted red. Dead bodies will litter the streets and the scenes will be reminiscent of the disgusting, terrifying, nightmarish news reports coming out of Algeria during the height of the general violence right before the final breakdown of the French colonial regime.

America has said "No" to the black man's demand for liberation, and this "No" is unacceptable to black people. They are going to strike back, they are going to reply to the escalation of this racist government, this racist society. They are going to escalate their retaliation. And the responsibility for all this blood, for all this death, for all this suffering . . . well, it's beyond the stage of assigning blame. Black people are no longer interested in adjudicating the situation, in negotiating the situation, in arbitrating the situation. Their only interest now is in being able to summon up whatever it will take to wreak the havoc upon Babylon that will force Babylon to let

the black people go. For all other avenues have been closed.

The assassin's bullet which struck down Dr. King closed a door that to the majority of black people seemed closed long ago. To many of us it was clear that that door had never been open. But we were willing to allow the hopeful others to bang upon that door for entry, we were willing to sit back and let them do this. Indeed, we had no other choice. But· now all black people in America have become Black Panthers in spirit. There will, of course, be those who stand up before the masses and echo the eloquent pleas of Dr. King for a continuation of the nonviolent tactic. They will be listened to by many, but from another perspective: people will look back upon Dr. King and upon his successors with something of the emotions one feels when one looks upon the corpse of a loved one. But it is all dead now. It's all dead now. Now there is the gun and the bomb, dynamite and the knife, and they will be used liberally in America. America will bleed. America will suffer.

And it is strange to see how, with each significant shot that is fired, time is speeded up. How the dreadful days that we all somehow knew were coming seem to cascade down upon us immediately, and the dreadful hours that we thought were years away are immediately upon us, immediately before us. And all eternity is gone, blown away, washed away in the blood of martyrs.

Is the death of Dr. King a sad day for America? No. It is a day consistent with what America demands by its actions. The death of Dr. King was not a tragedy for America. America should be happy that Dr. King is dead, because America worked so hard to bring it about. And now all the hypocritical, vicious madmen who pollute the government of this country and who befoul the police agencies of this country, all of the hypocritical public announcements following the death of Dr. King are being repudiated and held in contempt, not only by black people but by millions of white people who know that had these same treacherous, political gangsters made the moves that clearly lay within their power to make, Dr. King would not be dead, nonviolence would prevail and the terror would not be upon us. These people, the police departments, the legislatures, the government, the Democratic Party, the Republican Party, those commonly referred to as the Establishment or the power structure, they can be looked upon as immediate targets and symbols of blame.

But it has been said that a people or a country gets the leaders and the government that it deserves. And here we have at the death of Dr. King a President by the name of Lyndon Baines Johnson who has the audacity to stand before this nation and mourn Dr. King and to praise his leadership and the nonviolence he espoused, while he has the blood of hundreds of thousands of people and the slaughtered conscience of America upon his hands. If any one man could be singled out as bearing responsibility for bringing about the bloodshed and violence to come, it would be Lyndon Baines Johnson. But not just Lyndon Baines Johnson. All of the greedy, profit-seeking businessmen in America, all of the conniving, unscrupulous labor leaders of America, all of the unspeakable bootlickers, the

big businessmen of the civil rights movement and the average man on the streets who feels hatred instilled in his heart by this vicious and disgusting system—the blame is everywhere and nowhere.

Washington, D.C., is burning. My only thought at that is: I hope Stokely Carmichael survives Washington. Chicago is burning, Detroit is burning and there is fire and the sound of guns from one end of Babylon to the other.

Last night I heard Lyndon Baines Johnson admonishing his poeple, admonishing black people to turn away from violence, and not to follow the path of the assassins. And of all the corn pone that he spouted forth one thing struck me and I felt insulted by it. He was ringing changes on a famous statement made by Malcolm X in his speech, "The Ballot or the Bullet." Malcolm X had prophesied that if the ballot did not prevail in gaining black people their liberation, then the bullet would be made to prevail. And Lyndon Johnson said last night that he was going to prove to the nation and to the American people that the ballot and not the bullet would prevail. Coming from him, it was a pure insult.

Those of us in the Black Panther Party who have been reading events and looking to the future have said that this will be the Year of the Panther, that this will be the Year of the Black Panther. And now everything that I can see leaves no doubt of that. And now there is Stokely Carmichael, Rap Brown, and above all there is Huey P. Newton. Malcolm X prophesied the coming of the gun, and Huey Newton picked up the gun, and now there is gun against gun. Malcolm X gunned down. Martin Luther King gunned down.

I am trying to put a few words on tape because I was asked to do so by the editor of this magazine, to try to give my thoughts on what the assassination of Dr. King means for the future, what is likely to follow and who is likely to emerge as a new or a prevailing leader of black people. It is hard to put words on this tape because words are no longer relevant. Action is all that counts now. And maybe America will understand that. I doubt it. I think that America is incapable of understanding *anything* relevant to human rights. I think that America has already committed suicide and we who now thrash within its dead body are also dead in part and parcel of the corpse. America is truly a disgusting burden upon this planet. A burden upon all humanity. And if we here in America . . . .

Violent and Non-Violent Civil Disobedience

SYDNEY HYMAN

What is missing from this inventory of conditions under which the people in society may rebel by violent or non-violent means? Locke does not extend his inventory to cover conditions, first, when men are properly appointed to make laws, but the laws are felt to be unjust by a segment of society; second, when existing laws are faithfully executed, yet on that very account, what is felt to be unjust is felt all the more keenly; third, when there is no "long train of abuses," only specific abuses—in the eyes of some people, but not in the eyes of others; and fourth, when the cause of the abuses to be remedied lies not so much in government or in its agents, but in the broad reaches of society itself or in a sector of society.

Reprinted from The Politics of Consensus, pp. 173–78. Copyright 1968 by Random House Inc. Reprinted by permission of the publisher.

Are the items missing from Locke's inventory covered by Thoreau in the latter's essay "On the Duty of Civil Disobedience"? Thoreau himself spent one night in jail in punishment for his act of civil disobedience, and the experience triggered a one-shot literary explosion whose literary brilliance obscured its own gaps and internal contradictions. It is apparent from Thoreau's own text, for example, that he did not have to consider the propriety of going or not going to jail. He went to jail because he could not figure out a way of not going. It just happened. Even so, it just happened as a private event which went virtually unnoticed by his fellow townsmen and with no visible effect on them. He was piqued on that account, but only mildly so, since his main interest was not with society. Rather he seemed ready to secede from the society of Massachusetts in order to concentrate on his true main interest, namely, himself.

In any event, his was a very simple case of civil disobedience, from whence the questions arise: Is it possible to generalize the simple case? Does it comprise a theoretical argument for civil disobedience as a mode of resistance to all injustice regardless of particular circumstances—or without taking into account the consequences? Thoreau stammered when put to the test of these questions. On the one side, he observed that all injustice need not be resisted. "If the injustice is part of the necessary friction of the machine of government, let it go, let it go." It will wear itself out. On the other side, he observed that there were times when the injustice was so great that no calculus of consequences was required, since no consequence outweighed the obligation to resist the injustice: "When . . . a whole country is unjustly overrun and conquered by a foreign army, and subject to military law, I think that it is not too soon for honest men to rebel and revolutionize. What makes this duty the more urgent is the fact that the country so overrun is not our own, but ours is the invading army." The two statements, taken in combination, thus amount to an admission that the author had no rules for civil disobedience that were universally applicable. What was to be done or left undone depended on the facts of particular cases.

Gandhi came out at the same point, though he seemed to have a unified set of ideas about civil disobedience. Among other ideas, he asserted that the state, being essentially a coercive agency, could never claim inalienable, unchallengeable authority for itself—even if it secured the tacit consent or acquiescence of most of its citizens. The authority it could claim could only be of a conditional nature, subject to the way it bore itself in the presence of the individual. The individual was thus in a superior moral position to the state because *he* is a person and the state is *no* kind of entity.

Nevertheless, Gandhi ceaselessly tested his ideas against the dialectic experience, and he was forced as an honest man constantly to revise his constructs. In doing so, he tried to avoid the waspish moralism which raises every single issue, however local and specific, to the status of an eternal principle for which men must contend. He tried to show how important and how difficult are the conditions under which men can really succeed in consistently invoking eternal principles to justify civil disobedience. Yet he also rejected the spirit of a narrow legalism which reduces important issues of basic human rights to a frame where the formal letter of the law crushes the spirit of equity.

He emphasized that social and political conflicts could best be handled when the contestants respected the moral worth of each other, distinguished between measures and persons, conducted their battles in a spirit of self-criticism, and abstained from crude forms of coercion. While he upheld the "natural right" of every man to act according to his conscience in opposition to an external authority, he strongly stressed the need of the civil disobedient to maintain the bond of his connection with *society*. He must actively engage in philanthropic and other programs to ameliorate the lot of the victims of injustice. At the same time, to qualify on rare occasions to violate the unjust laws of the *state*, he must first show himself to be generally obedient to the laws of the state. He must prepare himself for the act of civil disobedience not with a burst of emotional enthusiasm, but by a cool cross-examination of his own motives—this, in order to reinforce his fearlessness, his moral strength, and the authenticity of his character as a civil resister.

On a related ground, Gandhi counseled against "organized" mass civil disobedience, seeing in it the means by which large numbers of people could be manipulated by a few. If mass civil disobedience was to remain undefiled by distortion and fraud, it must be, said he, a natural coming together of individuals who clearly recognized what was wrong in the order of things around them, and who prepared themselves for the heroic resistance and sacrifice required to change things for the better. Only so could there be preserved an attitude of mind on the part of the civil resister himself that left room for his opponent to be "converted" to the former's point of view. In short, everything Gandhi said—and revised— makes one point. Eevery case of civil disobedience is a hard case which must be assessed on its own terms.

If it is impossible to take into account all the variables that are present in all cases of civil disobedience, a few propositions seem to be generally valid as norms for civil disobedience where the people live under a constitutional government (as against a tyranny).

First, if the civil disobedient is not to corrupt or be corrupted by civil disobedience, he must be wholly aware that his act is directed toward a given, specific law, and not toward law generally. He must bear the burden of proving that his pinpointed law-breaking was in fact justifiable by the inherent injustice of the particular law itself. His act of civil disobedience must be a public instead of a private act. The primary function of the act must be to educate and persuade, and for this reason he must carefully choose his pedagogical technique if he is to get his message across to the audience he wants to educate and persuade. He must willingly suffer the legal punishment awaiting his illegal act. He must prove that he resorted to civil disobedience only because he has exhausted every available constitutional means in his search for a relief from what he feels is unjust, or only because the constitutional means as they exist on paper are in fact inoperative in practice because he was denied access to them. He must make it clear that he is not protesting in the abstract, but that in breaking the law his object is to bring to birth the terms of a new law which will remove the grounds for the injustice that aroused his protest. In short, his object must be to uphold the concept of law by establishing it on a more just basis sustained by a new consensus about what is just.

Yet when all this is said, there remains an ambiguous algebraic equation to be solved.

On the one side stands the fact that law is the organ of society. There could be no law and hence no society if groups of people in it breached laws at will according to their subjective sense of justice or ethics. Even if the shell of the law and society remained, what went on inside it could resemble the condition in Nazi Germany where a statute authorized judges to punish "according to the healthy sentiment of the people." The law, if it is to be anything more than a name for a capricious tyranny, must strive for consistency, so that men in society can plan their conduct for the future in a less uncertain way. This means that individualism, even an ennobled individualism, must bow before the law rather than aim at its disruption. It also means that no society can endure which does not attempt to curb the civil disobedience which threatens the fabric of law. On the other side stands the fact that a moral advance in society often depends on individuals who are ready to accept martyrdom by resorting to non-violent civil disobedience, and whose punishment awakens a community consciousness into changing unjust laws. The unknown x standing in between the two sides of the equation is, as said already, the difficulty of knowing when in a particular case the law must be enforced for the sake of order in society, and when individuals have a "higher title of right" to violate a law for the sake of justice in society.

Does the difficulty say that a politics of consensus is irrelevant to the matter? It says the opposite. It is only a politics of that kind, and the process of constitutional morality it expresses, which can consolidate the support of the community either on the side of order in society, or on the side of people who violate the laws for the sake of justice in society. It is only such a politics which can effectively decide the question whether or not a civil disobedient is in the right when he breaks the law with the object of changing it from what it is to what it ought to be.

3

THE POTENTIAL RECRUITS:

PASSIONATELY COMMITTED,
PASSINGLY CONCERNED,
INCREASINGLY ALIENATED,
BASICALLY APATHETIC?

Several significant and increasingly articulate groups in the United States are now demanding either inclusion in the system, or political change. These groups include university and college students, black citizens, poor people, women, Indians, Chicanos—in fact all who do not currently share equitably in the benefits of American democracy. A growing number now demand quick solutions to complex problems, while also demonstrating a distaste and, in some cases, a contempt for the "accepted" methods of social change. Although a majority of these groups have tended until recently to support the Democratic party, presumably because of the party's alleged propensity to speak for the powerless and underprivileged, this support has not necessarily meant actual involvement in the decision-making processes of party politics. Black citizens have generally been purposely excluded; the poor have been ignored for racial and economic reasons, as well as because of their own apathy; students have usually been involved only on the fringes (icing the soda pop at political rallies) and in ancillary roles; and the others have been left out for a variety of reasons.

Judging from the events of the seven years that have passed since the Berkeley Free Speech Movement of 1964, student activism appears to have two overriding, and complimentary, objectives. The first is for students to gain greater influence in the decision-making apparatus of university and college administrations, and the second is to exercise some influence in solving the unresolved domestic and world problems outside the campus. Pursuit of the first objective has led, in many institutions, to establishing a more democratic base for rules and procedures, revision of curricula to achieve more "relevance," and establishment of Black Studies departments and courses. Concern for the second objective and militant reactions to such issues as war, conscription, and racism have brought something new to American education—some of our campuses have been converted into bases of political operations and social change.

The Skolnick Report to the National Commission on the Causes and Prevention of Violence recently observed that the student protest movement has passed through two general phases. Before 1965, the movement usually accepted the legitimacy of both the American political system and the university, even while expressing concern, dissent, or protest. After 1965, the movement came to reject the system and began to popularize such concepts as "participatory democracy," to be attained by revolution if need be. The reason for the movement's increasing radicalism is a widely shared frustration and moral indignation over certain events, such as the escalation of the War in Indochina, the brutal use of police on campuses, and the cooperation of university officials with the so-called military-industrial complex. Thus the second objective of student activism, the remaking of society and, perhaps, the world, has become more important than the first.

The second group that has felt disenchantment with the American political system consists of those black citizens who have responded to the call for "black power." Samuel Lubell observed in 1964 that "if American society fails to treat Negroes as individuals, then they will remain a separate group—more accurately a subnation—in our midst." [1] The Kerner Commission's observation four years later that "our nation is moving toward two societies, one black, one white," [2] indicates that the situation has been getting worse, rather than better. Increasing frustration and militancy on the part of black citizens are the natural results of these trends.

Black militancy has progressed through at least two general stages. Until about 1965, the emphasis was upon civil rights and working within the system to achieve better conditions for black citizens. But, although nonviolent actions led to the first effective national civil rights laws since Reconstruction, the effects of these laws were disappointingly limited, and the lives of most blacks remained virtually unchanged. So it became apparent to large numbers of black Americans that only direct action outside the system, to bring about fundamental changes in American life and to end the evils of white racism, could succeed where the civil rights movement had failed. But before there could be such change, blacks had to become conscious of their problems and achieve racial dignity, unity, and most importantly, black power.

The concept of black power was first introduced in 1966 when, following the shooting of James Meredith in Mississippi, Stokely Carmichael called upon black citizens to build a power base:

[1] Samuel Lubell, *White and Black: Test of a Nation* (New York: Harper and Row, Publishers, 1966), p. 217.

[2] *Report of the National Advisory Commission on Civil Disorders* (New York: Bantam Books, Inc., 1968), p. 1.

We are going to build a movement in the country based on the color of our skins that is going to free us from our oppressors and we have to do that ourselves.[3]

Black power is essentially a concept of self-help, by which blacks can develop their own independent bases of economic, social, and political power. It is also a rejection of "gradualism" and anything that implies black dependence upon whites. But it is not considered, at least by the more moderate black spokesmen like Charles Hamilton, as an end in itself. Moreover, the moderates recognize that getting rid of racial injustice demands a cooperative effort by all citizens. As Martin Luther King said, "Anyone not working at it is *sleeping through a revolution*." [4]

The third group that has suffered from a lack of concern for its plight is made up of the American poor, or what Michael Harrington calls the "other America." The fact that the poor number from 15 to 25 per cent of our population means that they could, if united and militant, force important concessions from the majority. But the poor are also typically the least organized and, because of a feeling of powerlessness, are the least inclined to participate in politics.

It is indeed a paradox that the wealthiest country in world history has such a large group of economically deprived people. While we have raised the average, individual income of the industrial worker and the middle-class professional, we have done relatively little to guarantee any kind of minimum level of living for our poor. We are, for example, the only large industrial country that does not have a system of family allowances. Moreover, the much-criticized welfare system, which has been in operation since the 1930's, may only have contributed adversely to the condition of the poor by creating a permanently dependent class of those who do receive public assistance. Thus the gap between rich and poor has become wider, as the general standard of living has risen to unprecedented levels in America.

Recent developments in "poor power" have included the 1968 Poor People's Campaign to Washington, the tenants' strikes in the urban ghettoes, the attempts to "sit in" on sessions of state legislatures, and the work of the Welfare Rights Organization. Again, the choice seems to be between working within the system, or seeking solutions outside. It should be noted, however, that so far the most effective efforts to unify the poor have either been led by outsiders such as Saul Alinsky or Father Groppi, or have been part of racial or ethnic movements.

A fourth group which has been bypassed by the system to a certain extent is that majority-minority, the women. Although not all women may feel as oppressed as others, women do suffer discrimination in employment, politics, education, government, social clubs, and other activities. Moreover, as Betty Friedan has explained, women are treated as inferior, childlike, emotional, and incapable of

---

[3] Quoted in George A. Shanker, "Black Power," *Pace*, XIX, 4 (Fall-Winter, 1968), 10.

[4] Martin Luther King, Jr., "Remaining Awake Through a Revolution," *The Grinnell Magazine*, I, 3 (Summer, 1968), 19.

doing anything but raising children, performing household tasks, and providing companionship and inspiration for husbands.

The new feminist movement, or "women's lib," is now developing along two lines—the first, or more moderate, is presently working for the elimination of sex discrimination through lobbying, court action, and encouraging more women to run for public office. The second is much more radical and calls variously for separatism, the rejection of marriage, or the complete restructuring of society to eliminate male domination. The large majority of the new feminists, however, are committed to the moderate position of the National Organization for Women: "NOW is dedicated to the proposition that women, first and foremost, are human beings, who, like all other people in our society, must have the chance to develop their fullest human potential."[5] One dedicated feminist has predicted, "If the 1960's belonged to the blacks, the next ten years are ours."[6]

Two other groups that feel ignored or excluded by the American political system, to the point of attempting to change their situations, are the Indians and the Mexican-Americans. Although it is particularly difficult to generalize about the former group because of the great diversity of cultural affiliations, and aspirations of American Indians, the contemporary Indian "renascence" (as one authority calls it) appears to have two basic objectives—"the improvement of material standards of living and general welfare of Indian groups by means of increased formal education of Indians in professions and vocations to better serve Indian communities; emphasis on Indian identity in terms of reactivating or encouraging perpetuation of tribal languages, customs, and tribal residential communities."[7] Whatever may be said about contemporary Indian nationalism, it must be remembered that Indian citizens are only a very few generations removed from having been victimized by one of the most ruthless programs of repression ever conducted against any group of people in history.

"Brown power" signifies the movement for recognition by the Chicanos [young Mexican Americans], who now make up the second largest minority in the United States. They are also one of the poorest minorities, with one third of the Mexican-Americans of the Southwest living below the official poverty line. As with other such groups, the Chicanos are caught between two worlds—one demanding assimilation into American society, and the other dictating cultural isolation. Ignored by the system, however, many Chicanos find, as do black militants, that power can come only through cultural identity and direct action that challenges the system. As the Mexican-American poet, A. Arzate, has written, "Now must be the time to change, and with my forming hands, create my real self."[8]

[5] Quoted in Caroline Bird, Born Female: The High Cost of Keeping Women Down (New York: Pocket Books, 1968), p. 176.

[6] Lucy Komisar, "The New Feminism," Saturday Review, LIII, 8, (February 21, 1970), 55.

[7] Stuart Levine and N. Laurie, The American Indian Today (Baltimore: Penguin Books, Inc., 1968), p. 195.

[8] "Tio Taco is Dead," Newsweek, LXXV, 26 (June 29, 1970), 22.

These, then, are the leading groups that now provide recruits for the new politics. All of the disadvantaged demand change of the "system," in various ways, and in differing degrees. Whether or not these groups will receive their due from America remains to be seen. But the idea that the submerged consist of only small numbers of radicals or malcontents, as the leaders of the establishment are often inclined to believe, should be recognized as an unfounded, as well as dangerous, myth.

In this section, the readings have been chosen with a view toward presenting the widest possible range of opinions concerning the ideas, aspirations, and activities of the potential recruits for the new politics. The students are represented by Daniel Sisson, and the reaction to "student power" is discussed by Hans Morgenthau. Nathan Wright offers an eloquent appeal for black power, and Michael Harrington describes the "invisible land" of the poor in the selection from his now classic work, *The Other America*. The "new feminism" of the 1970's is described by Lucy Komisar; the "colonialism" of the Bureau of Indian Affairs is criticized in the report of the Citizens' Advocate Center. Finally, the newly developing phenomenon, "Chicano power," is described by Stan Steiner and Robert Littell in two articles that appeared recently in *The New Republic* and *Newsweek*. Although by no means exhaustive, these selections do at least present some of the more significant attitudes of the groups currently interested in the new politics.

one

STUDENTS: "WHAT DO THEY MEAN?"

The Dialogue: Youth and Society

DANIEL SISSON

This conference is meeting at a time when communication between youth and the adults in society is tenuous indeed. In fact, for millions of young people the dialogue has already broken down in what they regard as a society gone mad. It would appear from the recent turbulence that the adult society has failed to communicate its most important ideals to the young, especially in the ghetto areas.

But for many more of today's young people who still feel a bond with society, the great trinity of peace, justice, and freedom are merely ideas espoused by an older generation determined to hold onto its privilege and power. Though they are often told that all three exist in American society, the young see massive violence and injustice as daily occurrences in the lives of millions. Equality too is becoming synonymous with class warfare, as its denial issues forth in a young man bitterly saying, "Violence is as American as cherry pie!"

Reprinted, by permission from the Center Occasional Paper, "Students and Society," I, 1 (1967). A publication of the Center for the Study of Democratic Institutions in Santa Barbara, California.

These blatant contradictions cannot be denied, but many are more subtle and mask growing differences between the generations. Hypocrisy reigns in a social system that tells young people to discipline themselves while their elders do as they please. Parents complain that their children are unmanageable, that they cannot understand them, and further that they cannot influence them. What they really mean is that communication has broken down, that there is no dialogue between the generations.

Still this does not prevent the same adults from telling youth to fight for their country's freedom, while what they truly want them to do is fight for an economic system. The most recent draft legislation calls upon nineteen-year-olds to give their lives in Vietnam while those over twenty-six enjoy the "good life" at home. Meanwhile, disenfranchised youth vainly asks the government to change its policy.

The frustrations of youth do not stop there, though adults subtly seek to soften the blows. They remind the young that spiritual involvement develops character. Then the allurements of a materialistic society are held out to them, and made easier to obtain. Many are seduced, and it is no coincidence that Madison Avenue now considers the young as its greatest potential source of exploitation. For advertisers—those who write the message—the accent is on *youth,* and the media tell them what inflection they must use.

The culmination of such hypocrisy and cant is the feeling among young people that they are being manipulated and coerced into accepting a value system not their own. In a land where the individual once reigned supreme the young are denied the right to search for their own identity. Instead they are urged to conform to a rigid social pattern owned and operated for the benefit of adults. Communication proceeds in a straight line from adults to children. There is no feedback and hence no dialogue.

Almost every institution in society seems determined to thwart a youth's ambition to realize his potentiality. Education, politics, religion, the economic system—all calculate to bring the young into its fold. Yet something has gone wrong. The young are not falling into the "bag" as their adults wish them to. A full-scale rebellion is possible: youth pitted against their elders.

Ordinarily a rebellion among the young would suggest chaos; it would mean that society was in danger of disintegrating. In this instance I do not so much feel that we have reached the nadir of civilization as that we have descended to the lowest level of communication. Young people have simply turned the adults off. The dialogue is going.

Youth everywhere are rejecting the institutions that have dominated their lives, while the adults are demanding ever more loudly that they had better "come around." Simply taking one example—the adults' attitude toward drugs—it is not implausible to estimate that by 1980 85 per cent of the young will be felons while the other 15 per cent will be Fascists, trained to keep them under control.

But though the rebelling young have in many instances ceased communicating with adults, they are doing so with their peers in new and significant ways. The rebellion may turn out to be a blessing in disguise for the society. Young people who are throwing off the yoke of puritan constraint become open, and thus when among their peers are able to begin conversation more readily. Bizarre [*sic*] modes of dress and other aspects of physical appearance are thrusts against conventional society. The symbolic rejection of the gray-flannel suit is a step toward the promotion of dialogue.

The young people most successful in articulating their problems are the students and the hippies. And it is upon them that the success or failure of the dialogue depends. They must carry the dialogue to those in power who will listen; in short, they must set its tone.

Their ability to reach this end will rest upon the reforms that they can bring about in political and educational institutions. The success of the dialogue will also hinge upon the very nature of their efforts. Indeed it is possible that efforts of students to elevate the level of dialogue in society may prove to be their most important contribution.

The students, largely because adults have abandoned the dialogue, are going to have to aid in the re-birth of the dialogue in this society. Of necessity they are going to have to take radical action, but radical in the context of the dialogue. Their theory, strategy, programs, and solutions must be subjected to the reality of the dialectic —and in every instance keeping the good of society in mind.

What matters most is that the dialogue be built up, and that the invidiual, the faction, the coalition be encouraged to seek solutions to their problems by this method.

Disruption of constructive dialogue results in intellectual dogmatism. Students, for example, who refuse to form a coalition except on their own terms, who refuse to compromise at any level, frustrate the dialogue even while they labor under the illusion of communication. The refusal to listen, the intransigent style, the extremist position, the total conviction of one's own righteousness—all characterize the authoritarian personality and the lust for power.

These are the very traits which the young find repugnant in adults.

This polarization sets the scene for violence: verbal as well as physical. And violence whether it is calculated to insult or to cause bodily injury is by definition the foregoing of reasonable discussion.

Students in positions of leadership today must remember that soon new leaders will arise and a new generation of students will take their place. Their ideas may be as radically different from ours as ours differ from those of earlier generations. Thus it seems only sensible to begin a process—the dialogue, if you will—that will enable us, the students of the 1960's, to communicate with those who will follow.

Truth and Power

HANS J. MORGENTHAU

If one must admit the failure of these essays, insofar as they had an immediate political purpose, to influence political action, one cannot help noticing either that the experience of their futility is not a private, personal matter but coincides with a collective experience of futility that pits American youth not only against American politics

Reprinted from Hans J. Morgenthau, Truth and Power: Essays of a Decade, 1960–70 (New York: Frederich A. Praeger, Inc., 1970), pp. 433–39. Copyright 1970 by Praeger Publishers, Inc. Reprinted by permission of the publisher.

and society but against the modern world itself. And that American revolt, in turn, is but a national manifestation of a world-wide revulsion against the world as it is. The student revolt, expressing itself positively in attempts at creating a new culture and negatively in aimless destructiveness and revolutionary tantrums, has its most profound roots in the seeming meaninglessness of life as it is led throughout the world and, more particularly, in the United States. What does a man live for? What is his purpose in life? What is the meaning of death, which appears to wipe out that life as though it had never existed? What, in one word, is the truth about the human condition?

Man has always had to ask such questions, and in the past religion, reason, and science have endeavored to lay his questioning to rest. Yet the different systems of truth provided by these three methods of comprehending man and his world have tended to cancel each other out. Religion did not pass the test of reason, science discredited the metaphysical systems engendered by reason, and science has given us mastery over a monstrous world that needs religion and reason to give it meaning. That world is doubly monstrous because it sacrifices human ends to technological means, as well as the needs of the many to the enrichment and power of the few, and thereby diminishes the stature of man and threatens his very existence.

The universities have provided us with that mastery over nature, but they have been unable to give it meaning and harness it to human purposes. They claim to be dedicated to the disinterested search for truth about man, society, and the universe. But they have transformed themselves, through the very dynamics of their undertakings, into gigantic and indispensable service stations for the powers-that-be, both private and public. They serve society but do not sit in judgment on it. The student who enters the university with those questions about man and the universe on his lips finds himself in the presence of an institution that, to paraphrase Tolstoy, is like a deaf man answering questions nobody has asked. The university pretends to be the mouthpiece of the truth, the whole truth and nothing but the truth. But in actuality,

insofar as what it presents as the truth is really true, it is largely irrelevant to what concerns man, young and old, and much of what it presents as truth is either not truth at all or truth only by accident, arrived at because it furnishes the powers-that-be with ideological rationalizations and justifications for the *status quo*.

When the student turns from the university as the pretended source of truth and experiences it as one social institution among many, he comes face to face with another gap between pretense and reality. Social institutions pretend to serve the individual, and the university even pretends to do so *in loco parentis*. However, for whatever services they render, they exact a price, which, in turn, impairs or even negates the services themselves. Social institutions, in the measure that they are mechanized and bureaucratized, diminish the individual, who must rely upon others rather than himself for the satisfaction of his wants, from the necessities of life to his spiritual and philosophic longings. What he once controlled himself others now control, and in the measure that they do, they diminsh his freedom.

Thus, modern society suffers from a profound ambivalence. It pretends to take care of needs that formerly the individual himself had to struggle to take care of, and to a high degree it lives up to that pretense. Yet the institution that takes care of man's needs also has the power to withhold that care. If it does, the individual's needs are left without care, insofar as he has no alternative means to satisfy them through his own individual efforts; and the sphere in which such individual efforts can be effective has been reduced by the mechanization and bureaucratization of social institutions below the minimum necessary for the satisfaction of the individual's elemental needs. In one word, the individual, to a high and unprecedented degree, is at the mercy of the institutions established for the purpose of meeting his needs.

When the student turns to the economic sphere, he faces a contradiction between the objective conditions conducive to an economy of abundance and economic practices carried over from the traditional economy of scarcity. On the one hand, he is surrounded and well-nigh engulfed by the hedonism of the *status quo* as the prevailing economic attitude, the *status quo* being synonymous with the continuing increase of material wealth enjoyed by a substantial majority of the people. An ever greater national product, ever higher personal incomes, ever more extensive social benefits, ever more amenities of life, an ever greater variety of novelties, and change for its own sake of the cogs and bolts of a hardly moving social machine—such are the goals in which the purpose of America seems to exhaust itself. . . .

Not only American youth is repelled by this conspicuous irrationality. At a conference on "Culture and Society" held in Belgrade in the winter of 1969, one participant expressed dismay at a similar prospect for his society: "If the social development is not directed energetically toward a radical change of the social role and importance of the intellectual and cultural factors, I doubt whether it will be possible to achieve on our soil anything more important than a belated Balkan variant of modern technological-consumer civilization." In America that intellectual dismay becomes moral outrage. For while the orgy of wasteful production and distribution devours the resources of the nation, society appears to be unable to relieve hunger and stamp out poverty. While in 1967 the Bureau of the Census classified more than 25 million Americans as poor and, hence, in want of food, farmers are allowed to burn potatoes in order to get higher prices, and the government pays farmers for not producing. As school lunches for the poor tend to be perverted into subsidies for middle-class children [1] and farmers, so the agricultural support program tends to make the rich farmer richer and leave the poor farmer poor.[2] The regulatory agencies intended to protect the consumer have become the protectors of the economic forces they were created to regulate. The traditional liberal remedies have turned out to be not only unsuccessful but irrelevant to the issues at hand.

These experiences of a gap between pretense and performance culminate in the political sphere. The student has been told that his is a government of the people, by the people, for the people. Yet three basic experiences contradict that statement. First, the experience of the bureaucratization and mechanization of social life and the consequent diminution of the human person, to which we have referred before, is particularly pronounced in the political sphere. For the very political relationship—that is, one man imposing his will upon another—of necessity diminishes the latter's stature as a person. Yet contemporary political relationships are marked by an

[1] See Robert Sherill, "Why Can't We Just Give Them Food?" *The New York Times Magazine*, March 22, 1970, pp. 29, 91–103.
[2] See Willian Robbins, "Farm Policy Helps Make the Rural Rich Richer," *The New York Times*, April 5, pp. 1, 56.

unprecedented discrepancy in power between the wielder of power and its object. That power overwhelms the individual not only by its irresistibility, but also, because of its mechanized and bureaucratized nature, by its unfathomable anonymity. He lives in something approaching a Kafkaesque world, insignificant and at the mercy of unchallengeable and invisible forces.

Furthermore, the student not only feels helpless in the face of the powers-that-be but also appears incapable of influencing them. Students have demonstrated for freedom of speech in totalitarian countries; they have demonstrated against the Vietnam war and in support of racial justice in the United States and elsewhere. But what has been the result of all their demonstrations? Totalitarian governments still allow freedom of speech only to the rulers, the Vietnam war is still going on, and racial justice is still a postulate rather than a fact. The Chicago Democratic Convention of 1968 was experienced as the epitome of the sham of democracy.

This experience of futility is powerfully reinforced and made definitive by a third factor: the lack of a viable alternative to the dominant philosophy, regime, and policies. That is as true of the Soviet Union as it is of France, as true of Japan as it is of the United States. What difference does it make for whom one votes, when the policies of different persons and parties are virtually interchangeable?

Take the classic case of the 1964 presidential elections. Most of us thought that it was as clear-cut a case of two different personalities, two different political philosophies, and two different political programs as one could wish. But those who voted for the loser were pleasantly surprised to find that his political program, at least on the international scene, was in good measure executed by the victor who had opposed that political program in the election campaign. As Senator Goldwater put it in the fall of 1969, when asked how he felt about President Johnson's executing his program: "Well, he did it after he had read my speeches."

Thus the world into which the student is born, and into which he is supposed to fit himself to find his life's fulfillment, must appear to him as a world of make-believe, a gigantic hoax where nothing is as it appears to be and upon which what he feels, thinks, aspires to, and does has no effect except to provide inducements for harassment and repression. All the while, that meaningless and unbending world carries on under the shadow of an atomic cloud, which, if present trends continue, is likely to make an end to all of us. The virtual assurance of atomic destruction under present conditions compounds in the long run the senselessness of human existence that the practices of society bring home every day. The reaction of the activist youth has been threefold. It attacks universities as the weakest and most easily accessible outpost of the "establishment." It challenges the "establishment" at its fringes, as in the draft and the windows, furniture, and offices of public and corporate buildings. It tries to create a new culture in which man will come into his own, satisfying his emotions and expanding his consciousness.

However, while the destruction of a university is easy—a couple of hundred determined students can do it—it is also irrelevant to the distribution of power in society. One can even assert that insofar as the university has been faithful to its mission to speak truth to power, it has been a thorn in the side of the powers-that-be. Thus the destruction of the university may for a fleeting moment satisfy the emotions of the destroyers, but it performs no useful political or social function. The same conclusion applies to challenging the "establishment" at its fringes. The fringes are expendable and easily repaired. The demonstrated futility, in terms of the distribution of power in society, of the attacks upon the university and upon the fringes of the "establishment" by the very same token reveals for all to see the "establishment's" unchallengeable power.

It is a different matter with respect to the attempts at creating a subculture different from, and opposed to, the prevailing culture. If such a subculture were able to impose a new system of values and new modes of thought and action upon the material conditions of society, it would indeed thereby create a new society. Yet as far as one can see, what the proponents of a subculture seek is not to make rational and humane use of those material conditions but either to destroy them or to escape from them. Insofar as they do the latter —returning to a state of nature both physical and emotional—they may at best save themselves as individuals. But they do nothing—except set an example for some—for society at large.

Thus far we have spoken of what youth can do to society. However, given the weakness, both in terms of power and purpose, of youth, it is much more important to ask, given its unchallengeable power, what society may do to youth and the rest of us. Society has essentially two choices: It can face the issues its own dynamics has created

by perverting and faulting its original purpose of equality in freedom, to which it is still rhetorically committed, and thereby renew itself, or it can try to maintain the *status quo* with all means at its disposal, even at the expense of its original purpose. The preservation of the *status quo* then becomes the ultimate purpose.

There can be no doubt, in view of the record, that American society has chosen the latter alternative. Regardless of the libertarian and reformatory rhetoric, its policies, both at home and abroad, have served the defense of the *status quo*. Abroad, the United States has become the antirevolutionary power *par excellence*, because our fear of Communism has smothered our rational insight into the inevitability of radical change in the Third World. Our interventions in Indochina and the Dominican Republic are monuments to that fear. At home, our commitment to making all Americans equal in freedom has been at war with our fear of change and our conformist subservience to the powers-that-be.

Our commitment to the American purpose of equality in freedom has won a battle in enforcing the rights of the black Americans at least in certain respects, a step forward that appears rather big as compared with the conditions of twenty years ago and rather insignificant as compared with the present conditions of the blacks in education, employment, and housing. What the change in the status of the blacks amounts to is the willingness of the powers-that-be to coopt blacks in such numbers and such conditions as not to endanger the over-all distribution of power within American society. When the powers-that-be perceive, rightly or wrongly, that the danger point is being approached, they call a halt to change and man the bastions of the *status quo*. Thus, the American purpose is about to lose the war, because the powers-that-be will allow the *status quo* to be dented, but not endangered.

The extent of the repression in store for the dissenters will depend upon the subjective estimate of the seriousness the powers-that-be place upon the threat to the *status quo*. Considering the thus far marginal nature of the threat, society will need only resort to marginally totalitarian methods. The dissenters will people our prisons, our graveyards, our Bohemias or—as utter

cynics—our positions of power. Those last will not be unlike the Marxist-Leninists of the Soviet Union: They will mouth a litany of slogans which they not only do not believe in but which they also despise. Such a society can carry on for a while, like a body without a soul, but sooner or later it must either recover its soul—that is, the purpose that has given it life—or disintegrate from within. Perhaps, then, a new society, with a new purpose, will be built upon the ruins of the old; or perhaps nothing will be left but ruins for later generations to behold.

two

BLACKS: "I'M BLACK, GODDAMNIT, BUT I'M BEAUTIFUL"

Black Power and Urban Unrest

NATHAN WRIGHT

What is said here concerning self-development and self-respect is designed chiefly as an in-group discussion for black people. It may have signifi-

Reprinted from Nathan Wright, Jr., *Black Power and Urban Unrest: Creative Possibilities* (New York: Hawthorn Books, 1967), pp. 58–69. Copyright © 1967 by Nathan Wright, Jr. Reprinted by permission of the publisher.

cance for others who listen in on this family discussion, as well.

Perhaps the central concern of the current issue of Black Power—for the good of the Negro and for the larger good of this whole nation and of our world today—is the self-development and the growth into maturity of the black people of America.

Black people have been the sleeping giants of this land. Among all Americans, their power, insights and experience, potentially ready to enrich this nation, have been least developed. In words of cosmic import which speak to black people in uniquely immediate terms, "we have not yet become what we shall be."

The black people of America are this nation's most rich and ready asset —its greatest raw material—as once the unmined earth and its untouched forests, fields and rivers were. In former years this nation built its greatness upon the utilization, not unmixed with wastefulness, of the vast physical resources which had lain untapped. Today, the new frontier of this nation's destiny lies in the development and utilization to the full of its infinitely greater human resources. What greater and potentially more useful reservoir of undeveloped and unutilized human resource does this nation have than in the black people of this land?

THE NEED FOR SELF-DEVELOPMENT

The great difficulty which we have had in coming into our own in America has only, in these recent days of impetus toward Black Power, begun to be made plain. We have operated, for at least the last crucial period of thirty years, on the assumption that Negroes needed to be led into their wanted place of maturity in American life.

This assumption should perhaps have been seen to be fictitious on its face. It is simply naive to believe that any person or any group of people may grow into maturity save in terms of their own self-development. Human growth cannot be produced from without: it must always be developed from within. Thus, thanks to the undoubtedly

divine accident of the current focus on Black Power, black boys and girls, and black men and women—long lulled into a feeling of functionlessness and little worth—are awaking to realize that only through self-development can they become the people of power and of majesty and of might which their bearing of the image of their creator has destined them to be.

There is, on the part of the Negro, a manifest need for self-development. Yet, of recent years, we as black people have assumed that a slave mentality of dependence upon others, as we had in former years, was appropriate for the twentieth-century destiny to which we are called. This crippling dependence upon others has hung like an albatross on our necks. It has led us to the state of stagnation and bewildered consternation which we find, with a few notable exceptions, pervading the life of the black people of America today.

The experience of all rising ethnic groups in this our beloved land has been that each rising group in American life must do for itself that which no other group may do for it. Each rising group has had to devise, to engineer, and to control in its own way its own plan, however crude or inept it may seem to have been, for its own particular growth into freedom, into self-development, into self-sufficiency and into self-respect.

This path of self-development has been—since the well-known rejection by the American people in 1776 of the King George Plan for Colonial Development—the one and only truly American way. There has never been in the American experience a German-American plan for Jewish development. Nor has there been in the American experience a Polish plan for Italian development. Yet the black people of America have been led in these recent decades to believe that their due fulfillment and their appropriation of their due inheritance in America could come best, or even only, from a white American plan for black freedom. This is incongruous on its very face. The issue of Black Power for black people—and for the good of American life as a whole—speaks to the need for black people to move from the stance of humble and dependent and impotent beggars to the stature of men who will take again into their own hands, as all men must, the fashioning of their own destiny for their own growth into self-development and self-respect. Now herein precisely lies the singular difference between the impetus toward Black Power on the one hand and what we have known as the civil rights movement on the other.

While the civil rights movement has emphasized what black people have been due, the emphasis of black self-development is on what black people may give to America. The thrust of Black Power is toward national fulfillment through the utilization of the potentialities and latent gifts of all. Both Black Power and the civil rights movement must have their vital and necessary places. The civil rights movement has in its own invaluable way emphasized what the American Negro has been due as an American from the day of each black man's birth. Without the efforts of the civil rights movement, particularly over these past thirty and more years, it would be difficult to speculate on where we, and this nation as a whole, might be. The civil rights movement, with its interracial dialogue, needs to grow and to flourish. We must never indulge in the vain luxury of criticizing what our leaders—with the

aid of others—have done for us in the past.

What we must do, however, for the days ahead in the light of newly perceived conditions is to establish new and more realistic priorities in terms of the business of self-development. While pushing and participating in the absolutely worthwhile interracial program in the field of civil rights, the black people of America ought long ago to have been addressing themselves to the far more basic business of the development by black people of black people for the growth into self-sufficiency and self-respect of black people. This is the main and previously neglected business to which we must address ourselves. It is to this top priority concern of self-development that the issue of Black Power calls the black people of America today.

In the past, we've needed help; and we have received it. But we lacked even more the fundamental necessity of self-help, and self-initiative. It is by this alone we as a people may grow into that self-direction and self-sufficiency which is encumbent upon all who could claim the respect due to responsible and mature men. It is by black self-development that this nation may come most fully into its own. The absence of black self-development has taxed the resources of the nation and limited national destiny.

Now what, exactly, do me mean by self-development? We mean, for one thing, that we as black people must put behind us the "Hand me something" philosophy. Some of us will remember the hard years of the depression. In Philadelphia, we are told, they sang a song which said that:

"Jesus Christ will lead me and
F.D.R. will feed me."

And they asked, "What need have we, then, to fear?" Now such a philosophy, in part, may be said to be good for any time. But a part of it also is appropriate only on a limited and temporary basis. It is said that if you give a man a fish, you feed him for a day. But if you teach him to fish and then *let him fish in the stream,* you feed that man for a lifetime.

Black Power in terms of self-development means that we want to fish as all Americans should do together in the main stream of American life. It means that we must reject the assumption that long-term relief is a reasonable option for any man. This assumption must no longer be allowed. It is a minimum moral imperative for men to be thrust into and sustained in substantial jobs. At this point, we as black people must not equivocate. We must make it clear that long-term relief is weakening and damaging to all poor people, and especially so to us as a racial group. We must demand the abolition of its use in such a way. When people ask us about what substitute we would offer, we must tell them that this involves a second step, which we shall get to next. In principle, the welfare system presently is an effective curse upon the poor. Once this is clearly and unequivocably established, we may then address ourselves to the need to devise ways for human rehabilitation. This will call, understandably, for resourcefulness. Finding ways for bringing all America's human potential to its flower is a basic moral imperative for our nation and is a duty which must be met by all of us.

Black Power means black development into self-sufficiency for the good of Negroes and for the good of the whole nation. We want—as others must want—to replace the helping hand which now aids us with our own hand—to sustain ourselves and not be burdens on all others.

Black self-development means something more, as well. It means that we want to put into glorious use the latent resources that we have for devising new ways of bringing fulfillment to all of life. From our position of powerlessness we have learned that only through an immediate and equitable extension of power can the black and white poor of our land be transformed from crippling liabilities into tangible assets. Poverty will begin to be abated most effectively when the particular and precious insights of black people are used in devising anti-poverty efforts.

Black self-development also means that we as black people must take the initiative—using the brainpower and the other resources of all, under our own leadership—in building black unity, black pride and black self-confidence for the larger good of this whole nation. A strong, independent press oriented to the needs of black people will help us to achieve this.

Black people have much to give to America. But it is only as black people first have confidence, pride and self-respect that they can give to America the rich gifts which it needs and must demand of us.

SELF-RESPECT AND RESPECT BY OTHERS

Undoubtedly the most crucial part of black self-development is the building of black men's self-respect.

Of all Americans, the black people of this land are by far the most intensely loyal. No one has ever questioned this. We are the unique products of this our native land; and in every respect—for good *and* for ill—we have sought to emulate and to fulfill all that is American.

In this endeavor, we have even gone so far as to adopt the white American disdain for all that pertains to blackness. The sad fact is that in America black people have been taught that to be like other Americans they must come to hate themselves. And this we all too often do with tragic vengeance. Doubtless many Negroes decry Black Power because of a cultural perception of incongruity between "power" and "blackness." Negroes are culturally conditioned to see themselves as childlike, immature and powerless. But the Scriptures tell us that we must love God with all our hearts and our neighbors *as ourselves.* How can we love our neighbors when we do not love and respect ourselves?

An eminent young Negro psychiatrist, from whom we shall be hearing increasingly in the days ahead because of his aggressive professional advocacy of the philosophy of Black Power, reminds us of the therapeutic need for the development of black men's self-respect. He writes: "The Negro community's high rate of crimes of violence, illegitimacy and broken homes can be traced in part to the Negro's learned self-hatred as well as to his poverty." He believes that the kind of so-called integration which white people have offered to the black community "may have negative effects upon the Negro and may undermine his obvious need for strong positive group identification."

No man can instill pride and self-respect in another man. The same is true with ethnic groups. Every ethnic group, like every family, devises means of instilling group pride. Each idealizes its past and glorifies its ventures. So must the black people of America do.

Instead of hating ourselves—as any group which dwells on its weaknesses might do—we must accentuate the positive aspects of who and what we are. Every Negro in America must come to grow each day in self-esteem and self-respect. This must be encouraged at every hand for the good of ourselves and for the greater good of all.

Not long ago I looked a black man in the face. His complexion was darker than mine. His lips were thicker than mine. His nose was flatter and his hair had a tighter kink. I might add that he was a black man's man in that he stood up for black pride through black self-development and Black Power. And as I looked that black man in the face, I could only smile, for I realized that I was looking at one of the handsomest men on earth! We must have pride in ourselves.

When we look at black women who have dignity and a sense of pride in themselves, can there be any real doubt as to the superlative virtue of Black Power? A black man, who might have been any or all of us, recently said this: "When I was a child I was led to understand something of the nature of my heritage. I came to understand that from my relatively recent ancestral past the blood of black kings and princes flowed through my proud black veins. I knew also that the blood of proud Indian chieftains was mixed therewith. This to me was a source of undiluted pride. Then I came to know that in a more recent past the blood of white aristocracy, the very flower of white manhood, made its somewhat mixed contribution to the determinants of my life. This latter fact gave me, understandably, no greater sense of pride. But from my youth up," he concluded. "I have grown in the recognition that black men, and women and young people needed to appropriate the proud black heritage which is theirs, perhaps in a sense above all Americans, to have."

Negroes must, then, be proud of the variegated blackness which is theirs. When once we have come to have pride in what we are, and have been and must come to be, then—and only then—will others come to respect us for what we signify first and foremost to ourselves.

We hear all kinds of economic and political and psychological theories about the nature of racial prejudice. But the more I read and reflect upon them, the more I tend to believe that fundamentally they are straining at a relatively commonplace mechanism. When so-called racial prejudice is looked at in the context of Black Power as self-development, it may be explained in an elementary and far more creative way in terms of the dynamics of family life.

Look, for example, at the well-known story of the Prodigal Son. The brother in that classic story could not forgive an apparent blemish in his brother's life. Whether the defects we see in those close to us are imaginary or real, the family or in-group rejects with an irrational vengeance those who fail to measure up to the family's patterns or its agreed-upon purposes or goals.

In this light, the American black man's failure to stand securely by himself, however difficult the task, may provide sufficient explanation for his rejection by the American national family. In this sense, the black American may be perceived as a permanent and potentially significant part of the American household, with so-called racial

prejudice being the family's intensive reaction to the failure of one whom they wish to uphold the basic and continuing family tradition of self-development. To carry the parable further, we may have squandered a generation's treasure of time seeking after the elusive fruits of some degree of integration when we had not first developed sufficient pride in what we are to integrate as equals.

We need to have pride in ourselves. No one may give this to us. It is a matter of self-development.

THE REDEMPTION OF AMERICAN LIFE

Self-development, as I have said, may bring about the fulfillment of American life through the nation's answer to the Negro's incessant pleas.

The Negro people of America want far more desperately than any other Americans for this nation to come into its own. This means that the black of this land are, like the Jews of old, a people peculiarly elected to transmit and to perform no less than a sacred trust.

It is for us as black people to take the initiative in calling this nation as a whole to growth into maturity. The past and present apparent immaturity of the Negro is part and parcel of a wholesale national immaturity. Immaturity has begotten immaturity. Neither a nation nor a family may become what it should be without an equitable extension of relationships of power. Fail to encourage growth into self-sufficiency, and the family suffers as a whole. So it is with us.

We who are black people want this nation to grow up into the fulness of mature wisdom and power and might. This can come to the nation as a whole only as it comes to its each and every part.

It is for us who are black people to take the initiative in saving the nation of which we are an inextricable part. We must take the initiative to save the nation from the path of economic self-destruction, as it spirals its staggering costs for a kind of welfare system which we must reject in favor of far less costly and more fulfillment-laden efforts at genuine rehabilitation.

Black Power speaks—by its insistence upon equitable power relationships—to the precarious and perilous plight of those who are too powerful and to the needs of all in America of every color and every condition who are destined to become less than they should be by a debilitating absence of power.

In some sense of the word, all channels for the operation of cosmic purposes are woefully unworthy of their task. This is said in this instance of a young man whom we shall not name but who might be described as rash and wonderful, irratic [sic] and magnificent, as perhaps demagogue and perhaps also prophet and who in his own seemingly immature and yet undoubtedly brilliant way has raised for our generation an issue which may hold the key to the resolution of so many problems in almost every area of our corporate and personal life. If the devil himself had raised in these recent months the issue of power, it could hardly be less grace-laden for us and for our world.

Not long ago I sat with a group of men who to me were as great as they were serious and perplexed. They were alarmed at the recent turn of events, in which people long working together, apparently in unity for the good of all in America, had turned their backs or retreated in the area of civil rights. Some of these men spoke in terms of gloom and of dismay. We all listened attentively, and then one clergyman present suggested that there was at least one person in the room who did not accept the spirit of the conversation. He was asked the reason why. His answer came in a way that should give our hearts cause for rejoicing.

He said that for years he had hoped that somehow and in some way the issues in the area of civil rights and of race relations and of every form of inequity for any and all people could be made far more clear than they had been. People with so many mixed and different motives were working together for apparently good and noble purposes in an effectively neutralizing way. Yet there were no sharp and plain criteria for finding out just exactly where the battle lines could be clearly drawn. Then came the issue of power, and for him light came suddenly out of darkness. Those, he said, who worked for the immediate and equitable extension of power were on the side of a God who sought to be revealed in the here and now as a God of power, of majesty and of might. Those who would withhold or make light of the need for the equitable extension of power were, whatever their verbal protestations, fundamentally on the other side.

He went on to explain that whether the backlash grew or diminished, from the day of that revelation, it mattered very little. For to him, nothing short of the long-awaited day of the Lord had come, where the sheep might be separated from the goats. If those who are for more equitable power, he said, were only few in number, as they might appear at this hour to be, then with the battle lines clearly and unmistakably drawn we might—with the prophet Elisha—at last look up into the heavens and recognize as we see the host of heaven and the chariots of fire that "They that are with us are more than they who are against us."

We move on to one more brief story before we close. Joseph, in the classic biblical story, was sold by his brothers into Egyptian slavery. Several things happened which are suggestive of the black people's role in terms of both self-development and the moral and social development of this nation. Like Joseph, we as black people have been rejected and enslaved in various ways. In our rejected state, like Joseph we have developed resources which might well have a saving value for those who have rejected us. We have been pushed out to the margins of American life; and from our peculiar vantage point of a kind of dramatic distance we can see more clearly than other Americans what life is like down at the center of the stage. By many signs which need not be named, this nation, like Joseph's brethren who came to him in Egypt seeking succor, may be crying out at this time for the saving gifts which it is the destiny of black men alone at this crucial hour to give.

Doubtless the import of all what we have been saying here has begun in a way to be made plain. The task of self-development is our burden and ours alone as the central task, as the main business which is before us. This we must accept and aggressively and forthrightly implement not only for our needed self-respect but also for the respect and acceptance of others, which must inevitably follow upon our growth into self-esteem and into self-respect.

This nation needs us, as does our world. We must take our hats from our hands, and we must stand on our feet. The old, if we but open our eyes to see it, has passed away. The new day is at hand. We must put away childish things, and assume the proud demeanor of men.

three

POOR: "THE POOR YE SHALL HAVE WITH THEE ALWAYS"

The Other America

MICHAEL HARRINGTON

There are perennial reasons that make the other America an invisible land.

Poverty is often off the beaten track. It always has been. The ordinary tourist never left the main highway, and today he rides interstate turnpikes. He does not go into the valleys of Pennsylvania where the towns look like movie sets of Wales in the thirties. He does not see the company houses in rows, the rutted roads (the poor always have bad roads whether they live in the city, in towns, or on farms), and everything is black and dirty. And even if he were to pass through such a place by accident, the tourist would not meet the unemployed men in the bar or the women coming home from a runaway sweatshop.

Then, too, beauty and myths are perennial masks of poverty. The traveler comes to the Appalachians in the lovely season. He sees the hills, the streams, the foliage—but not the poor. Or perhaps he looks at a run-down mountain house and, remembering Rousseau rather than seeing with his eyes, decides that "those people" are truly fortunate to be living the way they are and that they are lucky to be exempt from the strains and tensions of the middle class. The only problem is that "those people," the quaint inhabitants of those hills, are undereducated, underprivileged, lack medical care, and are in the process of being forced from the kind into a life in the cities, where they are misfits.

These are normal and obvious causes of the invisibility of the poor. They operated a generation ago; they will be functioning a generation hence. It is more important to understand that the very development of American society is creating a new kind of blindness about poverty. The poor are increasingly slipping out of the very experience and consciousness of the nation.

If the middle class never did like

Reprinted with permission of The Macmillan Company from The Other America: Poverty in the United States, pp. 11–14, 21–24. Copyright 1962 by Michael Harrington.

ugliness and poverty, it was at least aware of them. "Across the tracks" was not a very long way to go. There were forays into the slums at Christmas time; there were charitable organizations that brought contact with the poor. Occasionally, almost everyone passed through the Negro ghetto or the blocks of tenements, if only to get downtown to work or to entertainment.

Now the American city has been transformed. The poor still inhabit the miserable housing in the central area, but they are increasingly isolated from contact with, or sight of, anybody else. Middle-class women coming in from Suburbia on a rare trip may catch the merest glimpse of the other America on the way to an evening at the theater, but their children are segregated in suburban schools. The business or professional man may drive along the fringes of slums in a car or bus, but it is not an important experience to him. The failures, the unskilled, the disabled, the aged, and the minorities are right there, across the tracks, where they have always been. But hardly anyone else is.

In short, the very development of the American city has removed poverty from the living, emotional experience of millions upon millions of middle-class Americans. Living out in the suburbs, it is easy to assume that ours is, indeed, an affluent society.

This new segregation of poverty is compounded by a well-meaning ignorance. A good many concerned and sympathetic Americans are aware that there is much discussion of urban renewal. Suddenly, driving through the city, they notice that a familiar slum has been torn down and that there are towering, modern buildings where once there had been tenements or hovels. There is a warm feeling of satisfaction, of pride in the way things are working out: the poor, it is obvious, are being taken care of.

The irony in this (as the chapter on housing will document) is that the truth is nearly the exact opposite to the impression. The total impact of the various housing programs in postwar America has been to squeeze more and more people into existing slums. More often than not, the modern apartment in a towering building rents at $40 a room or more. For, during the past decade and a half, there has been more subsidization of middle- and upper-income housing than there has been of housing for the poor.

Clothes make the poor invisible too: America has the best-dressed poverty the world has ever known. For a variety of reasons, the benefits of mass production have been spread much more evenly in this area than in many others. It is much easier in the United States to be decently dressed than it is to be decently housed, fed, or doctored. Even people with terribly depressed incomes can look prosperous.

This is an extremely important factor in defining our emotional and existential ignorance of poverty. In Detroit the existence of social classes became much more difficult to discern the day the companies put lockers in the plants. From that moment on, one did not see men in work clothes on the way to the factory, but citizens in slacks and white shirts. This process has been magnified with the poor throughout the country. There are tens of thousands of Americans in the big cities who are wearing shoes, perhaps even a stylishly cut suit or dress, and yet are hungry. It is not a matter of planning, though it almost seems as if the affluent society had given out costumes to the poor so that they would not offend the rest of society with the sight of rags.

Then, many of the poor are the wrong age to be seen. A good number of them (over 8,000,000) are sixty-five years of age or better; an even larger number are under eighteen. The aged members of the other America are often sick, and they cannot move. Another group of them live out their lives in loneliness and frustration: they sit in rented rooms, or else they stay close to a house in a neighborhood that has completely changed from the old days. Indeed, one of the worst aspects of poverty among the aged is that these people are out of sight and out of mind, and alone.

The young are somewhat more visible, yet they too stay close to their neighborhoods. Sometimes they advertise their poverty through a lurid tabloid story about a gang killing. But generally they do not disturb the quiet streets of the middle class.

And finally, the poor are politically invisible. It is one of the cruelest ironies of social life in advanced countries that the dispossessed at the bottom of society are unable to speak for themselves. The people of the other America do not, by far and large, belong to unions, to fraternal organizations, or to political parties. They are without lobbies of their own; they put forward no legislative program. As a group, they are atomized. They have no face; they have no voice.

Thus, there is not even a cynical political motive for caring about the poor, as in the old days. Because the slums are no longer centers of powerful political organizations, the politicians need not really care about their inhabitants. The slums are no longer visible to the middle class, so much of the

idealistic urge to fight for those who need help is gone. Only the social agencies have a really direct involvement with the other America, and they are without any great political power.

To the extent that the poor have a spokesman in American life, that role is played by the labor movement. The unions have their own particular idealism, an ideology of concern. More than that, they realize that the existence of a reservoir of cheap, unorganized labor is a menace to wages and working conditions throughout the entire economy. Thus, many union legislative proposals—to extend the coverage of minimum wage and social security, to organize migrant farm laborers—articulate the needs of the poor.

That the poor are invisible is one of the most important things about them. They are not simply neglected and forgotten as in the old rhetoric of reform; what is much worse, they are not seen.

One might take a remark from George Eliot's *Felix Holt* as a basic statement of what this book is about:

> . . . there is no private life which has not been determined by a wider public life, from the time when the primeval milkmaid had to wander with the wanderings of her clan, because the cow she milked was one of a herd which had made the pasture bare. Even in the conservatory existence where the fair Camellia is sighed for by the noble young Pineapple, neither of them needing to care about the frost or rain outside, there is a nether apparatus of hot-water pipes liable to cool down on a strike of the gardeners or a scarcity of coal.
>
> And the lives we are about to look back upon do not belong to those conservatory species; they are rooted in the common earth, having

to endure all the ordinary chances of past and present weather.

Forty to 50,000,000 people are becoming increasingly invisible. That is a shocking fact. But there is a second basic irony of poverty that is equally important: if one is to make the mistake of being born poor, he should choose a time when the majority of the people are miserable too.

J. K. Galbraith develops this idea in *The Affluent Society,* and in doing so defines the "newness" of the kind of poverty in contemporary America. The old poverty, Galbraith notes, was general. It was the condition of life of an entire society, or at least of that huge majority who were without special skills or the luck of birth. When the entire economy advanced, a good many of these people gained higher standards of living. Unlike the poor today, the majority poor of a generation ago were an immediate (if cynical) concern of political leaders. The old slums of the immigrants had the votes; they provided the basis for labor organizations; their very numbers could be a powerful force in political conflict. At the same time the new technology required higher skills, more education, and stimulated an upward movement for millions.

Perhaps the most dramatic case of the power of the majority poor took place in the 1930's. The Congress of Industrial Organizations literally organized millions in a matter of years. A labor movement that had been declining and confined to a thin stratum of the highly skilled suddenly embraced masses of men and women in basic industry. At the same time this acted as a pressure upon the Government, and the New Deal codified some of the social gains in laws like the Wagner Act. The result was not a basic transformation of the American system, but it did transform the lives of an entire section of the population.

In the thirties one of the reasons for these advances was that misery was general. There was no need then to write books about unemployment and poverty. That was the decisive social experience of the entire society, and the apple sellers even invaded Wall Street. There was political sympathy from middle-class reformers; there were an élan and spirit that grew out of a deep crisis.

Some of those who advanced in the thirties did so because they had unique and individual personal talents. But for the great mass, it was a question of being at the right point in the economy at the right time in history, and utilizing that position for common struggle. Some of those who failed did so because they did not have the will to take advantage of new opportunities. But for the most part the poor who were left behind had been at the wrong place in the economy at the wrong moment in history. . . .

Today the situation is quite different. The good jobs require much more academic preparation, much more skill from the very outset. Those who lack a high-school education tend to be condemned to the economic underworld— to low-paying service industries, to backward factories, to sweeping and janitorial duties. If the fathers and mothers of the contemporary poor were penalized a generation ago for their lack of schooling, their children will suffer all the more. The very rise in productivity that created more money and better working conditions for the rest of the society can be a menace to the poor.

But then this technological revolution might have an even more disastrous consequence: it could increase the ranks of the poor as well as intensify the disabilities of poverty. At this point it is too early to make any final judgment, yet there are obvious danger signals. There are millions of Americans who live just the other side of poverty. When a recession comes, they are pushed onto the relief rolls. (Welfare payments in New York respond almost immediately to any economic decline.) If automation continues to inflict more and more penalties on the unskilled and the semiskilled, it could have the impact of permanently increasing the population of the other America.

Even more explosive is the possibility that people who participated in the gains of the thirties and the forties will be pulled back down into poverty. Today the mass-production industries where unionization made such a difference are contracting. Jobs are being destroyed. In the process, workers who had achieved a certain level of wages, who had won working conditions in the shop, are suddenly confronted with impoverishment. This is particularly true for anyone over forty years of age and for members of minority groups. Once their job is abolished, their chances of ever getting similar work are very slim.

It is too early to say whether or not this phenomenon is temporary, or whether it represents a massive retrogression that will swell the numbers of the poor. To a large extent, the answer to this question will be determined by the political response of the United States in the sixties. If serious and massive action is not undertaken, it may be necessary for statisticians to add some old-fashioned, pre-welfare-state poverty to the misery of the other America.

Poverty in the 1960's is invisible and it is new, and both these factors make it more tenacious. It is more isolated and politically powerless than ever before. It is laced with ironies, not the least of which is that many of the poor view progress upside-down, as a menace and a threat to their lives. And if the nation does not measure up to the challenge of automation, poverty in the 1960's might be on the increase.

II

There are mighty historical and economic forces that keep the poor down; and there are human beings who help out in this grim business, many of them unwittingly. There are sociological and political reasons why poverty is not seen; and there are misconceptions and prejudices that literally blind the eyes. The latter must be understood if anyone is to make the necessary act of intellect and will so that the poor can be noticed.

Here is the most familiar version of social blindness: "The poor are that way because they are afraid of work. And anyway they all have big cars. If they were like me (or my father or my grandfather), they could pay their own way. But they prefer to live on the dole and cheat the taxpayers."

This theory, usually thought of as a virtuous and moral statement, is one of the means of making it impossible for the poor ever to pay their way. There are, one must assume, citizens of the other America who choose impoverishment out of fear of work (though, writing it down, I really do not believe it). But the real explanation of why the poor are where they are is that they made the mistake of being born to the wrong parents, in the wrong section of the country, in the wrong industry, or in the wrong racial or ethnic group. Once that mistake has been made, they could have been paragons of will and morality, but most of them would never even have had a chance to get out of the other America.

There are two important ways of saying this: The poor are caught in a vicious circle; or, The poor live in a culture of poverty.

In a sense, one might define the contemporary poor in the United States as those who, for reasons beyond their control, cannot help themselves. All the most decisive factors making for opportunity and advance are against them. They are born going downward, and most of them stay down. They are victims whose lives are endlessly blown round and round the other America.

Here is one of the most familiar forms of the vicious circle of poverty. The poor get sick more than anyone else in the society. That is because they live in slums, jammed together under unhygienic conditions; they have inadequate diets, and cannot get decent medical care. When they become sick, they are sick longer than any other group in the society. Because they are sick more often and longer than anyone else, they lose wages and work, and find it difficult to hold a steady job. And because of this, they cannot pay for good housing, for a nutritious diet, for doctors. At any given point in the circle, particularly when there is a major illness, their prospect is to move to an even lower level and to begin the cycle, round and round, toward even more suffering.

This is only one example of the vicious circle. Each group in the other America has its own particular version of the experience, and these will be detailed throughout this book. But the pattern, whatever its variations, is basic to the other America.

The individual cannot usually break out of this vicious circle. Neither can the group, for it lacks the social energy and political strength to turn its misery into a cause. Only the larger society, with its help and resources, can really make it possible for these people to help themselves. Yet those who could make the difference too often refuse to act because of their ignorant, smug moralisms. They view the effects of poverty—above all, the warping of the will and spirit that is a consequence of being poor—as choices. Understanding the vicious circle is an important step in breaking down this prejudice.

There is an even richer way of describing this same, general idea: Poverty in the United States is a culture, an institution, a way of life.

There is a famous anecdote about Ernest Hemingway and F. Scott Fitzgerald. Fitzgerald is reported to have remarked to Hemingway, "The rich are different." And Hemingway replied, "Yes, they have money." Fitzgerald had much the better of the exchange. He understood that being rich was not a simple fact, like a large bank account, but a way of looking at reality, a series of attitudes, a special type of life. If this is true of the rich, it is ten times truer of the poor. Everything about them, from the condition of their teeth to the way in which they love, is suffused and permeated by the fact of their poverty. And this is sometimes a hard idea for a Hemingway-like middle-class America to comprehend.

The family structure of the poor,

for instance, is different from that of the rest of the society. There are more homes without a father, there is less marriage, more early pregnancy and, if Kinsey's statistical findings can be used, markedly different attitudes toward sex. As a result of this, to take but one consequence of the fact, hundreds of thousands, and perhaps millions, of children in the other America never know stability and "normal" affection.

Or perhaps the policeman is an even better example. For the middle class, the police protect property, give directions, and help old ladies. For the urban poor, the police are those who arrest you. In almost any slum there is a vast conspiracy against the forces of law and order. If someone approaches asking for a person, no one there will have heard of him, even if he lives next door. The outsider is "cop," bill collector, investigator (and, in the Negro ghetto, most dramatically, he is "the Man").

While writing this book, I was arrested for participation in a civil-rights demonstration. A brief experience of a night in a cell made an abstraction personal and immediate: the city jail is one of the basic institutions of the other America. Almost everyone whom I encountered in the "tank" was poor: skid-row whites, Negroes, Puerto Ricans. Their poverty was an incitement to arrest in the first place. (A policeman will be much more careful with a well-dressed, obviously educated man who might have political connections than he will with someone who is poor.) They did not have money for bail or for lawyers. And, perhaps most important, they waited their arraignment with stolidity, in a mood of passive acceptance. They expected the worst, and they probably got it.

There is, in short, a language of the poor, a psychology of the poor, a world view of the poor. To be impoverished is to be an internal alien, to grow up in a culture that is radically different from the one that dominates the society. The poor can be described statistically; they can be analyzed as a group. But they need a novelist as well as a sociologist if we are to see them. They need an American Dickens to record the smell and texture and quality of their lives. The cycles and trends, the massive forces, must be seen as affecting persons who talk and think differently.

I am not that novelist. Yet in this book I have attempted to describe the faces behind the statistics, to tell a little of the "thickness" of personal life in the other America. Of necessity, I have begun with large groups: the dispossessed workers, the minorities, the farm poor, and the aged. Them, there are three cases of less massive types of poverty, including the only single humorous component in the other America. And finally, there are the slums, and the psychology of the poor.

Throughout, I work on an assumption that cannot be proved by Government figures or even documented by impressions of the other America. It is an ethical proposition, and it can be simply stated: In a nation with a technology that could provide every citizen with a decent life, it is an outrage and a scandal that there should be such social misery. Only if one begins with this assumption is it possible to pierce through the invisibility of 40,000,000 to 50,000,000 human beings and to see the other America. We must perceive passionately, if this blindness is to be lifted from us. A fact can be rationalized and explained away; an indignity cannot.

What shall we tell the American poor, once we have seen them? Shall we say to them that they are better off than the Indian poor, the Italian poor, the Russian poor? That is one answer, but it is heartless. I should put it another way. I want to tell every well-fed and optimistic American that it is intolerable that so many millions should be maimed in body and in spirit when it is not necessary that they should be. My standard of comparison is not how much worse things used to be. It is how much better they could be if only we were stirred.

four

WOMAN: "WHAT DOES SHE WANT? DEAR GOD, WHAT DOES SHE WANT?"

The New Feminism

LUCY KOMISAR

A dozen women are variously seated in straight-backed chairs, settled on a couch, or sprawled on the floor of a comfortable apartment on Manhattan's West Side. They range in

Reprinted from Saturday Review (February 21, 1970), 27–30, 55. Copyright 1970 by Saturday Review, Inc. Reprinted by permission of the publisher.

age from twenty-five to thirty-five, and include a magazine researcher, a lawyer, a housewife, an architect, a teacher, a secretary, and a graduate student in sociology.

They are white, middle-class, attractive. All but one have college degrees; several are married; a few are active in social causes. At first, they are hesitant. They don't really know what to talk about, and so they begin with why they came.

"I wanted to explore my feelings as a woman and find out what others think about the things that bother me." Slowly, they open up, trust growing. "I always felt so negative about being a woman; now I'm beginning to feel good about it."

They become more personal and revealing. "My mother never asked me what I was going to be when I grew up." "I never used to like to talk to girls. I always thought women were inferior—I never *liked* women." "I've been a secretary for three years; after that, you begin to think that's all you're good for." "I felt so trapped when my baby was born. I wanted to leave my husband and the child."

Repeated a hundred times in as many different rooms, these are the voices of women's liberation, a movement that encompasses high school students and grandmothers, and that is destined to eclipse the black civil rights struggle in the force of its resentment and the consequence of its demands.

Some of us have become feminists out of anger and frustration over job discrimination. When we left college, male students got aptitude tests, we got typing tests. In spite of federal law, most women still are trapped in low-paying, dead-end jobs and commonly earn less than men for the same work—sometimes on the theory that we are only "helping out," though 42 per cent of us support ourselves or families.

Others have discovered that the humanistic precepts of the radical movement do not always apply to women. At a peace rally in Washington last year, feminists were hooted and jeered off the speakers' platform, and white women working in civil rights or anti-poverty programs are expected to defer to the black male ego. Many of us got out to salvage our own buffeted egos. However, most of the new feminists express only a general malaise they were never able to identify. . . .

If women need more evidence, history books stand ready to assure us that we have seldom existed except as shadows of men. We have rarely been leaders of nations or industry or the great contributors to art and science, yet very few sociologists, political leaders, historians, and moral critics have ever stopped to ask why. Now, all around the country, women are meeting in apartments and conference rooms and coffee shops to search out the answers.

The sessions begin with accounts of personal problems and incidents. For years, we women have believed that our anger and frustration and unhappiness were "our problems." Suddenly, we discover that we are telling *the same story!* Our complaints are not only common, they are practically universal.

It is an exhilarating experience. Women's doubts begin to disappear and are replaced by new strength and self-respect. We stop focusing on men, and begin to identify with other women and to analyze the roots of our oppression. The conclusions that are drawn challenge the legitimacy of the sex role system upon which our civilization is based.

At the center of the feminist critique is the recognition that women have been forced to accept an inferior role in society, and that we have come to believe in our own inferiority. Women are taught to be passive, dependent, submissive, not to pursue careers but to be taken care of and protected. Even those who seek outside work lack confidence and self-esteem. Most of us are forced into menial and unsatisfying jobs: More than three-quarters of us are clerks, sales personnel, or factory and service workers, and a fifth of the women with B.A. degrees are secretaries.

Self-hatred is endemic. Women—especially those who have "made it"—identify with men and mirror their contempt for women. The approval of women does not mean very much. We don't want to work for women or vote for them. We laugh, although with vague uneasiness, at jokes about women drivers, mothers-in-law, and dumb blondes.

We depend on our relationships with men for our very identities. Our husbands win us social status and determine how we will be regarded by the world. Failure for a woman is not being selected by a man.

We are trained in the interests of men to defer to them and serve them and entertain them. If we are educated and gracious, it is so we can please men and educate their children. That is the thread that runs through the life of the geisha, the party girl, the business executive's wife, and the First Lady of the United States.

Men define women, and until now most of us have accepted their definition without question. If we challenge men in the world outside the home, we are all too frequently derided as "aggressive" and "unfeminine"—by women as readily as by men.

A woman is expected to subordinate her job to the interests of her husband's work. She'll move to another city so he can take a promotion—but it rarely works the other way around.

Men don't take women's work very seriously, and, as a result, neither do most women. We spend a lot of time worrying about men, while they devote most of theirs to worrying about their careers.

We are taught that getting and keeping a man is a woman's most important job; marriage, therefore, becomes our most important achievement. One suburban housewife says her father started giving her bridal pictures cut from newspapers when she was six. "He said that was what I would be when I grew up."

Most femininsts do not object to marriage per se, but to the corollary that it is creative and fulfilling for an adult human being to spend her life doing housework, caring for children, and using her husband as a vicarious link to the outside world.

Most people would prefer just about any kind of work to that of a domestic servant; yet the mindless, endless, repetitive drudgery of housekeeping is the central occupation of more than fifty million women. People who would oppose institutions that portion out menial work on the basis of race see nothing wrong in a system that does the same thing on the basis of sex. (Should black and white roommates automatically assume the Negro best suited for housekeeping chores?) Even when they work at full-time jobs, wives must come home to "their" dusting and "their" laundry.

Some insist that housework is not much worse than the meaningless jobs most people have today, but there is a difference. Housewives are not paid for their work, and money is the mark of value in this society. It is also the key to independence and to the feeling of self-reliance that marks a free human being.

The justification for being a housewife is having children, and the justification for children is—well, a woman has a uterus, what else would it be for? Perhaps not all feminists agree that the uterus is a vestigial organ, but we are adamant and passionate in our denial of the old canard that biology is destiny.

Men have never been bound by their animal natures. They think and dream and create—and fly, clearly something nature had not intended, or it would have given men wings. However, we women are told that our chief function is to reproduce the species, prepare food, and sweep out the cave —er, house. . . .

The species must reproduce, but this need not be the sole purpose of a woman's life. Men want children, too, yet no one expects them to choose between families and work. Children are in no way a substitute for personal development and creativity. If a talented man is forced into a senseless, menial job, it is deplored as a waste and a personal misfortune; yet, a woman's special skills, education, and interests are all too often deemed incidental and irrelevant, simply a focus for hobbies or volunteer work.

Women who say that raising a family is a fulfilling experience are rather like the peasant who never leaves his village. They have never had the opportunity to do anything else.

As a result, women are forced to live through their children and husbands, and they feel cheated and resentful when they realize that is not enough. When a woman says she gave her children everything, she is telling the truth—and that is the tragedy. Often when she reaches her late thirties, her children have grown up, gone to work or college, and left her in a bleak and premature old age. Middle-aged women who feel empty and useless are the mainstay of America's psychiatrists— who generally respond by telling them to "accept their role."

The freedom to choose whether or not to have children has always been illusory. A wife who is deliberately "barren"—a word that reinforces the worn-out metaphor of woman as Mother Earth—is considered neurotic or unnatural. Not only is motherhood not central to a woman's life, it may not be necessary or desirable. For the first time, some of us are admitting openly and without guilt that we do not want children. And the population crisis is making it even clearer that as a symbol for Americans motherhood ought to defer to apple pie.

The other half of the reproduction question is sex. The sexual revolution didn't liberate women at all; it only created a bear market for men. One of the most talked-about tracts in the movement is a pamphlet by Ann Koedt called "The Myth of the Vaginal Orgasm," which says most women don't have orgasms because most men won't accept the fact that the female orgasm is clitoral.

We are so used to putting men's needs first that we don't know how to ask for what we want, or else we share the common ignorance about our own physiology and think there is something wrong with us when we don't have orgasms "the right way." Freudian analysts contribute to the problem. The realization that past guilt and frustration have been unnecessary is not the least of the sentiments that draws women to women's liberation.

Feminists also protest the general male proclivity to regard us as decorative, amusing sex objects even in the world outside bed. We resent the sexual sell in advertising, the catcalls we get on the street, girlie magazines and pornography, bars that refuse to serve unescorted women on the assumption they are prostitutes, the not very subtle brainwashing by cosmetic companies, and the attitude of men who praise our knees in miniskirts, but refuse to act as if we had brains.

Even the supposedly humanistic worlds of rock music and radical politics are not very different. Young girls who join "the scene" or "the movement" are labeled "groupies" and are sexually exploited; the flashy pornosheets such as *Screw* and *Kiss* are published by the self-appointed advocates of the new "free," anti-Establishment life-style. *"Plus ça change. . . ."*

We are angry about the powers men wield over us. The physical power —women who study karate do so as a defense against muggers, not lovers. And the social power—we resent the fact that men take the initiative with women, that women cannot ask for dates but must sit home waiting for the phone to ring.

That social conditioning began in childhood when fathers went out to work and mothers stayed home, images perpetuated in schoolbooks and games and on television. If we were bright students, we were told, "You're smart —for a girl," and then warned not to appear *too* smart in front of boys—"Or you won't have dates."

Those of us who persisted in reaching for a career were encouraged to be teachers or nurses so we would have "something to fall back on." My mother told me: "You're so bright, it's a pity you're not a boy. You could become president of a bank—or anything you wanted."

Ironically, and to our dismay, we discovered that playing the assigned role is precisely what elicits masculine contempt for our inferiority and narrow interests. *Tooth and Nail,* a newsletter published by women's liberation groups in the San Francisco area, acidly points out a few of the contradictions: "A smart woman never shows her brains; she allows the man to think himself clever. . . . Women's talk is all chatter; they don't understand things men are interested in."

Or: "Don't worry your pretty little head about such matters. . . . A woman's brain is between her legs. . . . Women like to be protected and treated like little girls. . . . Women can't make decisions."

The feminist answer is to throw out the whole simplistic division of human characteristics into masculine and feminine, and to insist that there are no real differences between men and women other than those enforced by culture.

Men say women are not inferior, we are just different; yet somehow they have appropriated most of the qualities that society admires and have left us with the same distinctive features that were attributed to black people before the civil rights revolution.

Men, for example, are said to be strong, assertive, courageous, logical, constructive, creative, and independent. Women are weak, passive, irrational, overemotional, empty-headed, and lacking in strong superegos. (Thank Freud for the last.) Both blacks and women are contented, have their place, and know how to use wiles—flattery, and wide-eyed, open-mouthed ignorance—to get around "the man." It is obviously natural that men should be dominant and women submissive. Shuffle, baby, shuffle.

Our "sexist" system has hurt men as well as women, forcing them into molds that deny the value of sensitivity, tenderness, and sentiment. Men who are not aggressive worry about their virility just as strong women are frightened by talk about their being castrating females. The elimination of rigid sex-role definitions would liberate everyone. And that is the goal of the women's liberation movement.

Women's liberation groups, which have sprung up everywhere across the country, are taking names like Radical Women or the Women's Liberation Front or the Feminists. Most start as groups of ten or twelve; many, when they get too large for discussion, split in a form of mitosis. Sometimes they are tied to central organizations set up for action, or they maintain communications with each other or cosponsor newsletters with similar groups in their area.

Some are concerned with efforts to abolish abortion laws, a few have set up cooperative day-care centers, others challenge the stereotypes of woman's image, and many are organized for "consciousness-raising"—a kind of group therapy or encounter session that starts with the premise that there is something wrong with the system, not the women in the group.

The amorphousness and lack of central communication in the movement make it virtually impossible to catalogue the established groups, let alone the new ones that regularly appear; many of the "leaders" who have been quoted in newspapers or interviewed

on television have been anointed only by the press. . . .

Today, Betty Friedan says, the movement must gain political power by mobilizing the 51 per cent of the electorate who are women, as well as seeking elected offices for themselves. "We have to break down the actual barriers that prevent women from being full people in society, and not only end explicit discrimination but build new institutions. Most women will continue to bear children, and unless we create child-care centers on a mass basis, it's all talk."

Women are beginning to read a good deal about their own place in history, about the determined struggles of the suffragettes, the isolation of Virginia Woolf, and the heroism of Rosa Luxemburg. The Congress to Unite Women, which drew some 500 participants from cities in the Northeast, called for women's studies in high schools and colleges. . . .

Free child care is likely to become the most significant demand made by the movement, and one calculated to draw the support of millions of women who may not be interested in other feminist issues. About four million working mothers have children under six years of age, and only 2 per cent of these are in day-care centers.

Even Establishment institutions appear to reflect the new attitudes. Princeton, Williams, and Yale have begun to admit women students, though on an unequal quota basis—and not to the hallowed pine-paneled halls of their alumni clubhouses.

Nevertheless, most people have only a vague idea of the significance of the new movement. News commentators on year-end analysis shows ignored the question or sloughed it off uncomfortably. One said the whole idea frightened him.

Yet, the women's movement promises to affect radically the life of virtually everyone in America. Only a small part of the population suffers because it is black, and most people have little contact with minorities. Women are 51 per cent of the population, and chances are that every adult American either is one, is married to one, or has close social or business relations with many.

The feminist revolution will overturn the basic premises upon which these relations are built—stereotyped notions about the family and the roles of men and women, fallacies concerning masculinity and femininity, and the economic division of labor into paid work and homemaking.

If the 1960s belonged to the blacks, the next ten years are ours.

five

INDIANS: THE VANQUISHED AMERICANS?

The Indian and His Keepers: Inside a Closed Room

EDGAR S. CAHN, Editor

The Indian is never alone. The life he leads is not his to control. That is not permitted. Every aspect of his being is affected and defined by his relationship to the Federal Government—and

Reprinted by permission of The World Publishing Company from Our Brother's Keeper: The Indian in White America edited by Edgar S. Cahn. A New Communities Press book. Copyright © 1969 by New Community Press.

primarily to one agency of the Federal Government: the Bureau of Indian Affairs.

From birth to death his home, his land, his reservation, his schools, his jobs, the stores where he shops, the tribal council that governs him, the opportunities available to him, the way in which he spends his money, disposes of his property, and even the way in which he provides for his heirs after death—are all determined by the Bureau of Indian Affairs acting as the agent of the United States Government.

The Bureau of Indian Affairs came into being symbolically and functionally as a division of the War Department in 1834. The Bureau defined Indians as sovereign nations with whom one entered into peace treaties and enforced promises to cease hostilities.

In time, treaties came to be unnecessary. The Indian could simply be regulated and ruled by act of Congress as a subject people. In 1849 the Bureau of Indian Affairs was transferred from the War Department to the Department of the Interior, where it remains to this day. Since then, the Indian has been defined in terms of the land areas reserved for a conquered people. The Bureau's relationship to the Indian became defined in terms of the administration of Indian land, the discharge of treaty obligations respecting that land, and the implementation of those duties owed a conquered and subject people. The Bureau became the army of occupation exercising all powers necessary to govern the conquered Indian territories. Certain of those powers remain to this day. Laws on the books give the Federal Government and the Bureau authority to abrogate treaties with any tribe with whom the United States is at war; prevent the introduction of all goods into Indian country, in the public interest; prohibit the issuance of food rations to the head of any Indian family with children between the ages of eight and 21 who do not attend school; and to authorize the use of vacant army posts and barracks for Indian schools.

And then in 1924, came a new definition: Indians were granted citizenship. The Bureau's responsibilities were broadened to include both the discarge of previous treaty obligations, and the administration of programs created by Congress to give the "new citizen" proper training.

The granting of citizenship to Indians expanded, rather than limited, the BIA's control. New resources were put at the Bureau's disposal, and new programs guaranteed further extension of the Bureau's reach into every aspect of the Indians' individual and communal lives. The Bureau must then be comprehended as a system permeating every dimension of Indian life and every element of Indian activity. More than just the sum of its parts or an aggregate of responsibilities, the relationships between the Indians and the Bureau of Indian Affairs together comprise a total and separate world.

As trustee, governor and benefactor of the Indian, the Bureau of Indian Affairs is a pervasive presence in the Indian world. The Indian's life can be measured in encounters with his Keepers as they make their appointed rounds. The BIA domain touches most states and covers more than 50 million acres which belong to the Indians. The BIA effectively governs the 400,000 Indians on the reservations, and heavily influences the lives of 200,000 living elsewhere. At the huge and fort-like Pine Ridge, South Dakota reservation, an observer likened the Bureau's presence to the British occupation of equatorial Africa.

"The Bureau of Indian Affairs is *the* economic and political force. . . . Bureau personnel attend most public meetings and usually call them to get the Sioux to agree to some program or other, *and* direct them as well. The school teachers are federal employees in the Bureau. The local Indian who drives the school bus is a Bureau employee. The social worker who calls at an Indian home is part of the same federal bureaucracy. Tribal projects are supervised by Bureau officials. . . .

"After living on the Pine Ridge Reservation for a few months, one cannot help falling into the habit of looking back over one's shoulder now and then," the observer concluded.[1]

The Bureau, unique among federal agencies, is the federal, state and local government of the Indians, and supplants or dominates the private sector as well. It is realtor, banker, teacher, social worker; it runs the employment service, vocational and job training program, contract office, chamber of commerce, highway authority, housing agency, police department, conservation service, water works, power company, telephone company, planning office; it is land developer, patron of the arts, ambassador from and to the outside world, and also guardian, protector and spokesman. Based in Washington, D.C., the Bureau's 16,000 employees are located in outposts extending like tentacles westward from the Potomac.

The BIA Commissioner has his own "cabinet" in Washington—six departments or branches, each with a staff: Community Services, Economic Development, Education, Administration, Engineering and Program Coordination. This structure is duplicated on a regional level in Area Offices, headed by Area Directors. It is duplicated a third, and even a fourth, time at the reservation —or agency and sub-agency—level. Be-

hind every official looking over every Indian's shoulder, there are several layers of officials looking over each others' shoulders.

The authority of the Bureau in every realm of Indian life is absolute both as a legal and practical matter. A Harvard Law Review article summed it up:

"Although the normal expectation in American society is that a private individual or group may do anything unless it is specifically prohibited by the Government, it might be said that the normal expectation on the reservation is that the Indians may not do anything unless it is specifically permitted by the Government." [2]

The BIA defines who is an Indian. It defines tribes, and can consolidate tribes at will. The Shoshone and Bannock peoples, for instance, have been forced to live together at Fort Hall Reservation, Iowa, and deal with the Bureau as one tribe. The Bureau decides how tribal membership is determined and supervises admission to tribal rolls.

Nowhere is the BIA's authority better demonstrated than in its power over tribal and individual Indian trust property. The use of Indian land is controlled by the Bureau, as are sales, exchanges and other land transactions. The Bureau prescribes the number of cattle which may graze on a parcel of land. It approves leases, controls prices, terms and conditions. Often the leasing process is initiated not by the owner of the land, but by the person desiring to lease it. Leases have been approved without the owner's consent and *only* the Bureau—not the tribe or individual

[1] Robert K. Thomas, "Powerless Politics," *New University Thought,* Vol. 4, p. 51, 1967.

[2] Warren H. Cohen, Philip L. Manle, "The Indian: The Forgotten American," *Harvard Law Review,* Vol. 81, No. 8, p. 1820, June 1968.

owner—is empowered to cancel a lease. Under certain circumstances the Bureau can sell timber on Indian land without the owners' consent, and get grant rights of way and permission to build roads, pipelines and even dams.[3]

Even the Indian's personal property is controlled by the Bureau. The Indian may be an adult—and perfectly sound in mind and body. But he still can be treated by the Bureau as legally incompetent to manage his own affairs.

Mere supposition by a Bureau official that an Indian might prove indiscreet in handling money, might be exploited, or might at some future point be unable to provide for himself—any of these is considered reason enough to relieve the Indian of control over his possessions. Once the Indian is deemed incompetent he cannot even draw money from his own bank account without obtaining approval from a BIA guardian. The decision is virtually unchallengeable.

The Indian can, however, count on being treated as "competent" for at least one purpose—to sell his land. He may not be competent to lease it or to mortgage it, but if he needs money he will find the BIA most willing to help sell his land. When an Indian is hungry and desires welfare assistance, the Bureau may devise an acceptable pretext for authorizing the sale or may simply declare his land—land held in trust for him and his heirs forever—an "available asset" which he must utilize before qualifying for welfare. Once he

has sold the land, the Bureau insists that the Indian spend the money from it before qualifying for welfare—but with restrictions. The money becomes subject to BIA control; it is doled out to the Indian at the welfare rate, which is usually below subsistence level.

In its own fashion, the Bureau looks after the education of its younger wards. The BIA operates boarding schools for some Indians, and contracts with local schools for the rest. But what lawyers call in loco parentis—"parents by proxy" —has disturbing implications when children are taken from their parents and transported as far as 6,000 miles from Alaska to Oklahoma boarding schools. The Bureau decides where Indian schools will be built and who will attend them. In the case of a Bureau school in Oregon, no Oregon Indian children or Indian children from the Northwest are permitted to attend. The Bureau can close a school and dispose of it without consent of the tribe it serves whenever it is judged that "the good of the service will be promoted thereby." [4]

Tribes must secure the consent of the Bureau to meet and discuss their constitutions. The Bureau decides whether a tribe's chosen form of government is acceptable, and nearly all tribal government decisions must be reviewed by BIA officials.

Even when exercised illegally, the total power of the Bureau is virtually unchallengeable and unreviewable. Where the normal citizen has three avenues of redress—political, judicial, administrative—the Indian has none.

Politically he is impotent. He lacks significant voting power. Even where there are sufficient concentrations of

---

[3] U.S. v. Creek Nations, 295 U.S. 103, 110 (1935); 25 C.F.R. 151.1 et seq. (1968); 25 U.S.C. §§ 415, 415 (c) (1964); 25 C.F.R. §§ 131.5 (a); 25 C.F.R. § 131.2; 25 C.F.R. §§ 131.14; 25 C.F.R. §§ 141.7 (1968); 25 U.S.C. § 373 (1964).

[4] 25 U.S.C. § 292 (1964).

Indians to have some impact they are frequently disenfranchised. Every politician loves to pose with Indians, but very few feel compelled to listen to them.

The Indian has no effective administrative remedy. The Indian Affairs Manual, which explains and sets forth the procedures and rules that govern Indians, fills 33 volumes which stack some six feet high. And this manual is not available to the Indian—except at some BIA office, if they choose to let him glance at it. There are more than 2,000 regulations, 389 treaties, 5,000 statutes, 2,000 federal court decisions and 500 opinions of the Attorney General which state, interpret, apply or clarify some aspect of Indian law.

Even the Bureau is confounded by its rules. In 1957 the BIA Commissioner wrote: "The uncertainty of our position and the generally adamant, but in the main equally uncertain, knowledge on the part of Indian people concerning their 'treaty rights' make is necessary that such 'rights' be clarified without further delay to facilitate program planning with individual groups." That day of clarification has not come.

The Bureau has a difficult time following its own rules and regulations. Nothing has changed since 1961 when the Task Force on Indian Affairs, in its report to the Secretary of the Interior, criticized "the slow rate at which the Bureau performs its abundant paperwork. Items initiated in the field often must move through a network of reviews and appeals all the way to the Secretary's office, with numerous side trips to specialists and solicitors."

The frustration of this jungle of rules and writ is magnified for the Indian, because normally he cannot obtain a lawyer to help him understand them. Despite a federal law which requires that Indians be provided with legal representation by the U.S. Attorney, very few are in fact provided. Further, no tribe can hire a lawyer without the approval of the Federal Government.

The Bill of Rights was extended to Indians in 1968, but even so, hired lawyers representing Indians at times have been barred from a reservation. For the overwhelming majority of Indians there are still no lawyers available, and without lawyers, rights are just cruel, unfulfilled promises. Even the courts, the forum of last resort and the ultimate source of protection against injustice, become, as a practical matter, unavailable to Indians.

The BIA's plenary and unreviewable power to govern, to assist and to fulfill solemn promises has a tremendous potential for good, but it has equal potential for harm. In practice, the exercise of this power has been used primarily to frustrate the purposes for which it was intended: the social, political and economic self-realization of the Indian.

The failure to accomplish the goals sought for the Indians stems from a perversion of the Federal Government's relationship with the Indian. All Bureau responsibilities and powers stem from its unique obligation to stand as trustee for the nation to honor and implement promises to the Indians.

Other people besides Indians have trustees; other persons besides Bureau officials have fiduciary obligations. Such relationships exist between banker and depositor, lawyer and client, doctor and patient. That relationship does not normally imply any stigma of inferiority or incompetence. But in discharging its trustee responsibilities, the Bureau has perverted its ties to the Indian to a most narrow relationship—that of a competent to an incompetent, a parent to a child, a guardian and his ward.

Felix Cohen, one of the nation's experts on Indian law, noted that in the white man's business world a trustee has no control over his beneficiary's person, but merely attends to the interests of his properties. "In the Indian's world, the same principles should apply; there is no legal basis for the common view that the Indian Bureau may deal with Indian trust property as if it were the owner thereof, or use such power over lands and funds to control Indian lives and thoughts. . . .

"Over the years, any order or command or sale or lease for which no justification could be found in any treaty or act of Congress came to be justified by BIA officials as an act of 'guardianship,' and every denial of civil, political, or economic rights to Indians came to be blamed on their alleged 'wardship.' Under the reign of these magic words nothing Indian was safe. The Indian's hair was cut, his dances were forbidden, his oil lands, timber lands, and grazing lands were disposed of, by Indian agents and Indian commissioners for whom the magic word 'wardship' always made up for any lack of statutory authority."

Constant use of that concept has given it permanence and acceptance in public opinion, but as Cohen notes, "it remains an illusion, unsupported by legal authority." [5]

Through the pervasiveness of the Bureau's role, the exercise of power and administration of programs by the BIA have come to ensure that every effort by the Indian to achieve self-realization is frustrated and penalized; that the Indian is kept in a state of permanent dependency as his price of survival; and that alienation from his people and past is rewarded and encouraged for the Indian

But somehow, the Indian persists in defining himself—as a man, a divinely created being:

> "The gods and the spirits of the Sacred Mountains created Man. He was made of all rains, springs, rivers, ponds, black clouds, and sky. His feet are made of earth and his legs of lightning. White shell forms his knees, and his body is white and yellow corn; his flesh is of daybreak, his hair darkness; his eyes are of the sun. White corn forms his teeth, black corn his eyebrows, and red coral beads his nose. His tears are of rain, his tongue of straight lightning, and his voice of thunder. His heart is obsidian; the little whirlwind keeps his nerves in motion, and his movement is the air. The name of this new kind of being was 'Created from Everything.' " [6]

[5] Lucy Kramer Cohen, ed., *The Legal Conscience: Selected Papers of Felix S. Cohen,* pp. 331–333.

[6] Philip Hyde and Stephen C. Jett, ed., *Navajo Wildlands: As Long as the Rivers Shall Run.*

CHICANOS: THE FORGOTTEN MINORITY

Side by Side—And a World Apart—In Uvalde, Texas

ROBERT LITTELL

Drive 85 miles west from San Antonio along U.S. 90, through the cactus-clumped hills of Edwards Plateau country, past road signs that say things like "This is God's country," and you'll come to Uvalde, a drowsy, churchgoing town of 10,400 that can stand as a metaphor for America as the *chicano* knows it. For more than anything else, the story of Uvalde is a tale of two cultures that live side by side—and a world apart.

Slightly fewer than half the people in Uvalde are Anglo—and their town has all the marks of Middle America: fadingly elegant houses (one of which was the home of FDR's first Vice President, the late John Nance Garner) set back from graceful streets, Rotarians, Lions, Kiwanians, a riding club called the Sheriff's Posse, a country club, a new civic center and an atmosphere of belonging.

For the Mexican-Americans in Uvalde, life is a perpetual struggle. With few exceptions, even the very few

who have managed to accumulate money live in the barrios, clusters of shacks assembled piece by salvaged piece amid unpaved, potholed roads that raise dust clouds during a dry spell and turn to mud after the first good rain. Many of the chicanos in the barrios live without sanitation, electricity, running water or heat; come winter, one family of seven moves into a covered trench for warmth.

Thirsty. At one corner of Uvalde is the "barrio of the thirsty ones." The municipal authorities do not supply water to this area because, as a technical matter, the section is just outside the city limits. Mrs. Juanita Gonzáles, her husband, Daniel, and their five children are among the thirsty ones. Mrs. Gonzáles—who is 48 but looks 68—and her family live in a tar-paper and sheet-metal shack with a dirt floor on which strips of linoleum have been laid.

A few steps from the house is the "casita"—the outdoor toilet. Open barrels are scattered around the yard to catch any rainfall. Daniel Gonzáles, 58, builds fences on nearby ranches. He earns $10 a day when he works, but gets work only half the time. When it rains, the family has water—but Gonzáles earns nothing.

Three times a week Mrs. Gonzáles loads a 10-gallon can onto a jerry-built wheelbarrow and trundles it down the ruts of Laredo Street to the Uvalde city cemetery. She drags the can through an opening in the shrubs, fills it quickly from a garden hose, then manhandles the can back through the bushes and rolls it home. Once Mrs. Gonzáles encountered an Anglo woman visiting a grave. The woman told her not to get water from the cemetery any more. So now Mrs. Gonzáles tries to go when nobody is around.

Wells: The thirsty ones survive by stealing water from the dead, but at least the water is pure. A few blocks farther on is another chicano barrio called the Burns Addition. People in this area—which is dotted with casitas—get their water from private wells. A few months ago, Texas Department of Health experts tested these wells and found coliform organisms, indicating the presence of human or animal fecal matter. John Burns, a wealthy Anglo who developed the tract and sells the water to the tenants for $3 a month, claims that the water is "the finest in the world." He puts chlorine in it "sometimes," and says that he is ordering two chlorinators for the system.

The Anglo Establishment in town centers around County Judge Leo Darley, the head of the county commissioners. Some white leaders deny that Uvalde suffers from hunger, malnutrition or substandard housing. And thus far, the county fathers—who never made a fuss about the $1,183,000 in agriculture subsidies that the Federal government paid out to landowners in the county last year—have refused offers from VISTA to help out in the barrios and resisted Federal food-stamp programs. Recently, they forced Jack "Bubba" Hays, who directs Head Start, Neighborhood Youth Corps and other programs in the area and has championed chicano causes, to move his headquarters out of Uvalde as the price of keeping his programs intact.

Boycott: The chicano movement in Uvalde is just beginning to stir. There have been a few protest marches down the dusty barrio streets, and in April about half the chicano students walked out of classes in a six-week school boycott. The demonstration ended without a single concession from the Anglo school board and with all the boycotters being left back. But the Mexican-American activists in the community remain undiscouraged. "Uvalde is going to be an interesting place to keep our eyes on," Gabe Tafolla, 27, a former Uvalde schoolteacher, told *Newsweek's* Kent Biffle. "I might be overoptimistic, but I just have to be this way or I would stop functioning. I feel certain that in five years, we will control the town." He shrugged. "Hell," he added quickly, "we can't be worse off."

Chicano Power

STAN STEINER

Up in the sky above the barrios of Los Angeles the leaflets fluttered like birds, strange birds in the smog. "In the spirit of a new people that is conscious of its proud historical heritage," said the airborne leaflets, "we, the Chicano inhabitants and civilizers of the northern land of Aztlan, whence came our forefathers, reclaim the land of our birth. Our blood is our power." Strollers who looked skyward that day might have thought it was a publicity stunt for a science fiction movie; or was Aztlan the name of a new brand of cigarettes? Few of the passersby would have believed that these were political leaflets, that quite seriously proclaimed the somewhat premature rebirth of the lost Kingdom of the Aztecs.

Aztlan! It was the ancient Kingdom of the Montezuma, Emperor of the Aztecs, that had vanished from history in 1513, when the Spanish Conquistadors conquered Mexico. In the spring of 1970 the word, Aztlan, has become a symbol of the political revolt of the Chicanos, as the young Mexican Americans call themselves, in the barrios throughout the Southwest.

Reprinted from Stan Steiner, "Chicano Power: Militance Among the Mexican Americans," The New Republic (June 20, 1970), 16–18. Copyright 1970 by Stan Steiner. Reprinted by permission of the Harold Matson Company, Inc.

"I see all over the Southwest [something] quite different from a melting pot. I see a boiling pot," says Dr. Ernesto Galarza, the "dean" of Chicano leaders in California, ex-farm worker, scholar and "grandfather of the Chicano movement."

The Chicanos of the Southwest have less voice in government than any people in the country, except for the Indians. It is estimated by Henry Quevedo, Nixon's adviser on Mexican American Affairs that there are eight to 10 million Chicanos, the country's second largest minority. Were representation in the US Congress proportionate to the population there would be from 15 to 25 Chicano congressmen. There are four.

In the Southwest there is not one large city—Phoenix, El Paso, Albuquerque, San Antonio, Denver, Tucson, Los Angeles, or even Fresno—with a Chicano mayor. There is not a state anywhere with a Chicano governor. There is one US senator, Joseph Montoya of New Mexico, where tradition insists on a bicultural split in that state's hyphenated politics. There is one Chicano in the legislature of California, Assemblyman Alex Garcia, though that state has more than two million Chicanos. There is not a single Chicano councilman in the City of Los Angeles, though an estimated one million Chicanos live in the metropolitan area alone. "Let's face it. Neither party has been particularly relevant to the barrios," says a highly placed Chicano official in the Nixon Administration; "We have been ignored by both parties."

A feeling of apathy has been the traditional response of the disenfranchised. "The word Politics like Sex was a bad word," wrote *El Chicano,* a barrio newspaper in the slums of San Bernardino, California. In the rural villages as dour an attitude was noted by the *New Mexican,* of Santa Fe: " 'Politics' remains a dirty word and accusation."

In their disdain of politics the barrio residents left the electoral system in the hands of the *jefe politico*—the local "political chief," or *Tio Tomas,* Uncle Tom. In his heyday the *jefe politico* traded the needs of the poor for votes. The "hidden vote" of the barrios has been a surreptitious protest vote for years. It has influenced political shifts in Texas, New Mexico and California. Senator John Tower of Texas owed his election in 1966, local barrio politicos claimed, to their "quiet campaign" of cross voting to register their dissatisfaction with the Democratic candidate. In New Mexico, Governor Cargo feels his first election was due to the "anger of the Hispano at being bossed by, then ignored by, the Democratic machines." In California the defeat of Humphrey in '68 was paced by a switch in barrio precincts from a 95 percent Democratic vote to a 35 percent Republican vote. It was "Dump the Democrats year," quipped California's most influential Chicano politico, Bert Corona, then head of the Mexican American Political Association (MAPA). "We were a 'captive audience,' " he recalled; "so we had to show them we are independent."

In one decade the Chicano population increased by 37 percent in Texas, 51 percent in Arizona, and 87 percent in California. So too, the Chicano vote has grown enormously. At least 400,000 new voters were registered in the barrios of California alone, during the fifteen years from 1950 to 1965.

It was the quiet discontent and the foreboding of an electoral revolt in the barrios that led to the formation by President Johnson in 1967 of the Inner-Agency Committee on Mexican American Affairs. The "benign neglect" of the Chicanos has since progressed from the vulgar to the sardonic. In the autumn of 1969 a bill, introduced by Senator Montoya to extend the life of the President's committee (rechristened the Cabinet Committee on Opportunity for the Spanish Speaking), passed the Senate and was sent to the House. It was "lost" for four months. Embarrassed by this denouement, its Senate sponsors instituted a hectic search for the missing bill. It was found in the House Foreign Affairs committee. Someone had assumed that "Mexican American Affairs" was a "foreign problem."

Popeye, immortalized in a larger than life statue blesses the town of Crystal City, Texas. He is the patron saint of the economy in the rural community, and in his hand he holds a can of spinach, the manna of this "Spinach Capitol of the Country." A quiet, dusty farmtown on the West Texas prairie, its 10,000 citizens are typically divided by the railroad tracks that run through the middle of its Main Street. On one side live the Mexican American farmworkers, who are 85 percent of the population, and on the other live the Anglo ranchers, who own 95 percent of the farms.

One year, in the mid-sixties, the Chicano decided to challenge City Hall. They elected their own mayor. Yet "nothing changed" in the town's landscape of power and poverty, says Jose Angel Guitierrez. A local boy, the son of a barrio doctor, he returned to Crystal City with a Master's Degree from St. Mary's University, in San Antonio, in his pocket and a plan for "social revolution" in his fist.

Guitierrez, while at the university, was the founder of MAYO, the Mexican American Youth Organization, then a Ford Foundation-financed group of student activists (funds have since been withdrawn because of the group's "political activities"). He brought his abstract idea of "Chicano nationalism" into practical politics. In Crystal City, he and his young adherents established an independent party, *La Raza Unida*, in an attempted "takeover" of the town's school board, the city council, and the county government. They envisioned an economic shake-up that would lead to the establishment of Chicano-owned shops and cooperatives.

"If it works here," he says, "it's the model for Texas—rural, city, anywhere." Within a few months *La Raza Unida* party startled Texas politicians by winning the school board election. Like many local activists young Guitierrez believes "integration is not possible," in Texas. "In the history of the country there has never been equality between Anglos and Chicanos," says Guitierrez; "self-determination will not be attained until there is power on both sides."

Onetime titular leader of the Democratic Party in West Texas, County Commissioner Albert Pena, of San Antonio (Bexar County) has thrown his political power behind the independent party of the young Chicanos. "These young people are the wave of the future. If things are going to change in Texas, they are going to do it. The Chicano is more determined and more militant. He is no longer asking, he is demanding. We already have a Chicano party, *La Raza Unida*, on the ballot in three Texas counties. It's the only way we can win."

The mobility of a barrio "swing vote," and the desire for political independence, has brought support to the young Chicanos from officials in Washington. "I see a Chicano party as a 'Declaration of Political Independence,' " says Henry Quevedo. "So I am all for such activity, if it helps the Chicano. We have had mainly 'walkout politics,' until now. That is, we voted against those we opposed. Now we are beginning to make affirmative choices, in our own interests. Chicanos will no longer vote for 'the good of the country.' Chicanos will vote for the good of Chicanos."

Not every *politico* in the barrios is quite as enthusiastic about the new politics of the young Chicanos. The most uncompromising critic is the bull-jawed, tall, and politically powerful congressman, Henry Gonzales, of Texas. In angry speeches on the floor of the House this spring, the Texas lawmaker attacked the formation of the Chicano party, *La Raza Unida*, in his district, as "reverse racism" . . . "as evil as the deadly hatred of the Nazis." Young Chicanos who delude themselves that "the wearing of fatigues and a beard makes (them) revolutionaries" are the "new racists," Congressman Gonzales said. He feared that the "politics of race"—"Only one thing counts to them, loyalty to *la raza*, above all"—might lead to race riots in the barrios of

Texas. "I stand for classless, raceless politics," the congressman concluded. His strong stand incurred the wrath of the young activists. Yet, none has dared oppose Gonzales' bid for reelection.

When the Texas congressman addressed students at St. Mary's University, a fist fight erupted and the young activists staged a walkout. The *Carta Editorial* of California, while praising the congressman's civil rights record, noted its "sorrow" that "his lack of understanding of his own people" had introduced "the generation gap" into the barrios. "The youth are angry," wrote the California journal, "not only at the *gringos,* they are angry at their parents, at Congressman Gonzales' generation, who they feel let them down"; scolding in the Congressional Record, "will not stop them, they will be heard, even if their language sounds uncouth to our ears. . . ."

And yet, even some of the Chicano activists view the independent parties with suspicion. Gilbert Ballejo, a barrio organizer in Albuquerque, where he ran as an independent for the local school board, is dubious; "Like everything else, a third party can be manipulated. Like the vote, it too, can give an illusion of power where there is none."

In Denver, at the barrio bastion of the Crusade for Justice, where the *Plan de Aztlan* was originally proposed, its young, politically astute leader, Rololfo "Corky" Gonzales, scoffs at these doubters and critics. He has urged the formation of a National Independent Chicano Party; not a third party, "in the Anglo sense," Gonzales insists. It will be "a revolutionary party by and for La Raza." "Nationalism," he argues, "transcends political barriers, religious barriers, social and class bar-riers. We need a party of all our people. We will use it to unite our people. . . . There are more Chicanos in Illinois than in Colorado. There are more Chicanos in Michigan than in New Mexico."

"Corky" Gonzales is an exemplar of the "New Breed" of young Chicanos. In his office, with the *Virgin de Guadalupe,* patron saint of La Raza, on the wall behind him, and a poster of Che Guevara at his side, he muses about the improbabilities of politics. As a youth Gonzales had been a National and International Amateur boxing champion; he entered politics to become Colorado's state chairman of the *Viva Kennedy* campaign for whom he turned out the largest precinct majorities in the state. Later, he was chairman of the Denver War On Poverty Board.

On his desk he no longer has the picture of the murdered President, with its message, "To Corky—John F. Kennedy." Instead he has the poems of Lorca. He talks now in poetic images: "We don't need anymore godlike leaders. We don't need any more paper tiger *politicos.* We don't need any more Anglo hypocrisy. We need people who have *machismo,* who have beautiful hearts, who have free Chicano minds."

At the Chicano Youth Liberation Conference, which the Crusade for Justice holds each spring, the 2500 delegates from hundreds of student and youth clubs, and barrios as far away as Alaska, heard Gonzales propose a "Congress of Aztlan," to inaugurate programs of economic development, community health plans, an "independent Chicano school system," "free Chicano universities," law enforcement "by ourselves" for the "independent nation of Aztlan." He urged "An Appeal to the United Nations" for a plebiscite to be held in the Southwest. "Chicanos are already a nation," a policy statement of the conference declared. If they do not have their own land, they are merely in the position of the "Jews before Israel was recognized.

Late last February, two hundred civic and community, veteran and patriotic, conservative and militant groups gathered at the Congress of Mexican American Unity in East Los Angeles. "We here in Aztlan [the Southwest]," they said, "understand full well that our own liberation as well as that of our *carnales* [brothers, or Soul Brothers] in Anahuac [old Mexico] is basically one of delivering ourselves from the exploitation and repression of imperialist forces."

The six hundred delegates were not a haphazard group of motley radicals without a constituency. Every element of barrio life, with few exceptions, was represented. At the beginning of the meeting 210 barrio groups were affiliated with the Congress of Mexican American Unity; by the time the resolutions had been voted there were 304 member organizations and local clubs.

"We have to speak with one voice," said Estaban Torres, the newly elected president of the Congress of Mexican American Unity. The young, university educated Torres, a former International Representative of the United Auto Workers, in Washington, D.C. ("Special Assistant for Latin America") had recently returned to the barrio in which he grew up. "I gave up my romantic job, my trips to Rio de Janeiro, to come home where I belong."

In years past the droning meetings of barrio groups like the Congress of Mexican American Unity were dubbed "Endorsement Conferences." Democratic and Republican candidates came before them, ate *enchiladas,* offered promises and were "endorsed." But, this year not a single Anglo politician, on either the Democratic or Republican ticket, was endorsed. The delegates voted for only Chicanos.

"Political sophistication has come of age in the barrios," was the pleased comment of Esteban Torres. "We are building a 'Chicano Power' bloc to deal with the power structure."

4

THE UNSOLVED ISSUES:

CAN THEY BE SOLVED—NOW?

Commonly shared by the recruits for the new politics is a belief that the American political system has either avoided, or overlooked, the most outstanding and pressing issues of our times. Hence the new politics is strongly issue-oriented and concerned with the creation and implementation of public policy designed to eradicate the great social, economic, political, and technological ills of our country. The old politics, with its primary commitments to compromise and expediency, is rejected because it has not demonstrated a genuine and effective concern for these "real" issues. Instead, the old politics has become concerned, in actual practice, with the maintenance of the status quo and support of the existing power groups and ideologies.

According to the reformers, we need more emphasis upon both issues and ideals, in order to make American politics relevant to the modern world. Carey McWilliams, lending his support to the student revolt, has called for a "new infusion of utopian idealism"[1] in the new politics of student activists. Stokely Carmichael and Charles Hamilton have said that the reason the two political parties now fail to give legitimate representation to the American population is that the "old ideological issues, once the subject of passionate controversy, . . . are of little interest today."[2] Thus, we often also find among the new politicians an abolitionist and crusading spirit that presents very simple answers to the most complex problems.

[1] Carey McWilliams, Foreword to Mitchell Cohen and Dennis Hale, eds., *The New Student Left: An Anthology*, p. xii.
[2] Stokely Carmichael and Charles V. Hamilton, *Black Power: The Politics of Liberation in America* (New York: Vintage Books, 1967), p. 42.

The various disaffected groups are interested in issues that demonstrate a common characteristic—they are so deep-seated and so controversial that they currently receive only superficial treatment by the old politics. Effective consideration of these issues might well require basic changes in the beliefs or procedures of our society, to the extent that we might have to reject some of the time-honored concepts that make up the "American way of life." The issues that are currently of greatest concern to the new politicians are racism, equal opportunity, poverty, war, and most recently pollution. Indeed, the extent of the concern for these issues might lead one to the conclusion that we may be faced with the prospect of profound, qualitative changes in the American political system, even if the reformers should attain only part of what they desire.

James Farmer said recently that "racism, like a miasma, is still breathed with the air"[3] in America. Farmer's view concurs with that of the National Advisory Commission of Civil Disorders, which in 1968 officially informed the American people that the United States is a racist society. Racism is defined as an orientation that "sets deep within the human mind the inherent belief in the inferiority of one dissimilar group in comparison with assumed superior qualities of one's own."[4] Such a belief is literally passed, largely unconsciously, from generation to generation as it becomes a cultural pattern within a society.

According to most experts, the United States is the only nation outside Africa in which skin color is the main designation of caste. This does not mean, of course, that every American white citizen shares in the myth of white supremacy. But it does mean that the institutions of American society operate as though all whites did share the myth. As the Kerner Commission stated:

> What white Americans have never fully understood—but what the Negro can never forget—is that white society is deeply implicated in the ghetto. White institutions created it, white institutions maintain it, and white society condones it.[5]

This is the racism that James Farmer, Dick Gregory, Stokely Carmichael, and Dr. Martin Luther King have condemned in America—the racism ingrained in the myriad of political, social, economic, religious, or educational institutions which make up American society. Thus many black leaders now assert that the real problem of America is not discrimination, but white racism, which after three and a half centuries continues to bring more grief and harm to more people than any other cultural defect in American society.

Equal opportunity is an ideal that has been denied to many groups throughout American history. As with other ideals, its denial demonstrates the great

---

[3] James Farmer, "Are White Liberals Obsolete in the Black Struggle?" *The Progressive*, XXXII, 1 (January, 1968), 14.

[4] Barry N. Schwartz and Robert Disch, *White Racism: Its History, Pathology and Practice* (New York: Dell Publishing Co., 1970), p. 1.

[5] *Report of the National Advisory Commission on Civil Disorders*, p. 2.

gap which lies between rhetoric and practice in American social thought. According to theory, every human being should have the opportunity to develop to his or her fullest potential. Nonetheless, this opportunity has been arbitrarily denied to millions of citizens solely on the basis of race, sex, religion, and ethnic background since before the country was founded. Compared to other areas of the world, America possesses a relatively classless society—yet we have imposed distinctions on our people as rigid as any that exist elsewhere.

Denial of opportunity is most obviously demonstrated in regard to racial minorities. But what of discrimination against religious minorities, Indians, Mexican-Americans, women, and others? The kind of discrimination which treats the least capable member of a racial, sexual, religious, or ethnic group as better, or more entitled to the benefits of society, than the most capable member of another group, even if the latter individual may be more capable than most members of the dominant group, is purely arbitrary and unjust. This, however, is what has happened in America, despite the widely held belief in the dream of equal opportunity.

Poverty, as the prophets have said, has always been with us, and probably always will be. According to the classic liberal Protestant ethic, hard work, initiative, virtue, and talents will not go unrewarded in a society that encourages self-help and free enterprise. By a process of natural selection, or "survival of the fittest," the best will rise to the top, and be rewarded with money, recognition, and political power. A society like the United States, which has accepted this theory, can in good conscience ignore the poor and the powerless by reasoning that intellectual, racial, sexual, or ethnic inferiority (sometimes referred to as simple "laziness") is the real reason some do not enjoy all the benefits that society bestows upon its "deserving" members. This "ethic" still permeates American thought, because it offers a convenient rationalization for the great inequities that obviously continue to exist in this country.

Poverty has long been an anachronism in the United States, whereas effective concern for its existence is of recent origin. The popular reaction to Michael Harrington's *The Other America* in 1962, for example, indicates that only within the last decade have we manifested general, widespread concern for the poor and the powerless. Although the number of poor persons in the United States is impossible to ascertain with certainty, the Census Bureau recently estimated that there were 24.3 million in 1969, over one third of whom were nonwhite. The figure represents approximately 12 per cent of the population, or a drop from the 22 per cent of 1959. Although the income of nonwhites rose in the 1960's, the proportion of poor nonwhites remained virtually unchanged over the same period. As yet, one-third of minority group members are classified as living in poverty, compared to only 10 per cent of whites. Poverty, then, is shared much more widely by the same group that suffers most from the ill effects of racism and the denial of equal opportunity.

It is indeed a remarkable turn of events that has forced the United States, in a very few years, to emerge from a state of virtual inaction in world affairs to a position of world leadership. But even more remarkable is the change that has occurred in popular thinking about the American position in the world. We have come to accept, almost as a commonplace, a role that leads to intervention in the affairs of states all over the world, the development and constant expansion of the most powerful military system that has ever existed, and involvement in a succession of undeclared wars. Moreover, the American nation has tended to regard itself as fulfilling a kind of mission that requires it to repel any actual, alleged, or anticipated Communist aggression, and to promote the peace of the world. Thus, we can justify the maintenance of a peacetime draft, involvement in the longest war in American history, undercover manipulation of the affairs of other states, participation in a never-ending arms race, and continued support of what has been called "Pentagon capitalism," or the military-industrial complex.

James Madison once observed that a standing army was "one of the greatest mischiefs that can possibly happen . . ." to a country. More recently, and more in tune with post-war developments, President Eisenhower warned that we "must guard against the acquisition of unwarranted influence . . . by the military-industrial complex." [6] Since the end of World War II, the United States has spent more than a trillion dollars for national security. Adding together the annual defense budget, and the costs of past wars, American military activities, past, present, and future, cost the taxpayer approximately 70 cents out of every dollar. In fact, the military has become the largest single activity in the country, with ties to almost every aspect of American life. The extent of this activity, and its effects on our lives, have led some observers to conclude that the United States is fast becoming a "militarized society." [7]

It is difficult to assess the domestic effects of the tremendous expansion of America's involvement in the world. But it is safe to say that one of the most serious effects has been the development of dangerous internal disruptions and conflicts among groups with opposing views. Another effect is that we obviously spend more of our resources on war and defense than we do on domestic concerns. We appear also to have accepted the kind of war ideology that condones the destruction of villages in Vietnam in order to save them from Communism, or which rationalizes massacres like that at My Lai 4 as simply inevitable consequences of the battle with the Communist conspiracy. Finally, we have come to accept the inevitability of an arms race, by which the United States has now accumulated enough power to deliver the equivalent of more than six tons of

[6] Quoted in James A. Burkhart, Samuel Krislov, and Raymond L. Lee, eds., *The Clash of Issues*, 3d ed. (Englewood Cliffs, N.J.: Prentice-Hall, Inc., 1968), p. 377.

[7] See Donald McDonald, "Militarism in America," *The Center Magazine*, III, 1 (January-February, 1970), 13–33.

TNT for every person living on this planet. It is no exaggeration to say that of all issues now facing this country, war is the most pressing and perhaps also the most imminently dangerous.

Of very recent interest is the issue of pollution, which has also been combined with concern for the "population bomb." The environmental crisis, as it is now called, has developed into a major problem, and unless concerted public action is soon taken on a broad scale, the world as a whole may someday be faced with disaster, at least if some of the experts' direst predictions should prove valid. As for the population explosion, at the present growth rate of 2 per cent a year, the number of people in the world will almost double to seven billion by the year 2000, and will double again by 2015. Unfortunately, the greatest increases will occur in the poorest, underdeveloped areas of the world, where they will have the most detrimental effects upon standards of living.

At the heart of the problem lies man's alleged need, or his desire, for an expanding economy. First, the Industrial Revolution, and then the great technological revolution of the twentieth century, have led to the unlimited exploitation of natural resources and contamination of the air, water, and land that have created the ecological crisis. In other words, pollution of the earth seems to be the price we pay for prosperity and technological progress. As a partial corrective, population planning may be required—self-limitation, reevaluation of our goals, and, perhaps, ultimately some type of governmental incentives appear to be the inevitable solutions. As Walter Sullivan has said, "In a world of proliferation—proliferation of human beings, of nuclear weapons, of food additives—unplanned, uncontrolled technological growth can no longer be tolerated." [8] Hence, the warnings of the ecologists are challenging, because, as we are told, "an increase in the gross national product must be construed, from the ecological point of view, as disastrous." [9]

The solution of all these problems, if solution is indeed possible, will require fundamental, and far-reaching, changes in our present thinking and ways of doing things. It is not enough simply to await gradual change or to hope that the "system," in its usual manner, can ultimately take care of the most pressing problems. These issues must be considered in a different light from other issues, for if they are not dealt with adequately and soon, the United States, and perhaps the world itself, may someday have to face disaster. The growing concern for these issues must, then, be considered as a very important feature of the new politics, not only because new groups are interested in the issues, but because the resolution of them requires new approaches, new concepts, and new procedures. In fact, we may eventually need to develop a whole new life

[8] Quoted in Roger P. Hanson, "Informing the Activist," *Journal*, VIII, 4 (January-February, 1970), 29.

[9] William Murdoch and Joseph Connell, "All About Ecology," *The Center Magazine*, III, 1 (January-February, 1970), 63.

style in this country. As one observer has said, "the world has become too dangerous for anything less than utopia." [10] In the words of Walter Lippmann, "the immediate but fundamental question is whether popular democracy is capable of voting, administering and enforcing the complicated reforms the technological age demands. Is popular democracy capable of reforming itself?" [11] The American political system is now facing its severest challenges—it can meet these challenges only if it is willing to recognize its weaknesses and failings and to act now to close the gap between stated goals and actual accomplishments.

Although the issues now of concern to those who would desire change in America are numerous, some of the most salient are presented in the following selections. The problem of white racism, as opposed to the "Negro problem," is discussed by Lerone Bennett in his article from *Ebony* magazine. Caroline Bird compares the issue of sex discrimination with racism in the selection from her recent book, *Born Female*. The political neglect of poverty and hunger is forcefully discussed by Nick Kotz; "state-management" by the Pentagon is explained by Seymour Melman. Finally the problems and consequences of the environmental crisis are described in the articles by Kenneth Boulding and Ellen Graham. The reader should be cautioned again, however, that this is only a sampling of the problems that currently face the American people and that demand solutions— *now!*

[10] Walter Sullivan, quoted in Hanson, "Informing the Activist," p. 29.

[11] Walter Lippmann, "Politics Lags Behind Spirit of Revolution," *The Minneapolis Tribune,* June 9, 1968, p. 4c.

RACISM: "YOU CAN'T KEEP A MAN IN THE GUTTER WITHOUT FALLING IN YOURSELF"

The White Problem in America

LERONE BENNETT, JR.

There is no Negro problem in America.

The problem of race in America, insofar as that problem is related to packets of melanin in men's skins, is a white problem. And in order to solve that problem we must seek its source, not in the Negro but in the white American (in the process by which he was educated, in the needs and complexes he expresses through racism) and in the structure of the white community (in the power arrangements and the illicit uses of racism in the scramble for scarce values: power, prestige, income).

The depth and intensity of the race problem in America is, in part, a result of a 100-year flight from that unpalatable truth. It was a stroke of genius really for white Americans to give Negro Americans the name of their problem, thereby focusing attention on symptoms (the Negro and the Negro community) instead of causes (the white man and the white community).

When we say that the causes of the race problem are rooted in the white America and the white community, we mean that the power is the white American's and so is the responsibility. We mean that the white American created, *invented* the race problem and that his fears and frailties are responsible for the urgency of the problem.

When we say that the fears of white Americans are at the root of the problem, we mean that the white American is a problem to himself and that because he is a problem to himself he has made others problems to themselves.

When we say that the white American is a problem to himself, we mean that racism is a reflection of personal and collective anxieties lodged deep in the hearts and minds of white Americans.

By all this, we must understand that Harlem is a white-made thing and that in order to understand Harlem we

Reprinted from Lerone Bennett, Jr., The White Problem in America (Chicago: Johnson Publishing Company, Inc., 1966), pp. 1–10. Copyright 1965 by Johnson Publishing Company, Inc. Reprinted by permission of the publisher.

must go not to Harlem but to the conscience of white Americans and we must ask not what is Harlem but what have you made of Harlem. Why did you create it? And why do you need it?

The validity of this approach has been underlined by many experts, including Gunnar Myrdal, who began his massive work on the Negro (*An American Dilemma*) by admitting, in so many words, that he had studied the wrong people. "Although the Negro problem is a moral issue both to Negroes and to whites in America," he wrote, "we shall in this book have to give *primary* attention to what goes on in the minds of white Americans. . . . When the present investigator started his inquiry, his preconception was that it had to be focused on the Negro people and their peculiarities. . . . But as he proceeded in his studies into the Negro problem, it became increasingly evident that little, if anything, could be scientifically explained in terms of the peculiarities of the Negroes themselves. . . . It is thus the white majority group that naturally determines the Negro's 'place.' All our attempts to reach scientific explanations of why the Negroes are what they are and why they live as they do have regularly led to determinants on the white side of the racial line. In the practical and political struggles of affecting changes, the views and attitudes of the white Americans are likewise strategic. The Negro's entire life, and, consequently, also his opinions on the Negro problem, are, in the main, to be considered as secondary reactions to more primary pressures from the side of the dominant white majority."

Scores of investigators have reached the same conclusions: namely, that the peculiarities of white folk are the primary determinants of the American social problem.

Consider, for example, the testimony of James Weldon Johnson, the great Negro leader:

". . . the main difficulty of the race question does not lie so much in the actual condition of the blacks as it does in the mental attitude of the whites."

Johnson also said:

"The race question involves the saving of black America's body and white America's soul."

White Americans have perceived the same truth. Author Ray Stannard Baker wrote:

"It keeps coming to me that this is more a white man's problem than it is a Negro problem."

So it seemed also to Thomas P. Bailey, a Southern white.

"The real problem," he wrote, "is not the Negro but the white man's attitude toward the Negro."

And again:

"Yes, we Southerners need a freedom from suspicion, fear, anxiety, doubt, unrest, hate, contempt, disgust, and all the rest of the race-feeling-begotten brood of vituperation."

Ralph McGill, another Southerner, made a similar observation.

"We do not have a minority problem," he said, "but a majority problem."

Of like tone and tenor was the perceptive statement of Thomas Merton, the Trappist monk.

"The purpose of non-violent protest, in its deepest and most spiritual dimension is then to awaken the conscience of the white man to the awful responsibility of his injustice and sin, so that he will be able to see that the Negro problem is really a *White* problem: that the cancer of injustice and hate which is eating white society and is only partly manifested in racial segregation with its consequences, *is rooted in the heart of the white man himself.* [Merton's emphasis.]

It is there, "in the heart of the white man himself," in his peculiarities, in his mental attitudes, in his need for "a freedom from suspicion, fear, anxiety, doubt, unrest, hate, contempt, disgust," that we must situate the racial problem. For here, as elsewhere, the proper statement of the problem, though not a solution, is at least a strong step in the right direction. For too long now, we have focused attention on the Negro, forgetting that the Negro is who he is because white people are what they are. In our innocence—and in our guile —we have spoken of Negro crime, when the problem is white crime; we have spoken of the need for educating Negroes, when the problem is the education of whites; we have spoken of the lack of responsible Negro leadership, when the problem is the lack of responsible white leadership.

The premise of this special issue is that America can no longer afford the luxury of ignoring its real problem: the white problem. To be sure, Negroes are not blameless. It takes two to tango and the Negro, at the very least, is responsible for accepting the grapes of degradation. But that, you see, has nothing to do with the man who is responsible for the degradation. The prisoner is always free to try to escape. What the jailer must decide is whether he will help escaping prisoners over the wall or shoot them in the back. And the lesson of American life is that no Negro—no matter how much money he accumulated, no matter how many degrees he earned—has ever crossed completely the wall of color-caste, except by adopting the expedient of passing. Let us come to that point and stand on it: Negroes are condemned in America, not because they are poor, not because they are uneducated, not because they are brown or black—Negroes are condemned in America because they are Negroes, that is, because of an idea of the Negro and of the Negro's place in the white American's mind.

When we say that the race problem in America is a white problem, we mean that the real problem is an irrational and antiscientific idea of race in the minds of white Americans. Let us not be put off by recitations of "social facts." Social facts do not make Negroes; on the contrary, it is the idea of the Negro which organizes and distorts social facts in order to make "Negroes." Hitler, who had some experience in the matter, said social facts are sustainers and not creators of prejudice. In other words: If we assume that Negroes are inferior and if we use that assumption as a rationale for giving Negroes poor schools, poor jobs, and poor housing, we will sooner or later create a condition which "confirms" our assumption and "justifies" additional discrimination.

No: social facts are not at the heart of the problem. In fact, social facts tell us more about whites, about their needs, insecurities, and immaturities, than about Negroes. Many Negroes are poor, but so are forty to fifty million American whites. Some Negro women have babies out of wedlock, but so do millions of middle-class American white women. Racists and millions of "normal" white Americans know this; but they are not and cannot be convinced *for their knowledge precedes facts.* Because the *idea of race* intervenes between the concrete Negro and the social fact, Negro intellectuals and white racists rarely, if ever, understand each other. What the white racist means by social facts is that there are "Negro social facts," that Negroes, by virtue of their birth, have within them a magical substance that gives facts a certain quality. He means by that that there is a Negro and a white way of being poor, that there is a Negro and white way of being immoral, that, in his mind, white people and black people are criminals in different ways. As a result of this magical thinking, millions on millions of white Americans are unable to understand that slums, family disorganization and illiteracy are not the causes of the racial problem, but the end product of the problem.

That problem, in essence, is racism. But we misunderstand racism completely if we do not understand that racism is a mask for a much deeper problem involving not the victims of racism but the perpetrators. We must come to see that racism in America is the poor man's way out and the powerful man's way in: *a way in* for the powerful who derive enormous profits from the divisions in our society; *a way out* for the frustrated and frightened who excuse economic, social, and sexual failure by convincing themselves that no matter how low they fall they are still higher and better than Harry Belafonte, Ralphe Bunche, Cassius Clay and Martin Luther King Jr., all rolled up into one.

We must realize also that prejudice on all levels reflects a high level of personal and social disorganization in the white community. On a personal level, particularly among lower-income and middle-income whites, prejudice is an avenue of flight, a cry for help from desperate men stifling in the pris-

ons of their skins. Growing up in a culture permeated with prejudice, imbibing it, so to speak, with their milk, millions of white Americans find that Negroes are useful screens to hide themselves from themselves. Repeated studies have shown that Negro hate is, in part, a socially-sanctioned outlet for personal and social anxieties and frustrations. From this standpoint, racism is a flight from the self, a flight from freedom, a flight from the intolerable burdens of being a man in a menacing world.

Not all white Americans are biased, of course, but all white Americans and all Americans have been affected by bias. This issue suggests that we need to know a great deal more about how white Americans exist with their whiteness, and how some white Americans, to a certain extent, rise above early conditioning through non-Communist radicalism or liberalism.

The racist impulse, which white Americans express in different ways but which almost all do express, either by rebelling against it or by accepting it, reflects deep forces in the dominant community. There is considerable evidence, for example, that the culture's stress on success and status induces exaggerated anxieties and fears which are displaced onto the area of race relations. The fear of failure, the fear of competitors, the fear of losing status, of not living in the "right" neighborhood, of not having the "right" friends or the "right" gadgets: these fears weigh heavily on the minds of millions of white Americans and lead to a search for avenues of escape. And so the second- or third-generation factory worker or the poor white farmer who finds himself at a dead end with a nagging wife, a problem child, and a past-due bill may take out his aggressive feelings and his frustrations in race hatred.

The concept of the Negro problem as a white problem suggests that there is a need for additional research to determine to what extent Negro hate is a defense against self-hate. It also suggests that attention should be directed to the power gains of highly-placed politicians and businessmen who derive direct power gains from the division of our population into mutually hostile groups. By using racism, consciously or unconsciously, to divert public discontent and to boost the shaky egos of white groups on or near the bottom, men of power in America have played a key role in making racism a permanent structure of our society.

It is fashionable nowadays to think of racism as a vast impersonal system for which no one is responsible. But this is still another evasion. Racism did not fall from the sky; it was not secreted by insects. No: racism in America was made by men, neighborhood by neighborhood, law by law, restrictive covenant by restrictive covenant, deed by deed.

It is not remembered often enough today that the color-caste vise, which constricts both Negroes and whites, was created by men of power who artificially separated Negroes and whites who got on famously in Colonial America. This is a fact of capital importance in considering the white problem. The first black immigrants in America were not slaves; nor, for the most part, were the first white immigrants free. Most of the English colonists, in the beginning, were white indentured servants possessing remarkably little racial prejudice.

Back there, in the beginning, Negro and white indentured servants worked together in the same fields, lived together in the same huts and played together after working hours. And, of course, they also mated and married. So widespread was intermingling during this period that Peter Fontaine and other writers said the land "swarmed with mulatto" children.

From 1619 to about 1660, a period of primary importance in the history of America, America was not ruled by color. Some, perhaps all, of the first group of African-Americans worked out their terms of servitude and were freed. Within a few years. Negroes were accumulating property, pounds, and indentured servants. One Negro immigrant, Richard Johnson, even imported a white man and held him in servitude.

The breaking of the developing bonds of community between Negro and white Americans began with a conscious decision by the power structures of Colonial America. In the 1660s, men of power in the colonies decided that human slavery, based on skin color, was to be the linchpin of the new society. Having made this decision, they were forced to take another, more ominous step. Nature does not prepare men for the roles of master or racist. It requires rigid training, long persisted in, to make men and women deny other men and women and themselves. Men must be carefully taught to hate, and the lessons learned by one generation must be relearned by the next.

The Negro and white working class of the 1660s, the bulk of the population, had not been prepared for the roles outlined in the new script of statutes. It was necessary, therefore, to teach them that they could not deal with each other as fellow human beings.

How was this done?

It was done by an assault on the Negro's body and the white man's soul.

Legislatures ground out laws of every imaginable description and vigilantes whipped the doubtful into line. Behind the nightriders, of course, stood God himself in the person of parsons who blessed the rupture in human relations with words from the Bible.

Who was responsible for this policy?

The planters, the aristrocrats, the parsons, the lawyers, the Founding Fathers—*the good people:* they created the white problem.

Men would say later that there is a natural antipathy between Negro and white Americans. But the record belies them. Negro and white Americans were taught to hate and fear each other by words, sermons, whips, and signed papers. The process continued over a period of more than 100 years, a period which saw the destruction of the Negro family and the exclusion of Negro workers from one skilled trade after another. Nor did white men escape. They saw, dimly, what they were doing to themselves and to others and they drew back from themselves, afraid. But they did not stop; perhaps they could not stop. For, by now, racism had become central to their needs and to

their identity. Moreover, they were moved by dark and turbulent forces within. The evidence of their deeds bred fear and guilt which, in turn, led to more anxiety and guilt and additional demands for exclusion and aggression. Propelled by this dynamic, the whole process of excluding and fearing reached something of a peak in the first decade of the Twentieth Century with a carnival of Jim Crow in the South and a genteel movement which blanketed the North with restrictive covenants. The net result was a system of color-caste which divided communities, North and South, into mutually hostile groups.

Since that time, investigators have focused almost all of their attention on the Negro community, with the resulting neglect of primary determinants on the white side of the racial line. By asserting that the Negro problem os predominantly a white problem, this issue summons us to a new beginning and suggests that anything that hides the white American from a confrontation with himself and with the fact that he must change before the Negro can change is a major part of the problem.

two

EQUAL OPPORTUNITY: BUT FOR WHOM?

Born Female: The Negro Parallel

CAROLINE BIRD

Early in the 1960s a male professor of anthropology at Vassar College startled his class by listing the parallels between the disabilities Negroes suffer by virtue of their skin color and the disabilities women suffer by virtue of their sex. To begin with, neither women nor Negroes could hide the respective facts of sex or race. Generalizations about Negroes and women as workers relegated both groups to inferior status on the job. Both groups were regarded as a labor reserve, denied equal hiring, training, pay, promotion, responsibility, and seniority at work. Neither group was supposed to boss white men, and both were limited to jobs white men didn't want to do.

Negroes were supposed to be better able to stand uncomfortable physical labor; women, boring details. Both had emerged from a "previous condition of servitude" that had denied them the

vote, schooling, jobs, apprenticeships, and equal access to unions, clubs, professional associations, professional schools, restaurants, and public places. Strikingly similar rationalizations and defense mechanisms accommodated both denials of the central American ideal of equal opportunity.

Both women and Negroes were held to be inferior in intelligence, incapable of genius, emotional, childlike, irresponsible, and sexually threatening. They were supposed to be all right in their places, and were presumed to prefer staying there. (If they didn't they were shamed, ridiculed, or slandered.) Both were viewed as treacherous, wily, "intuitive," voluble, and proud of outwitting their menfolk or white folk.[1]

Most people didn't see these similarities, because they did not think women were unfairly treated. "Discrimination" meant Negroes and, to a lesser extent, Jews. In 1967, for instance, the Public Affairs Pamphlet, *Job Discrimina-*

From Born Female by Caroline Bird. Copyright 1968 by Caroline Bird. Reprinted by permission of David McKay Company, Inc.

[1] Helen Hacker, "Women As A Minority Group," *Social Forces*, December 1951.

138

tion Is Illegal, made no mention at all of sex and described the Civil Rights Act of 1964 as outlawing discrimination on the basis of "race, religion, creed, or national origin," although the law read, "race, color, religion, sex or national origin."

But career women began to mention the parallel, if only as a bitter joke. "Like the Negro in our land, we [women] may be off the chains, but we're not off the hook and, by no means, off the plantation," Jane Trahey declared. "If you take James Baldwin's *Another Country,* and substitute the word 'woman' every time you come to Negro, you will simply have another very true book."

"Well, at least they don't say that women have a fine sense of rhythm," another woman said during a discussion of the jobs regarded as appropriate for women in her organization. The analogy was close enough to the surface to keep a classic "Pat and Mike" type of joke going the rounds.

"Have you heard the news about God?" the first man asked.

"No, what?" the straight man replied.

"She's black."

Marian Trembley, store manager of Macy's San Francisco, said she was able to "get down to brass tacks" with a Negro executive on her staff who complained of discrimination on the part of colleagues. "Look here," she told him, "I'm a minority, too. Let's sit down and talk about it."

Surprising as it sounds, Negroes up to now have had a broader choice of occupations than women. Because 11 percent of the labor force has been Negro, equal rights leaders have argued that 11 percent of the payroll of every big company ought to be Negro, too. In 1967, Dr. Edward Gross, Professor of Sociology at the University of Washington, applied this principle to test discrimination against women.

There are nearly two men working throughout the country for every woman, so if women were to demand their fair share of the jobs in each of the hundreds of occupations listed by the Census, there would be a woman engineer for every two men engineers, a woman company president for every two men company presidents, and a woman secretary for every two male secretaries. Obviously, of course, neither women nor Negroes are getting their "fair share." But when Dr. Gross studied the statistics he discovered that the sex ratios were more lopsided than the race ratios. If women were to be fairly represented in every occupation, two-thirds of those now working would have to change jobs. Thousands of secretaries, for instance, would have to become engineers. Race equality would be much easier to achieve. Less than half the Negroes would have to change jobs in order to give Negroes their fair share of every occupation. Part of the difference, of course, was that there were "bonafide sex qualifications" for some jobs. The EEOC maintained that there wasn't a job in the occupational list for which a Negro could not qualify, but it permitted employers to specify women for modeling or attending women's washrooms. Nevertheless, the jobs for which sex was a "bonafide qualification" were much too rare to account for the difference Dr. Gross found in segregation by race and sex.

The minority status of women went unnoticed because they are, as Helen Hacker said, "the only minority in history which lives with the master race."

In comparing the two "minorities," she said that women are more important to the "master race" of white men than Negroes, and they arouse more ambivalent feelings. Men, after all, have to live with women, but whites can choose to live with Negroes or deal with them at arm's length as they please. Hostility between the races can, after all, be managed, if only by such morally repugnant devices as South African apartheid, but hostility between men and women threatens family solidarity. Historically, principled opposition to woman suffrage has come from people who sincerely feared that families would break up if wives were given a chance to vote independently of their husbands at the polls.

The comparison between women and Negroes is suggestive in many areas. For instance, the conspicuous absence of women in certain fields seems proof that women just don't care about them. But something more than sex may be involved. Chemical, steel, and railroad companies which limit women workers frequently turn up on lists of companies charged with discrimination against Jews and Negroes. One of the few things Negroes, Jews, and women have in common is that they rarely head industrial enterprises. Could it be that for some reason or other these industries put more emphasis than others on employing people who "look like us"?

Or take the moves under way to make men's and women's colleges coeducational. Usually these plans are discussed in terms of changing relations between men and women. Issues of sex morality are argued. But Negro colleges are beginning to recruit white students, and Ivy League colleges are going out of their way to recruit Negro applicants. Can it be that there is a rebellion afoot against "face validity" of every kind?

Comparison between women and Negroes sheds new light on the handicaps they both face in the job market. Both are fired before white men and hired after them. Both are arbitrarily limited to the lower-paying, least productive, less-skilled jobs and sometimes the same ones. For many years, for instance, Southern textile mills reserved for white women those jobs that were filled in the North by Negro men. It is not surprising to learn from the Bureau of Labor Statistics that women average 2.4 years less than men on the jobs they hold, while Negro men average two years less than white men. The gap between the races in job tenure is similar to the gap between the sexes. The similarity is worth noting because it suggests reasons why neither Negroes nor women gravitate to steady work. Both are fired before white men, of course, but both are also more apt to quit because they move away or can't get transportation to the job. Women and Negroes often do not have as much control over where they live as white men.

The frequent moves that rising executives have to make are a special hardship for Negroes; it is much easier for white men to find a convenient place to live in a new town. Career women have the same problem. If they are married, they are rarely in a position to choose a residence on the basis of convenience to their work. . . .

Negroes who fit the Southern stereotype used to be approved, by Southerners, as "good Nigras." Myrdal found that leading whites sometimes consulted "old, practically illiterate ex-servants while cold-shouldering the upper-class

Negro." "Uncle Tom" Negroes who accept these favors often criticize the Negro race more harshly than do whites.

"Good" or "real" women enjoy the same dubious advantage. Office "housekeepers" are often treated with much greater deference than women who make independent contributions to an organization. The opinions of a good secretary are frequently solicited and treated with a respect seldom accorded the opinions of professional women on the staff who are, of course, less apt to mirror the boss's opinions. "Most males do not enjoy working relationships on an equal basis with women who may bring additional talents to the task at hand," said a woman librarian. "It has been more comfortable to accept ideas if they come from women at the clerical level," she went on. And women who rise as office wives or housekeepers believe in the limited role of women in business as firmly as the remaining old-fashioned Uncle Tom Negroes accept the inferiority of the Negro race. Like the Uncle Toms, these "Aunt Janes" are often used by the management to keep their own kind in line. . . .

Hypocritical insistence that opportunity is really equal is the cruelest form of discrimination. It implies that the loser in any contest has lost through his own inabilities. And while women and Negroes realize that the cards are stacked against them, they are compelled by the prevailing rhetoric to act as if they had actually lost out in fair competition. Negroes and women who maintain their mental health develop some kind of defense against the imputation of incompetence. As employers complain, both groups need continual and massive injections of praise

and attention—injections that become a burden to the supervisory staff.

Myrdal has decribed sympathetically the efforts of superior Negroes to keep their emotional balance without "falling into the bitter complacency of the inferiority doctrine or by overdoing the equality doctrine and trying to build up a case that black is superior to white." A third temptation, Myrdal has said, is "to exaggerate the accusation against whites and so use caste disabilities to cover all personal failings." Women have used all three defenses against the doctrine of intrinsic inferiority. As their critics maliciously point out, career women gloat over every instance in which a woman outdoes a man, and blame most of their shortcomings on discrimination, yet they can be easily trapped into conceding that they are not as good as men.

Negroes and women both are popularly supposed to be troublesome employees because they tend to "take things personally." But so, of course, does anyone whose status is uncertain. The consolations of religion, the petty satisfaction of sabotage, withdrawal from competition ("I don't care"), mockery of the powerful boss and contravention of his purposes, and the pursuit of small advantage by devious means are characteristic outlets for resentment. Women clerical workers and Negro domestic or menial workers often exasperate their employers by their unwillingness to "see the point," and at some level of consciousness this provocation is deliberate. The tragedy of this response, immediately satisfying as it might be, is that it provides a rationale for discrimination.

The intuition ascribed to women and Negroes can be fully explained by the closer attention these groups are compelled to pay to the personal responses of their superiors. "Most middle- and upper-class whites get satisfaction out of the subserviency and humbleness of lower-class Negroes," said Myrdal. Most men in middle and top management got satisfaction out of the subserviency of the women who waited on them at home or work.

The "separate but equal" distinction between the sexes is drawn with all the ambiguities and ambivalences that mark the distinctions between the races, as well. The profusion of Negro organizations impressed Myrdal, and as a Swede he was inclined to attribute it in part to the over-organization of American life in general. He pointed out that Negroes excluded from professional organizations formed their own, and that the ones that were Negro could be distinguished by the term "National," where the white organizations called themselves "American."

But for every Negro counterpart organization there also seems to be a woman's counterpart organization, too, setting up an unbelievably awkward apparatus. There is a National Medical Association for Negro doctors, and an American Medical Women's Association for women doctors, in spite of the fact that the American Medical Association admits both Negroes and women. There are women's associations for accountants, architects, engineers, journalists, and on down through the alphabet of professions. There are social, fraternal, professional, political, and business organizations for women paralleling every kind of organization set up for men, and many of the men's groups have women's auxiliaries for their wives, as well.

The very names of women's organizations suggest all the ways in which

women have felt themselves segregated. There is an Advertising Women of New York and a Women Leaders Round Table, although women are admitted to the Advertising Club of New York and the Million Dollar Round Table of high-producing insurance salesmen. There is the Society of Woman Geographers, the Women's National Press Club, and Women World War Veterans, Inc.

The New York phone book yields Women for President and Other Public Office, Inc., Federation of Women Shareholders in American Business, Inc., Women's Architectural Auxiliary, Women's Association of Allied Beverage Industries, Women's Metropolitan Golf Association. There are the American Women in Radio and Television, and the American Women Buyers' Club. Semantically speaking, one of the most arresting is the organization of utility company home economists who call themselves the Electrical Women's Round Table.

The time-honored argument for segregated organizations has been that they give minority leaders and professional workers a chance to develop. Negro schools provided employment for Negro teachers, and women's colleges provided employment for women scholars. Women are sometimes accused of wanting to get into men's colleges or men's clubs because they want to get close to men in a sexual way or become men themselves. When psychological testers ask people which sex they would like to be if they could be born again, many more women than men want to change their sex. This need not be taken as evidence of rampant penis envy. It may simply reflect a desire to achieve male *status*. No one would look for murky psychological explanations if a similar survey should demonstrate that many more Negroes than whites wanted to change race. Straightforward economic reasons provide ample motivation.

Whites—and particularly white men—continue to impute a sexual motive to the ambitions of Negroes and women because they themselves see demands for equality as a sexual threat. If men are driven to success by the necessity to prove that they are "men," they're likely to feel that women who aspire to success are out to unman them. Psychiatrist John Dollard of Yale analyzed the complex sexual basis of white prejudice against Negroes in his *Caste and Class in a Southern Town*. The point here is that the sexual aspect of segregation or integration is much more important to men than to women.

The evasions, denials, and hypocrisies that arise whenever men discuss —or more often, pointedly ignore—the possibility of women assuming high-level jobs all have certain sexual implications. There is an etiquette to discussion of women in business that is akin to what Myrdal has called the "etiquette of race relations." If the topic is discussed at all, for instance, it is lost in clouds of verbiage. No one seems willing or able to speak plainly or see it as a simple moral issue the way Myrdal taught people to see the Negro "problem."

More often, the etiquette prescribes silence. If you don't talk about a situation, the presumption is that it does not exist or will go away. But as Freud has said, the repressed idea returns. The censored problem enriches gossip and speeds along the organizational grapevine. A major cosmetic company, for instance, was known to have few women above the secretarial level. Women knew about the company and passed the word to each other, but the com-

pany officers denied the charge. They had no written, formal policy about women, they insisted. It was just that "for some reason no qualified girls seem to have applied to us." Some companies used to complain that Negroes did not apply to them, either.

As long as the subject is taboo, complaints can be blamed on somebody else. Negroes who complain are "bad apples"; women who complain are dismissed as psychiatric cases or sexually unattractive. The party who brings the charge is expected to bear the burden of proof: Would *you* want your sister to marry a Negro? Would *you* let a woman operate on you? "Our Nigras were happy, it's those outside agitators who are stirring them up," some Southerners still maintain. "Women were contented until Betty Friedan got hold of them," Old Masculinists grumble.

Responsibility is frequently shifted to third parties, most of whom aren't asked to give an opinion. Manufacturers allege that Negro storekeepers would rather buy from white distributors. Employers say that women would rather work for a man than a woman. "I would be willing to put a Negro or a woman on the job. *I* am not prejudiced. But fellow workers or customers wouldn't stand for it." Women can thank students of racial and religious discrimination for pointing out that policy-makers usually have the power to overcome these third-party objections if they are willing to take a stand.

Another advantage of ignorance is that motive can be safely imputed to the victims. Thus there is no Negro problem because Negroes love us. There is no woman problem because women love us. Women executives wouldn't be comfortable in the executive dining room with all those men. Women don't want to sell outside the office. Negroes would rather go to "their own" church than mix with the whites. Women and Negroes don't want better jobs because they seldom ask for them. Women "like" detail work.

Myrdal accused white Southerners of turning a deliberate blind eye to the Negroes they claimed to know and love so that they could maintain their view of them. Men were accused of the same wishful thinking. "It has always been a part of male vanity to contend that marriage is the only real goal of a girl's life," Pauline M. Leet, Director of Special Programs at Franklin and Marshall College, a men's college in Lancaster, Pennsylvania, told a meeting of students. Mrs. Leet was pioneering a strenuous program of coaching high-school dropouts to get them into college and keep them there. She intended to stir up the complacent Franklin and Marshall undergraduates, and drew an analogy between attitudes toward race and sex to make her point. "If you could be privy to some of the feelings girls have when they exchange names, you might not be so smug," Mrs. Leet warned the students. Her speech moved some undergraduates to demand the admission of women to a college that has been educating men only for 179 years.

Both women and Negroes have been ignored when they step outside their "places." Legislators turned aside the demands of early suffragettes by refusing to lift their eyes from their desks when the petitioners appeared. Southerners discussed the Negro problem before Negro waiters because they were not supposed to hear table talk. Myrdal told the story of a Negro waiter who answered the obvious questions by saying, "No, I don't mind, I'm just a block of wood." Women complain that bosses and husbands accept them as "part of the furniture." The complaint that Southerners treated Negroes as "work objects" could be paralleled by the complaint that many men discuss women primarily as "sex objects."

Mrs. Leet advised the young men of Franklin and Marshall College that it was both difficult and important for them to understand women. Charging that anthologists have been "sexist" in omitting women poets, just as historians have been "racist" in ignoring the contributions of Negroes, she urged them to learn about women in the only way open to them—by associating with them as people. . . .

Men aren't usually impressed by such commentary. Women are different, they say. Women have a "special place," so different from the place of men that the very concept of equality is treacherous. Wherever that place is, even if above, as men sometimes maintain, it is always located with reference to the needs of men. "Who will do the cooking?" an alarmed member of Congress cried out when the draft of women was suggested in World War II. Southerners used to object to higher education for Negroes because educated "Niggers" wouldn't do dirty work.

And if the special place of women has disadvantages, there are supposed to be compensations. "Miss Jones is probably being treated unfairly (and stupidly) when she is passed over for a job in favor of a man with less ability, but I don't think she is morally wronged the way a Negro is wronged when his race is held against him," Sandford Brown, a senior editor of *The Saturday Evening Post,* wrote us after a lively conversation on the subject. "Our social mores relieve Miss Jones of certain economic obligations on account of her sex as well as assigning her certain disadvantages—and I don't think equality of opportunity for women can be a moral absolute unless there are changes to equalize the burdens between the sexes."

"Women have a better life as it is," another man put it. "Would you do away with chivalry?" Negroes are in a different situation, he said, because they have no compensation for their disabilities in the job market.

There is, of course, a compensation for Negroes, but it goes by the dirty word "paternalism." Southern traditionalists used to maintain that it was all right to keep the "Nigras" down because "we" take care of them. "It is a sign of social distinction to a white man to stand in this paternalistic relation to Negroes," Myrdal reported. Chivalry, too, was upper-class. Class leveling has made both attitudes suspect. The advantages of the carefree Negro existence are no longer a conversational staple of the South, not even among Southerners who call women "ladies."

Women can thank the Negro rights movement for alerting the literate population to the self-serving attitude that has imprisoned women as well as Negroes.

Like Negroes, women have been denied training, and then denied work on the grounds that they are not skilled. Both have been confined to low-paid, monotonous jobs which carry a high rate of absenteeism and turnover on the grounds that both groups have been too unstable to trust with more responsibility. Then when they have stayed away from work or quit in disgust or defeat, the charge of instability was proved. The hypothesis was confirmed.

Sexist and racist job assignments are similarly self-confirming. Negroes are allowed to become entertainers because they are supposed to be naturally funny. They are allowed to become firemen on trains because millenniums of exposure to the tropical sun are supposed to have conditioned them to withstand excessive heat. When they took the only jobs offered them, the lowly work they had to do was cited as evidence of their instability, just as the success of women in the monotonous clerical jobs to which they have been confined is cited as proof of a special aptitude for enduring boredom.

Most people now understand that Negroes who are not ambitious were responding rationally to the fact that ambition doesn't "pay" a Negro as it does a white, self-defeating as this attitude is. The Negro analogy helps contemporary feminists to see that what early suffragettes deplored as the apathy of women won't be overcome until society rewards women for trying instead of punishing them for their efforts to achieve.

"As long as American Negroes consciously or unconsciously saw themselves as an inferior race, they inevitably collaborated in their own exploitation," Ellen and Kenneth Keniston began their article "The American Anachronism: The Image of Women at Work" in the Summer 1964 issue of *The American Scholar.* But like Negroes, women sometimes refuse to collaborate in their own exploitation. On December 14, 1967, New York City women picketed the office of the EEOC with sandwich boards reading: WOMEN CAN THINK AS WELL AS TYPE and SEX SEGREGATION IS AS UNFAIR AS RACE SEGREGATION.

Meanwhile, of course, most women continued to rate themselves on how well they were accepted by men, just as Negroes used to rate each other on how close their skin color was to white. Both Negroes and women realized that things being what they were, the royal road to success lay in winning the favor of "The Man," as Negroes called the white boss. They saw more clearly than he that his favor was more important than their performance when it came to winning pleasanter work assignments, time off, minor points of prestige, and other small but realistic advantages open to workers in dead-end jobs.

Adoption of the dominant stereotypes doomed most Negroes and women to self-hatred. Any minority which takes most of its power, prestige, and values from the majority cannot organize in its own defense. There are anti-Semitic Jews, anti-Negro Negroes, and anti-women women. Negroes who rise because of extraordinary talent and application tend to think that most Negroes don't get ahead because they don't really try. "Upper-class Negroes are inclined to minimize the handicaps the Negro caste labors under," Myrdal wrote in *The American Dilemma.* "They are often as overbearing to common Negroes as they are weak and unassertive to whites." Achieving women solve the problem of differentiating themselves from the unaspiring women in their organizations in much the same unlovely way.

"Give women time!" gradualists urge when the disabilities of women are pointed out. "They're newly up from slavery!" These conservatives expect women, as they expect Negroes, to thrill to their escape from the literal and figurative slavery that would have been their lots if they had been born a century earlier. And if this is cold comfort, the gradualists promise a bright future for grandchildren, provided that no one upsets the applecart in the present.

Over the past century and a half, Negroes and women have had the same friends and the same enemies. Their enemies were conservatives, Southerners, male legislators, literal interpreters of the Bible, and Establishment politicians fearful of upsetting the known balance of power. Their friends were Marxists, intellectuals, the city-bred, preachers of the social gospel, and politicians looking for new votes.

On most fronts, the Negro rights movement was one step ahead of the feminist movement. Negroes got the vote before women. ("He can vote," a suffragette poster proclaimed, showing a rather unattractive Negro. "Why can't you?") Race discrimination in employment was outlawed before consideration was given to outlawing discrimination on the basis of sex.

The full employment of the mid-1960s brought the possibility of equal work opportunities to increasing numbers of Negroes and women. Acceptance of Negroes and women in jobs they had not previously held tended to break down the prejudice against them so that it could never again be quite so formidable a barrier. In World War II, white men got used to fighting and working alongside Negroes in the armed forces and in war plants. In 1968, the shortage of clerical help gave thousands of office workers the experience of working happily and cooperatively alongside colleagues of an unexpected race or sex.

In the executive talent shortage of the 1960s, some organizations encouraged women in the patronizing way they had encouraged promotable Negroes when the Negro rights movement was popular, but the efforts to see that qualified women were promoted were much more half-hearted than those promoting Negroes. In 1967, for instance, 15 percent of a group of companies queried by the Bureau of National Affairs said they had undertaken aggressive recruiting of promotable Negroes in response to Title VII, but only one company reported an aggressive policy of recruiting women.

"I'm not ready for a woman," a frank management consultant confessed in 1966 when a woman executive recommended a woman for a job he had open. "But boy, would I love to get hold of a good Negro!"

three

POVERTY: THE AFFLUENT SOCIETY, BUT . . .

Let Them Eat Promises: The Politics of Hunger

NICK KOTZ

Judging from past experience with other social legislation, a full-fledged national commitment will require a basic reorientation of attitudes concerning

Reprinted from Nick Kotz, Let Them Eat Promises: The Politics of Hunger in America (Englewood Cliffs, N.J.: Prentice-Hall, Inc. 1969), pp. 20–30, 240–48. Copyright 1969 by Nick Kotz. Reprinted by permission of the publisher.

federal aid to the poorest Americans. This nation has never decided that its government should guarantee every citizen an adequate diet. Food aid to the poor simply is not viewed by affluent Americans in the same light as aid to other segments of society—whether aid takes the form of crop subsidy payments, oil depletion allowances, ship building subsidies, government-guaranteed home loans, or a thousand other government benefits which touch various groups of Americans. This strange inconsistency of attitudes about federal benefits was dramatized in 1969 by arch-reactionary Representative Otto Passman of Louisiana, who told the House about attitudes in his congressional district toward food aid reform. Angered by discussion of more food aid to the poor, a constituent wrote Passman "humorously" recommending that the hungry poor would be better motivated to seek work and grow gardens if their federal food aid consisted of Army C rations placed in garbage dumps. The constituent concluded his letter by thanking Passman for "the wonderful [government] benefits you have provided this area."

Ben W. Heineman, chairman of the President's Commission on Income Maintenance Programs,[1] described this American attitude to the McGovern Committee: "It has been public policy to have the nonpoor decide what the poor need, and to provide them with these things rather than with money which could be misspent. It has generally been believed that dependency and poverty spring from faulty values, laziness, apathy, and the like, and the treatment of poor and dependent families should include rehabilitation, services, and guidance."

These attitudes are illustrated in high public office when an Agriculture Secretary (Orville Freeman) dismisses the idea of a cash assistance system for food aid on grounds that old people "would use the money to play bingo"

[1] President Lyndon Johnson appointed this study group in 1968. It was scheduled to present its recommendations in late 1969.

or a Presidential counselor (Arthur Burns) worries that even food stamps are not a foolproof way of feeding the poor because "they may buy potato chips and soft drinks." Such scornful attitudes toward the unworthiness and lack of capability of the poor have led to policies of providing minimum survival aid only after the most careful restraints are placed on the poor man's freedom.

After visiting the poor in America, Heineman rejected these hostile characterizations of the poor. "Given the extremely low income of many of our [poor] witnesses," said Heineman, "I was amazed at how they could manage at all. They often displayed incredible ingenuity in food preparation and provided as much variety and as balanced a diet as could be expected. Ingenuity, however, cannot compensate for the lack of cash to buy meats, fruits, vegetables, and milk."

Heineman, chairman of the board of Northwest Industries, and a man who has changed his own attitudes after studying welfare programs, concluded that "our current food programs are encroachments on individual freedom of choice."

As the politics of hunger gain momentum, it is natural that discussion should move toward broader issues of public welfare. If the poor are malnourished mainly because they lack money, then a more fundamental approach to their problems might be taken by radically revising the nation's patchwork welfare benefits or by providing a guaranteed annual income. From a practical standpoint, a food program provides only limited assistance if a family still lacks money for adequate clothing, housing, and medical care.

In a broader sense, one of the

greatest handicaps for the poor is their total sense of powerlessness, their feeling of complete impotence within the cycle of poverty and dependency. These feelings are augmented by a welfare system in which the dole is grudgingly given and regimentally supervised. The use of food stamps in itself can be a degrading experience which leads proud men to go hungry rather than be marked out as helpless. When the poor person goes to the grocery store, federal regulations require that he hand the food stamp book to the grocer, who then removes the proper amount of stamps. The objective of this regulation is to discourage trading or selling of food stamps. If the poor man's pride already suffers, not being trusted to tear out his own stamps is just one further indignity.

At the heart of the matter is whether the poor are to be given their survival money in such paternalistic fashion that they are degraded as human beings and limited in exercise of the freedom essential to ending their dependency. For the poor black in Mississippi, for example, the required relationship with a county welfare official often may be just as degrading as that with the plantation patron. "Dignity is very important," says Dr. Mayer. "Very poor Americans need to eat what other Americans eat so they feel they are a part or this country."

Of course old people will play bingo. Of course the poor will spend money foolishly or whimsically or indulgently, just as the middle class and the rich do. One cannot insure that the poor will spend money wisely any more than that the wealthy will use their multiple government subsidies wisely. The question is whether we in this counrty are willing to permit even the poorest, most unfortunate Americans the honor of not having to beg for existence, of not having to go through one line after another answering questions and identifying themselves as the poor who live at the will of the state. I would strongly argue that the poor in affluent America should be given this opportunity to succeed or fail, to feed their children or drink beer, to live more nearly as other Americans do.

The poorest Americans who have been buried in the Deep South, the Appalachian hills, the Indian reservations, the *barrios* of the Southwest, and the big city ghetto did not fail to make it in America simply because they lacked ambition or ability. The plantation system, the migrant system, the mining system, the Indian welfare system all created long odds against a man's breaking out of a cycle of abject, dependent peonage. On that basis alone, justice demands that every American be guaranteed a decent minimum income.

Arguments for a minimum income plan to replace present categorical aid programs can be advanced strictly in terms of cost effectiveness. The cost to America eventually should be less and the results better if men have enough money to fend for themselves. The public sector could devote its money more effectively toward job training and education than toward building an increasing bureaucratic structure to superintend welfare and food programs. The growth of even more patchwork programs seems inevitable as legislation is now introduced in Congress calling for a "clothing stamp" program.

"We ought not to be talking about giving people 'food stamps' or 'bed stamps' or 'rent stamps' at all, except as emergency and interim programs," said Yale Law School professor Edward Sparer, who served as a member of the Citizens' Board of Inquiry. "We ought to be talking about income and income maintenance programs."

Income maintenance advocate Heineman points to the history of the two-year struggle for food aid reform and suggests: "If we somehow solve the food problem, we must then solve the housing problem. If, after more hearings, new commissions, television documentaries, and renewed public indignation, we solve the housing problem, we will then have to solve the clothing problem and the medical problem and the transportation problem and so on and so on.

"It seems to me that we must recognize all of these problems for what they are—interrelated attributes of the lack of money income. Perhaps, if we do that, we can make a concerted attack on the basic problem, rather than take time-consuming, inefficient, and unsure routes such as the one we have followed in the past. For that path has put us where we are today."

Nixon Urban Affairs chief Moynihan hoped that the family allowance system would be a major step toward survival with dignity for the poor. Most of the original food aid reformers, while agreeing in principle with Heineman and Moynihan, are seriously concerned that the poor in America will continue to suffer hunger and malnutrition, if reasonable food aid reforms now are delayed any longer. The delay could continue for years while the country begins to debate the very broad and controversial subject of family allowances, income maintenance, minimum guaranteed income, or negative income tax. As Senator Walter Mondale told Heineman, "I don't want

children to starve during the ten years it is going to take us to debate income maintenance."

A reformed food stamp program would be a form of income maintenance and could easily be converted into such a plan if and when the nation approves it.

The promise of solving the hunger and malnutrition problem in America will not be kept if it is given only the same priority as other national promises on jobs, housing, and poverty. It will take the kind of commitment with which the United States builds a weapon system on schedule or decides in 1961 to go to the moon before 1970, and then, at the cost of billions of dollars, does just that.

Before the nation makes this kind of commitment it will have to answer the kind of question Apollo 8 Astronaut Frank Borman posed after his trip into space. "When we looked back over the lunar horizon at the earth," he said, "I found that I could take my thumbnail and put it up and cover the earth. You begin to realize our planet is a very fragile, a very small and very delicate piece of granite in the midst of a black nothing. And the thing that so concerns you is how in the world can the human beings that produced this technical marvel—a really mechanical miracle— how can we do all that and yet in all recorded history not have been able in some way to live together in peace and harmony."

This is a time of crucial questioning in America, and the answers we provide may determine the fate of a free American society. Seeing that government still fails to act, a Dr. Robert Coles questions: "Why must these children still go hungry, still be sick? Why do American children get born without the help of a doctor, and never see a doctor all their lives? It is awful, it is humiliating for all of us that these questions still have to be asked in a nation like this, the strongest, richest that ever was."

Perhaps these questions have to be asked because we have accepted too much at face value about ourselves; we have accepted too many assumptions about the essential benevolence of our institutions, without really analyzing how they really operate and how they affect all Americans.

The politics of hunger in America is a dismal story of human greed and callousness, of immorality sanctioned and aided by the government of the United States. But it is also a story that does provide hope that men can change things, that men do care about fulfilling this country's highest ideals and do care about their fellow human beings.

A few men and women forged at least the beginnings of a new politics of hunger. None of those food aid reformers are revolutionaries. None threatened to tear the country down if they could not change it. But all did threaten and continue to threaten the status quo of American institutions, and that kind of challenge is not popular with the institution rulers, whether in Washington, D.C., Washington County, Mississippi, or Washington state.

The institutions have malfunctioned badly when a few men in a few committees of Congress have held such outsized influence over food for the hungry poor. The institutions are functioning badly when the nation declines to challenge the power these few men exercise within their special preserves in the traditional system. The institutions need reshaping when a great

department of government and a few congressional committees can conspire together for years to subordinate the needs of hungry people to the needs of commercial agriculture. The institutions need rethinking when "local control" in America has for years given some men the option of deciding whether other men will eat or go hungry.

Our basic American institutions are on trial, and as John Gardner of the Urban Coalition has said, these institutions are caught in a savage crossfire between men who love only their rigidities and other men whose hatred of their imperfections blinds them to the promise of a free society in America. Our institutions may well be destroyed, he said, unless they are capable of change to meet human needs more adequately.

Students, in particular, are questioning the priorities, the values, and the honesty of their leaders.

Through the looking glass of America, one can see why the students are discontent. We do have the food; we do have the institutions for education and health; but we have not possessed the will to eliminate man's oldest scourge. Our ethics have become perverted when it is considered more important to starve a man to make him earn, than it is to insure that he and his children maintain good health and a zest for living.

Does the hunger issue indicate the corruption of our society and provide insight into the magnitude of our misallocated values? Or else, does this issue—raised by questioning citizens—reveal the possibilities for men to change the institutions, to meet the moral imperatives of a better society? Now only revealed, far from being resolved, it stands as a challenge both to those who criticize and deplore, and to those who claim America's system still can handle its problems.

"Something very like the honor of American democracy is at issue," President Nixon has said.

This nation oftentimes has not lived up to the ideals of its democracy. The struggle for a newer world and more perfect institutions may well fail. One can hope, though, that the modern politics of hunger will not end before many Americans respond to the plea of Senator Robert F. Kennedy after he had seen the hungry children of America.

"Someone wrote a number of years ago," he said, "that 'perhaps we cannot prevent this world from being a world in which children are tortured, but we can reduce the number of tortured children. If we do not do this, who will do this?' [2] It seems to me it is our responsibility, all of us."

[2] Albert Camus.

four

WAR AND RUMORS OF THE MILITARY— INDUSTRIAL COMPLEX

Pentagon Capitalism: The Political Economy of War

SEYMOUR MELMAN

Military industry and research help civilian industry via "spillover" in knowledge and design factors. True, the development of computers for civilian use

From *Pentagon Capitalism: The Political Economy of War*, pp. 172–77, 180–83 by Seymour Melman. Copyright 1970 by Seymour Melman. Used by permission of McGraw-Hill Book Company.

got something from the investment made in computers for military use. True, the commercial jetliner came, in part, from the Air Force's jet refueling tanker. True, we have nuclear energy capability that may be increasingly useful for civilian purposes. Do these economically meaningful "spillovers" justify the use of over three-fourths of the government's research and development budget for military and allied purposes?

None of these "spillover" effects justifies the gross depletion and deterioration in many of our civilian industries. I recorded the first draft of this book on a tape recorder that was made in Japan, not America. Americans did major theoretical work in solid-state physics and enormous work on its technological application. But those technological applications have been, mainly, military applications. That is why, for the first time, new, mass-produced, durable-goods products are designed, produced, and marketed outside the United States. The inexpensive transistor radio, TV set, and tape recorder are products of the electronics industry of Japan, a country where the young electronics engineers have no place to go except to civilian-industry employers.

Military priority produces domestic stability because of high-level economic activity. On the contrary, sustained military priority and the unavailability of resources for much civilian investment is producing insurrection at home. The "domestic stability" induced by large military forces is incompatible with the values of freedom in society.

Military priority over a long period makes impossible the reconstruction of cities and the investment in human capital and in new work places that is essential if thirty million Americans are to be economically developed. About 7.5 million American families live in poverty. One estimate of the capital outlay required for their economic development is $50,000 per family. Thus, a capital fund of $375 million is required to raise the impoverished of our own country to productive status. That capital fund, and the manpower it must repre-

sent, are both unavailable and inaccessible today and in the foreseeable future, so long as the present military priority is sustained.

Military-industrial firms are new industries with a high level of technical competence and represent a general enrichment of the technical and managerial resources of the nation. Close scrutiny suggests that managements of the subsidiaries of the national military-industrial firm are infused with a trained incapacity for operating civilian enterprises functioning in the civilian market place. Attempts by these managements to enter civilian markets have mainly failed. The failures did not result from personal incompetence. Rather they stemmed from the fact that the management methods, costs, and technological requirements for the military market are inappropriate in the civilian sphere. Thus, the management style, technology, equipment, and practices required for producing certain nuclear submarines at $12 per pound are hopelessly inappropriate for producing commercial oil tankers at less than $1 per pound.

Military-industrial firms can readily convert to civilian work if that is required. The evidence of the 1963–1964 period, when there were minor curtailments in military contracts, instructs us to the contrary. It will be necessary to motivate these organizations strongly to attempt possible conversion planning. Beyond that, it will be necessary to plan for salvaging the individuals involved in the military-industrial sector with appropriate retraining and relocation programs to aid them in transferring them to civilian work.

We might just as well maintain military priorities, for even if we tried to realign priorities, Congress would not allocate the funds needed. In 1939–1940, the Congress of the United States appropriated 42 percent of the federal budget for social welfare, community development, health, education, housing, and allied purposes. The same set of purposes recently received about 12 percent of Congressional appropriations. There is no science from which to forecast that if Congress could do it in 1940, it could not do it again today. There is nothing in the nature of Congress as an institution that precludes changing an order of priorities.

Concentration of decision-power in the federal government is inevitable and as in the Department of Defense, desirable, in the name of economic-industrial efficiency. Efficiency indeed. Under the guidance of the Secretary of Defense, the F-111 airplane was supposed to cost up to $3.9 million. The latest estimate is $12.7 million. This ratio between expected and actual costs is fairly typical of industrial performance for the Department of Defense. Wherever the customer or competitor constraints of a commercial market are operative, this sort of cost performance would compel either a change of management, or bankruptcy, or both. In the land of military-industry, gross inefficiency has become normal. And so the polite thing is to be learned about the programs for "cost effectiveness" and the miracles generated by "cost-benefit analysis," thereby detracting attention from staggering cost-excesses that would be self-penalizing elsewhere. There is little evidence to be found in these spheres of ordinary workaday economy and efficiency.

If university professors and students would work on research problems of interest to the Department of Defense, then all will be well for the national defense, and for the universities and for the nation as well. This is not necessarily true. There are strong grounds for supposing that long concentration on military priorities, with the proliferation of military research activity, threatens the integrity of the university and undermines the traditional function of the university: teaching people and generating new knowledge.

The operation of the Department of Defense and its connections with industry are in good order as long as this is under civilian control. Holders of the highest offices of the state-management are nominally civilians. They are not professional military officers and they ordinarily wear civilian clothes to work. However, the difference between "military" and "civilian" in the government becomes blurred when the largest part of the federal budget is controlled by the Pentagon, whose control systems ramify into industry, the universities, and other areas of American society.

Whatever else may be said about the state-management, a managerial type of government is a bearable price to pay for a welfare state in a technological society. The fact is, more than two-thirds of spending by the federal government is for current and past military operations. In 1968, only 12 percent of the federal budget was used for health, education, welfare, and community development. By preempting manpower and money in the name of defense, the state-management has led the way in restricting the money and manpower left over for the human care of human beings. Furthermore, there is little evidence to support the proposition that only a centralized, federally controlled managerial organization is able to plan and execute activities designed to improve the condition of life.

Whatever may be said about the power-expanding propensity of the state-management, its activities are finally controlled by the Congress. It is true that the Congress votes the money required by the state-management. But the state-management has found ways of participating in these Congressional decisions. On February 20, 1969, the Associated Press reported that the Pentagon spends about $4 million a year for a lobbying force of 339 men, or about one lobbyist for every two members of Congress. With such continuing representation on Capitol Hill, the Pentagon is in a fine position to get its message across. Also, the state-management can use its unequaled capital-investment capability so that location decisions for new industrial and base operations improve Pentagon popularity among important congressmen.

> Lockheed, the largest defense firm, last year opened a plant in Charleston, S.C., home of Representative L. Mendel Rivers, chairman of the House Armed Services Committee. Last year also, General Dynamics, second largest defense plant (sic), placed on electronics subsidiary in Camden, Ark., after Senator John L. McClellan, chairman of the Government Operations Committee, had visited the Fort Worth plant where General Dynamics makes the F-111 (TFX). Senator McClellan has said that he asked the president of General Dynamics to take a look at what Arkansas had to offer when he was being shown around Fort Worth by that gentleman. (The Nation, October 21, 1968.)

Apart from its large size, the Department of Defense is just another government bureaucracy. The size of its budget and its control over people give this bureaucracy very special capabilities. Most important is its production decision-power. This latter set of powers identify this bureaucracy as a self-expanding industrial management.

The very diversity of the state-management's operation gives the President more choices in policy-making. Constitutionally, the President of the United States is a key decision-maker with respect to use of American military power. However, the President's alternatives are, in turn, defined by the great importance of the Pentagon. The result is that military options dominate the array of options considered.

A state-management is inevitable on account of the complex technologies that are used in military systems. Actually, the state-management orders the characteristics of military technology. Military technology has no life of its own. It is instrumental to the state-management, which was created to serve particular political requirements as perceived by President Kennedy and his aides upon entering office. . . .

Managers from military contracting firms go to work in the Pentagon. With their corporate associations they can exert important policy pressure on the operation of the state-management. The critical consideration is not where individuals come from but which institution has crucial decision-power. The state-management decides on which submanagements in the Pentagon industrial empire get work orders. The state-management also decides which firms shall undergo the greatest expansion. These are the controlling production decisions and they are made at the state-management level.

Consider the parallel condition in

the ordinary multi-division industrial firm. In that environment, the central office characteristically draws upon management men from the various divisions of the firm. Thereby, the divisions of the firm do not control the central office. That is so because it is the central office that is the location of critical decisions on capital investment and other key production decisions. The state-management in the Pentagon is similarly related to the managements of the sub-firms in its industrial empire. Many people have assumed that movement of former "defense contractor" managers to the Pentagon is evidence of their control over the Pentagon; the unstated underlying assumption is that the various military contracting firms are, in fact, private and autonomous. That is precisely not the case. These firms' operations for the Pentagon are controlled by the state-management.

Since there is no profit calculation by the state-management on its own functioning, it is not capitalism. All the main attributes of industrial capitalism (other than the profit calculation) are present in the state-management. There is a hierarchical organization, separation of decision-making from production, and sustained pressure to enlarge decision-power of the management group. In the modern corporation, recorded profit has often ceased to be an autonomous indicator of the success of a management. Instead, profit has become a factor that is determined, within a wide range, by management decisions on allocation and size of key costs. The state-management gets the effect of profit-accumulation and investment (i.e., enlarging its decision-power) without an intervening process of selling products and accumulating an actual money profit. This management draws

on the continuous flow of fresh capital granted to it by the Congress of the United States.

The state-management has made extensive use of systems-analysis and other techniques for assuring economic and technical effectiveness. This common understanding, elaborately cultivated by the state-management since 1961, does not account for important parts of the state-management's performance. Here is a list of 65 major defense projects which were canceled during the period 1953 to 1968 because they were found to be unneeded or unworkable. These 65 projects cost more than $10.5 billion before they were canceled. This "Sorry, but we changed our mind" list, furnished by the Pentagon, shows the name of the project, the year it was started, and the year canceled, and the amount of money that had been invested by the time of cancellation. This list of canceled contracts does not include the F-111 airplane fiasco which involved an enormous investment, under direct control of McNamara's office, in airplanes that finally did not function according to plan and may cost American citizens several billion dollars when all the outlays have been finally calculated. . . .

During the 1960's the very period of the formal establishment of the state-management, the reliability of major new military systems costing tens of billions of dollars was lower than the reliability of systems constructed during the 1950's. During this period, a great deal of work had been done toward improving the reliability of, for example, the individual electronic components. How can the reliability of single components go up while the reliability of systems goes down? This can happen as a result or great increase in the complexity of these systems. The error of a system is not the sum of the errors of the linked components. Rather, the system error is the product of the errors of components. Thereby, sufficient increase in the number of linked components can, through the multiplicative effect of linked error, offset improvements in reliability of single components. Something of this sort must have happened to help produce the remarkable decline in reliability of weapons systems that was reported by Richard A. Stubbing in January, 1969. Mr. Stubbing has been an analyst on military systems for the Bureau of the Budget. His paper on reliability of electronics systems during the 1950's and the 1960's presented a vivid set of data from which he concluded: "Less than 40 percent of the effort [during the 1960s] produced systems with acceptable electronic performance—an uninspiring record that loses further luster when cost overruns and schedule delays are also evaluated."

By means of their influence on the operation of the Pentagon, military-industry firms seem to get away with large profits. It is true that many military-industry firms have earned unusually large profits on their investments—larger than has been the case in private industry. The Stubbing report on military-system reliability showed that military industry firms that have produced systems of lowest technical reliability had also earned highest rates of profit. To explain this, it is necessary to see the military-industry empire as one big firm dominated by the state-management. In that case "profits" are, in effect, grants of capital from the top management to the sub-managements—reflecting decisions to differentially enlarge or support subdivisions of the empire. This under-

standing of the matter explains the otherwise inexplicable decisions by the state-management (publicly recorded in May, 1969) to make considerable grants of capital to the General Dynamics and the Lockheed companies, after both of them had gone well beyond original cost estimates on particular military work. In both instances these grants of funds from the state-management represented decisions to maintain or enlarge the two enterprises as parts of the military-industrial system. (See the reports in *The New York Times* and *The Washington Post* of May 3, 1969.)

Waste is deplorable anywhere, but in military matters it is to be expected because of the essential nature of the undertaking. Therefore, one has to accept the abandonment of many projects along the way as simply part of the price one pays for trying to build a modern military defense. On September 3, 1968, *The Washington Post* headlined an article on Pentagon industrial procurement with "Much of Pentagon's $45 billion spending buys nothing." I do not agree with the judgment contained in that headline. Decision-power is being purchased by the state-management's industrial expenditures, even where these are related to goods that are finally scrapped.

Even though the Pentagon may itself be unduly ambitious in its new weapons proposals, there are nevertheless outside checks on its operations —for example, from the Bureau of the Budget, which works directly for the President. The Bureau of the Budget has had about three hundred staff members, of whom thirty, or 10 percent, have been assigned to the Department of Defense. That means that half of the spending activity by the federal government gets 10 percent of the surveillance. Evidently the Pentagon's budgets have been treated as sacrosanct and have been given almost automatic approval. Neither has there been any sustained check from the committees of the Congress, since these committees on Armed Services and Appropriations have not only included strongly pro-Pentagon members, but have operated with virtually no staff of their own to give them independent investigative and policy-formulating ability.

War is inherently wasteful. However, the program planning and budgeting systems introduced by the state-management and the widespread training of the Pentagon staff in cost effectiveness techniques are bound to restrain inappropriate, unplanned use of public funds. On December 8, 1966, it was disclosed that, during the previous year, the Pentagon had spent $20 billion on the war in Vietnam, that being exactly twice the budgeted expenditure. Furthermore, this doubled expenditure had not been previously announced (apparently, not even inside the government) and, as a result, had the effect of seriously upsetting important parts of the fiscal policy operations of the federal government. One Washington report had it that the $10 billion of additional spending was concealed to make the war seem cheaper than it was, particularly before the election in November, 1966. Finally, under law, the Department of Defense and every other government department can only spend the money allocated by the Congress for designated purposes. Where did the Pentagon get the $10 billion to spend for military operations in Vietnam that had not been voted for this purpose by the Congress? What laws were violated by the use of $10 billion of funds assigned to other purposes? Who was responsible for this violation of law, and what has been done, if anything, by the Department of Justice to bring the culprits to the bar of justice?

The Pentagon, even though it is a large organization, is nevertheless a part of the American system of government and is responsible to the President, the Congress, and, ultimately, to the American people. In November, 1967, the Senate Foreign Relations Committee commented on the near-absolute power acquired by the President to commit the United States to war. The Committee held:

> The concentration in the hands of the President of virtually unlimited authority over matters of war and peace has all but removed the limits to Executive power in the most important single area of our national life. Unless they are restored, the American people will be threatened with tyranny or disaster.

The concentration of authority, while formally in the hands of the President, is exercised through the Department of Defense. In the Pentagon the new state-management has a centrally important role as a concentration of decision-power at home and abroad.

I have reviewed many of the key propositions which are used to justify the operation of the Pentagon and its state-management. Under critical scrutiny these ideas turn out to be little more than a web of half-truths (and sometimes less than half-truths), precariously balanced on each other to give the aura of a solid ideology. When dealt with singly, the whole net of interlocked mythology crumbles, and we must simply face the facts: first, "defense" is no longer possible—that is, there is no reliable way of preventing destruction of the United States by a determined attacker; second, the American economy and society are depleted and not benefited by military priorities; and, third, these priorities are very serviceable for enlarging the decision-power of the state-management. Despite their invalidity, these ideologies are persistently advanced, owing to their contribution to the ideologues and to the state-management with which these men have identified themselves.

five

POLLUTION: "I WILL NOT HAVE MY EYES PUT OUT . . ."

Electricity vs. Clean Air in New York

ELLEN GRAHAM

This city, where one skyscraper can use as much electricity as an entire town, is experiencing the worst power shortage since the chaotic Northeast blackout of 1965. At the same time, New York's air is officially the worst in the country, with three times as much sulphur dioxide contamination as the Federal Government considers safe for human life.

The problems are directly related:

Reprinted from The Wall Street Journal *(August 21, 1970), p. 6. Copyright 1970 by Dow Jones and Company, Inc. Reprinted by permission.*

To solve either would make the other worse, a dilemma that is forcing city officials into a politically painful re-examination of their most fundamental priorities.

Any day now, Mayor John V. Lindsay must grasp that dilemma by one horn or the other. On his desk is a request, conditionally approved by a high-level city study committee, that would ease the power shortage at the expense of the air. Consolidated Edison Co., New York's electric utility, wants permission to double the generating capacity of its fossil-fuel plant at Astoria, Queens. Fossil-fuel plants burn coal, oil or natural gas, and even under the best of present conditions cannot be made perfectly clean.

The mayor's decision is expected to be influenced by an unusual public debate on the issue. His administration is sharply divided, and he has allowed each side to take its case to the public. The result has provided a rare opportunity to watch the municipal government make up its mind—an opportunity that is probably not being wasted on other cities whose power-air conflict is not yet so acute. What is a crisis today in New York is usually a problem tomorrow in Seattle.

The opposing positions, briefly, are these:

Con Edison and its government supporters argue that if you project the city's power needs to 1974 and beyond, then total the utility's present generating capacity and the capacity of new plants already planned, the amount of electricity available wouldn't be enough to handle emergencies that are certain to arise. The company contends that a large reserve is necessary because even theoretically comfortable reserves have a way of evaporating. This summer, for example, two massive generators broke down, reducing power capacity by 17%.

For the long run, Con Edison says, there may be alternatives, such as out-of-town sites or cleaner methods of generating power. But for now the company contends that it has studied—and eliminated—every other location but Astoria, and that no other plant could be readied in time for the power shortage it predicts for the summer of 1974. It's Astoria or nothing. Con Edison says.

The opposition, led by Jerome Kretchmer, the city's Environmental Protection Administrator, accuses Con Edison of shading the truth. Mr. Kretchmer says Con Edison's projections make no allowance for buying power from other utilities, even though it does this routinely. He says the company doesn't need the high reserves it claims it must have, and he contends the company hasn't really studied alternative sites and has put pitifully little money into research leading to new methods of generating power. His aides paint a picture of corporate venality, of a company going about business as usual and feeling no particular urgency to clean up the air if it means spending more money. They even hint that Con Edison has overblown the present power shortage to scare people into accepting the expansion.

Another fossil-fuel plant inside the city is absolutely intolerable, Mr. Kretchmer argues, because it would push sulphur dioxide contamination to the danger point. Already, he estimates, 1,000 to 2,000 New Yorkers die prematurely each year as a result of breathing sulphur dioxide, and the new plant would add 15,000 tons of it to the air annually. Moreover, he says, the expansion would raise nitrogen oxide levels 15%, greatly increasing the incidence of Los Angeles-type smog.

What the argument obscures is the possibility that both sides could be right. That is, expanding the Astoria plant may well add to pollution, and not expanding it may lead to more severe power shortages. Perhaps the crucial question is put into focus most clearly by D. Kenneth Patton, the city's Economic Development Administrator. Arguing on behalf of the expansion, Mr. Patton notes that 44% of the city's power is used in commerce and industry. If the Astoria plant isn't doubled, he says, the city won't be able to meet its goal of creating 300,000 jobs in the next decade.

Mr. Patton is facing the priority question when he implicitly argues that providing jobs is more important than healthy air. Likewise, Mr. Lindsay must answer fundamental questions having to do with the traditional values of progress and growth. What is progress? Can growth—in the form of new jobs, for example—continue forever in this city? Is there no limit to the number of people, cars, offices and air conditioners that can be stuffed into one place before the place collapses?

For decades, the values of America have been based on the value of the frontier, when resources seemed unlimited. In the modern version, progress is measured in row upon row of smokestacks, or assembly lines stacked with new cars. Only now is the realization dawning that this progress causes many of the little horrors of modern life—consider, for example, that the incidence of emphysema has doubled every five years since World War II.

Our definition of progress has also been shaped by the belief that through technological ingenuity we can perpetually modify our surroundings, without harmful consequence. We may fret that under a certain combination of events the city could fill with poisonous fumes, as London did in 1952, when 1,600 people were killed by smog. But we remain complacent about the subtle effects of low-level, long-lasting air pollution—the kind that adds daily to the threat of emphysema, bronchitis, asthma, cancer and heart disease. We don't want to give up our air conditioning.

Whatever the mayor decides, Astoria is clear proof that the "build and be damned" attitude about the environment has come to an end. Con Edison's present power shortages are in part the result of conservation and environmental opposition to its Storm King plant outside New York City on the Hudson River. Now, with Astoria, the opposition has spread to top-level members of the municipal government.

Astoria is important, too, because the buck will stop with Mr. Lindsay's decision. Having invited public discussion, he will find any decision extremely unpopular with large segments of the electorate. He must say, in effect, either, "We will have clean air, even at the expense of industrial growth, convenience and comfort," or, "We will continue to expand, but at the expense of the public's health."

It may be the most difficult and significant decision of his political career.

The Economics of the Coming Spaceship Earth

KENNETH E. BOULDING

The closed earth of the future requires economic principles which are somewhat different from those of the open earth of the past. For the sake of picturesqueness, I am tempted to call the open economy the "cowboy economy," the cowboy being symbolic of the illimitable plains and also associated with reckless, exploitative, romantic, and violent behavior, which is characteristic of open societies. The closed economy of the future might similarly be called the "spaceman" economy, in which the earth has become a single spaceship, without unlimited reservoirs of anything, either for extraction or for pollution, and in which, therefore, man must find his place in a cyclical ecological system which is capable of continuous reproduction of material form even though it cannot escape having inputs of energy. The difference between the two types of economy becomes most apparent in the attitude towards consumption. In the cowboy economy, consumption is regarded as a

Reprinted from Garrett DeBell, ed., The Environmental Handbook (New York: Ballantine Books, 1970), pp. 96–101. Originally published in Environmental Quality in a Growing Economy, by The Johns Hopkins Press for Resources for the Future, Inc. Copyright 1966 by the Johns Hopkins Press. Reprinted by permission of the publisher.

good thing and production likewise; and the success of the economy is measured by the amount of the throughput from the "factors of production," a part of which, at any rate, is extracted from the reservoirs of raw materials and noneconomic objects, and another part of which is output into the reservoirs of pollution. If there are infinite reservoirs from which material can be obtained and into which effluvia can be deposited, then the throughput is at least a plausible measure of the success of the economy. The gross national product is a rough measure of this total throughput. It should be possible, however, to distinguish that part of the GNP which is derived from exhaustible and that which is derived from reproducible resources, as well as that part of consumption which represents effluvia and that which represents input into the productive system again. Nobody, as far as I know, has ever attempted to break down the GNP in this way, although it would be an interesting and extremely important exercise, which is unfortunately beyond the scope of this paper.

By contrast, in the spaceman economy, throughput is by no means a desideratum, and is indeed to be regarded as something to be minimized rather than maximized. The essential measure of the success of the economy is not production and consumption at complexity of the total capital stock, including in this the state of the human bodies and minds included in the system. In the spaceman economy, what we are primarily concerned with is stock maintenance, and any technological change which results in the maintenance of a given total stock with a lessened throughput (that is, less production and consumption) is clearly a gain. This idea that both production and consumption are bad things rather than good things is very strange to economists, who have been obsessed with the income-flow concepts to the exclusion, almost, of capital-stock concepts.

There are actually some very tricky and unsolved problems involved in the questions as to whether human welfare or well-being is to be regarded as a stock or a flow. Something of both these elements seems actually to be involved in it, and as far as I know there have been practically no studies directed towards identifying these two dimensions of human satisfaction. Is it, for instance, eating that is a good thing, or is it being well fed? Does economic welfare involve having nice clothes, fine houses, good equipment, and so on, or is it to be measured by the depreciation and the wearing out of these things? I am inclined myself to regard the stock concept as most fundamental, that is, to think of being well fed as more important than eating, and to think even of so-called services as essentially involving the restoration of a depleting psychic capital. Thus I have argued that we go to a concert in order to restore a psychic condition which might be called "just having gone to a concert," which, once established, tends to depreciate. When it depreciates beyond a certain point, we go to another concert in order to restore it. If

all, but the nature, extent, quality, and it depreciates rapidly, we go to a lot of concerts; if it depreciates slowly, we go to few. On this view, similarly, we eat primarily to restore bodily homeostasis, that is, to maintain a condition of being well fed, and so on. On this view, there is nothing desirable in consumption at all. The less consumption we can maintain a given state with, the better off we are. If we had clothes that did not wear out, houses that did not depreciate, and even if we could maintain our bodily condition without eating, we would clearly be much better off.

It is this last consideration, perhaps, which makes one pause. Would we, for instance, really want an operation that would enable us to restore all our bodily tissues by intravenous feeding while we slept? Is there not, that is to say, a certain virtue in throughput itself, in activity itself, in production and consumption itself, in raising food and in eating it? It would certainly be rash to exclude this possibility. Further interesting problems are raised by the demand for variety. We certainly do not want a constant state to be maintained; we want fluctuations in the state. Otherwise there would be no demand for variety in food, for variety in scene, as in travel, for variety in social contact, and so on. The demand for variety can, of course, be costly, and sometimes it seems to be too costly to be tolerated or at least legitimated, as in the case of marital partners, where the maintenance of a homeostatic state in the family is usually regarded as much more desirable than the variety and excessive throughput of the libertine. There are problems here which the economics profession has neglected with astonishing singlemindedness. My own attempts to call attention to some of them, for instance, in two articles,[1] as far as I can judge, produced no response whatever; and economists continue to think and act as if production, consumption, through-put, and the GNP were the sufficient and adequate measure of economic success.

It may be said, of course, why worry about all this when the space-man economy is still a good way off (at least beyond the lifetimes of any now living), so let us eat, drink, spend, extract and pollute, and be as merry as we can, and let posterity worry about the spaceship earth. It is always a little hard to find a convincing an-swer to the man who says, "What has posterity ever done for me?" and the conservationist has always had to fall back on rather vague ethical principles postulating identity of the individual with some human community or society which extends not only back into the past but forward into the future. Unless the individual identifies with some com-munity of this kind, conservation is ob-viously "irrational." Why should we not maximize the welfare of this gene-ration at the cost of posterity? Après nous, le déluge has been the motto of not insignificant numbers of human so-cieties. The only answer to this, as far as I can see, is to point out that the welfare of the individual depends on the extent to which he can identify himself with others, and that the most satisfactory individual identity is that which identifies not only with a com-munity in space but also with a com-munity extending over time from the

past into the future. If this kind of identity is recognized as desirable, then posterity has a voice, even if it does not have a vote; and in a sense, if its voice can influence votes, it has votes too. This whole problem is linked up with the much larger one of the deter-minants of the morale, legitimacy, and "nerve" of a society, and there is a great deal of historical evidence to suggest that a society which loses its identity with posterity and which loses its positive image of the future loses also its capacity to deal with present prob-lems, and soon falls apart.[2]

Even if we concede that posterity is relevant to our present problems, we still face the question of time-discount-ing and the closely related question of uncertainty-discounting. It is a well-known phenomenon that individuals discount the future, even in their own lives. The very existence of a positive rate of interest may be taken as at least strong supporting evidence of this hypothesis. If we discount our own future, it is certainly not unreasonable to discount posterity's future even more, even if we do give posterity a vote. If we discount this at 5 percent per an-num, posterity's vote or dollar halves every fourteen years as we look into the future, and after even a mere hun-dred years it is pretty small—only about 1½ cents on the dollar. If we add another 5 percent for uncertainty, even the vote of our grandchildren re-duces almost to insignificance. We can argue, of course, that the ethical thing to do is not to discount the future at all, that time-discounting is mainly the result of myopia and perspective, and hence is an illusion which the moral

[1] K. E. Boulding, "The Consumption Con-cept in Economic Theory," *American Economic Review,* 35 (May 1945), 1–14; and "Income or Welfare?" *Review of Economic Studies,* 17 (1949–1950), 77–86.

[2] Fred L. Polak, *The Image of the Future,* vols. I and II, translated by Elise Boulding (New York: Sythoff, Leyden and Oceana), 1961.

man should not tolerate. It is a very popular illusion, however, and one that must certainly be taken into consideration in the formulation of policies. It explains, perhaps, why conservationist policies almost have to be sold under some other excuse which seems more urgent, and why, indeed, necessities which are visualized as urgent, such as defense, always seem to hold priority over those which involve the future.

All these considerations add some credence to the point of view which says that we should not worry about the spaceman economy at all, and that we should just go on increasing the GNP and indeed the gross world product, or GWP, in the expectation that the problems of the future can be left to the future, that when scarcities arise, whether this is of raw materials or of pollutable reservoirs, the needs of the then present will determine the solutions of the then present, and there is no use giving ourselves ulcers by worrying about problems that we really do not have to solve. There is even high ethical authority for this point of view in the New Testament, which advocates that we should take no thought for tomorrow and let the dead bury their dead. There has always been something rather refreshing in the view that we should live like the birds, and perhaps posterity is for the birds in more

senses than one; so perhaps we should all call it a day and go out and pollute something cheerfully. As an old taker of thought for the morrow, however, I cannot quite accept this solution; and I would argue, furthermore, that tomorrow is not only very close, but in many respects it is already here. The shadow of the future spaceship, indeed is already falling over our spendthrift merriment. Oddly enough, it seems to be in pollution rather than in exhaustion that the problem is first becoming salient. Los Angeles has run out of air, Lake Erie has become a cesspool, the oceans are filling up with lead and DDT, and the atmosphere may become man's major problem in another generation, at the rate at which we are filling it up with gunk. It is, of course, true that at least on a microscale, things have been worse at times in the past. The cities of today, with all their foul air and polluted waterways, are probably not as bad as the filthy cities of the pretechnical age. Nevertheless, that fouling of the nest which has been typical of man's activity in the past on a local scale now seems to be extending to the whole world society; and one certainly cannot view with equanimity the present rate of pollution of any of the natural reservoirs, whether the atmosphere, the lakes, or even the oceans.

5

FORCES AGITATING
AMERICAN SOCIETY:

TEMPORARY STIRRINGS OR
LONG TERM DISCORD?

The recitation of forces agitating American society is a well-known litany: rapid and virtually uncontrolled social change; population growth and generational conflict; racism; poverty in the midst of affluence; urban turmoil; a revolution in communication; a crisis in authority, community, and the concept of the sacred; and a host of problems stemming from a society geared to science and technology. Most of the disorganization arising from these forces is rather apparent, except that relating to the impact of an urban, industrial society upon the individual. The problems of the "new" industrial culture are subtle and perplexing.

There can be little quarrel with the statement that we live in an industrial, perhaps a postindustrial, society. It is also self-evident that in many ways our political, economic, and social institutions have failed to keep pace with technological change. For example, we learn how to crack the atom but fail to develop effective political and international controls over the use of thermonuclear power. Beyond this, the consequences of technology are more debatable.

Technology and industrialism are frequently used interchangeably. Technically speaking, this is in error since all cultures are to some degree technological in that they employ tools and other artifacts. In a broader sense, however, equating the industrial and the technological with our society is appropriate. No other society has placed as much stress upon the large-scale production of material goods. In fact, our emphasis is distorted. The standard of life has become a physical standard of living and the "good" life in reality has become the "goods of life."

Beyond the environmental consequences of an ever increasing emphasis upon goods, it would appear that there are societal and psychic implications. In a goods-oriented society, privatism seems to take a priority over group co-operation and the pursuit of social goals. The acquisition of goods becomes a central and unquenchable drive. So much so that more and more time is consumed in the hunt, and the end of the chase is akin to a greyhound catching the wooden rabbit. This is true because there are limits beyond which goods can contribute little or nothing to the improvement of the quality of life; in fact, an overabundance of goods may blur values and dim perspectives.

Probably the most obvious by-product of industrialism is urbanization. The factory system requires a modicum of group living; the assembly-line and mass production system demand a large concentration of population in specific places. The result of this gravitation is the rise of the metropolis—huge, sprawling, chaotic, ugly—in short, a world unplanned and unforeseen. Critics of urbanism go back to Jefferson who felt that democracy could be maintained best by a nation of small farmers: "Farmers are God's chosen people." Jefferson also believed that the growth of large cities and the ensuing group conflict threatened democracy.

Urbanism has its supporters as well as critics. There are those who argue that many of the ills of the city are imaginary. They question the indictments of impersonality and disorganization, pointing out that the concept of neighborhood in the city is often very personalized and the advantages of urban life far outweigh ruralism. Nonetheless, urbanization does create a new set of problems. When people begin living close together, for example, outhouses become a serious problem. The need increases for social services to cope with psychological and other tensions, and we have yet to assess the effect of "crowding" upon modern man.

Urbanization is not technology's only output. Technological changes affect values, attitudes, institutions, and behavior. For example, the bicycle built for two, and later the automobile, all but destroyed chaperonage. At the same time, the automatic clothes dryer and other devices altered the work life of the house-wife, and the conveyor belt changed the work of the workmen. In each case technology assumed new and unquestioned importance.

But what about the rate of technological change? Is there a point of no return? Over a half century ago, Henry Adams noted that the tensions and social vibrations resulting from the impact of technology had increased a thousand times between 1800 and 1900. Earlier Emerson noted the run-away effect of technology:

> Things are in the saddle,
> And ride mankind . . .
> Law for man, and law for thing;
> The last builds town and fleet,

> But it runs wild,
> And doth the man unking.[1]

Virtually everyone would agree that the momentum of technology is immeasurably greater today than when Emerson and Adams wrote.

Technology and its modern corollary, an urban, industrial society, have, in the minds of many, destroyed the guidelines and social institutions of the older, agrarian culture. At the same time, new institutions have not been created, "We are placed between two worlds; one dead, the other struggling to be born." In the words of Mathew Arnold:

> . . . for the world, which seems . . .
> so various, so beautiful, so new,
> Hath really neither joy, nor love, nor light,
> Nor certitude, nor peace, nor help for pain;
> And we are here as on a darkling plain . . .
> Where ignorant armies clash by night.[2]

The breakdown of older customs has caused great social and personal disorganization. Formerly the traditional society imposed formal and informal controls, which operated on the basis of personal, primary relationships. When these restraints break down the individual is thrust into an anonymous, lonely, and one-dimensional society. At the same time, new forms of social control emerge that reduce the margins of acceptable thought and behavior. As Herbert Marcuse writes, "Contemporary society seems to be capable of containing social change—qualitative change which would establish essentially different institutions, a new direction of the productive process, new modes of human existence." [3]

Large-scale production creates large organizations, which in turn prompt the growth of large governmental bureaucracies to regulate private power structures. Bigness spawns bigness and the individual comes to feel less secure and more and more submerged by giant collectivities—big business, big labor, big agriculture, big government. Within these bureaucracies rules and routine replace personal relationship and disciplined work rules and automated tasks drain significance and spontaneity. Work becomes separated from living and the individual finds himself detached from another activity that should provide purpose and meaning.

As a result a person often comes to look upon himself as an alien, "out of touch with himself" and isolated from others as his social and psychological

---

[1] Ralph Waldo Emerson, "Ode," *Selected Prose and Poetry*, ed. Reginald L. Cook (New York: Holt, Rinehart & Winston, Inc., 1950), p. 381.

[2] Mathew Arnold, "Dover Beach," *Selected Prose and Poetry*, ed. Frederick L. Mulhauser (New York: Holt, Rinehart & Winston, Inc., 1953), p. 90.

[3] Herbert Marcuse, *One-Dimensional Man* (Boston: Beacon Press, 1964), p. xii.

moorings are eroded. The individual no longer feels that he is captain of his fate or even a member of the crew. He tends to feel powerless and overwhelmed. Small wonder Jacques Barzun states, "Man is *not* flourishing."

A striking characteristic of contemporary technology is its capability to bring into being a totally new culture with an unprecedented cultural transmission system based upon electronic communication. The prime exhibit is, of course, television. Television, with its instant coverage, passive persuasiveness, and capacity to telescope time and distance has had an incredible impact upon American life; so great, in fact, that we cannot evaluate fully either the long-term or short-term effects. What is, for example, the influence of television on governmental institutions (the President's access to the country and preemption of prime time)? on politics (the selling of a candidate)? on aspirations (everything is possible now)? on consumption (wall-to-wall mattresses and instant coffee)? on culture (no one gets old or is old on television)?

Technology has its defenders as well as detractors. There are many who believe there is much of value in man's progress and the future is not necessarily bleak. These individuals assert that we are not doomed robots unable to alter the repressive and destructive effects of uncontrolled technological change. In fact, they insist it is preposterous to feel that technology must be our master rather than our servant. Furthermore, scientific advances provide more possibilities for change and for human control over human destiny than at any time in man's career on this planet. However, survival up until now has been unplanned: for the human race to continue in the future, it will have to do so by design.

A chorus of dissenting voices respond to the forces agitating American society. There are those who argue that many of our ills are more apparent than real, that there is nothing a few years of peace and tranquility cannot cure, that our problems are not as serious as they are reported, and that the United States is going as well or better than any other nation in solving the problems of freedom and equality in an industrial society. Others dissent, asserting that the problems facing us are real and will not go away. To these observers the solution lies in changing our national priorities, redirecting our society to make it more supportive and more oriented to the fullest development of every man's personality. A few contend that the whole technological basis of our society must be altered. Virtually all critics of contemporary society agree that we must humanize the industrial system and make it more responsive to human needs and human fulfillment.

The readings in this chapter are concerned with several aspects of the problems presented by technological development, urbanization, industrialization, and alienation in American society. Theodore Roszak deals with the effects of technocracy upon the citizen, and the resultant development of a "counter-culture" by the young people who reject the technocratic value system. Robert

Hutchins explains the impact of "big science" in the United States, and calls for a return to political philosophy. Robert Jay Lifton explains the meaning of the "Protean style of self-process," and Richard Neuhaus describes the development of a "revolutionary consciousness" in American life. All of these writers are concerned with the overall issue of man vs. modern civilization, and all agree that society must somehow be humanized.

one

TECHNOLOGY: "THINGS ARE IN THE SADDLE . . ."

Technocracy's Children

THEODORE ROSZAK

By the technocracy, I mean that social form in which an industrial society reaches the peak of its organizational integration. It is the ideal men usually have in mind when they speak of modernizing, up-dating, rationalizing, planning. Drawing upon such unquestionable imperatives as the demand for efficiency, for social security, for large-scale co-ordination of men and resources, for ever higher levels of affluence and ever more impressive manifestations of collective human power, the technocracy works to knit together the anachronistic gaps and fissures of the industrial society. The meticulous systematization Adam Smith once celebrated in his wellknown pin factory now extends to all areas of life, giving us human organization that matches the precision of our mechanistic organization. So we arrive at the era of social engineering in which entrepreneurial talent broadens its province to orchestrate the total human context which surrounds the industrial complex. Politics, education, leisure, entertainment, culture as a whole, the unconscious drives, and even, as we shall see, protest against the technocracy itself: all these become the subjects of purely technical scrutiny and of purely technical manipulation. The effort is to create a new social organism whose health depends upon its capacity to keep the technological heart beating regularly. In the words of Jacques Ellul:

> Technique requires predictability and, no less, exactness of prediction. It is necessary, then, that technique prevail over the human being. For technique, this is a matter of life and death. Technique must reduce man to a technical animal, the king of the slaves of technique. Human caprice crumbles before this necessity; there can be no human autonomy in the face of technical autonomy. The individual must be fashioned by techniques, either negatively (by the techniques of understanding man) or positively (by the adaptation of man to the technical framework), in order to wipe out the blots his personal

Reprinted from Theodore Roszak, The Making of a Counter Culture (Garden City, N.Y.: Doubleday and Company, Inc., 1969), pp. 5–11, 22–25. Copyright 1968, 1969 by Theodore Roszak. Reprinted by permission of the publisher.

determination introduces into the perfect design of the organization.[1]

In the technocracy, nothing is any longer small or simple or readily apparent to the non-technical man. Instead, the scale and intricacy of all human activities—political, economic, cultural—transcends the competence of the amateurish citizen and inexorably demands the attention of specially trained experts. Further, around this central core of experts who deal with large-scale public necessities, there grows up a circle of subsidiary experts who, battening on the general social prestige of technical skill in the technocracy, assume authoritative influence over even the most seemingly personal aspects of life: sexual behavior, child-rearing, mental health, recreation, etc. In the technocracy everything aspires to become purely technical, the subject of professional attention. The technocracy is therefore the regime of experts—or of those who can employ the experts. Among its key institutions we find the "think-tank," in which is housed a multi-billion-dollar brainstorming industry that seeks to anticipate and integrate into the social planning quite simply everything on the scene. Thus, even before the general public has become fully aware of new developments, the technocracy has doped them out and laid its plans for adopting or rejecting, promoting or disparaging.[2]

[1] Jacques Ellul, The Technological Society, trans. John W. Wilkinson (New York: A. A. Knopf, 1964), p. 138. This outrageously pessimistic book is thus far the most global effort to depict the technocracy in full operation.

[2] For a report on the activities of a typical technocratic brain trust, Herman Kahn's Hudson Institute, see Bowen Northrup's "They Think For Pay" in The Wall Street Journal, September 20, 1967. Currently, the Institute is developing strategies to integrate hippies and to exploit the new possibilities of programmed dreams.

Within such a society, the citizen, confronted by bewildering bigness and complexity, finds it necessary to defer on all matters to those who know better. Indeed, it would be a violation of reason to do otherwise, since it is universally agreed that the prime goal of the society is to keep the productive apparatus turning over efficiently. In the absence of expertise, the great mechanism would surely bog down, leaving us in the midst of chaos and poverty. As we will see in later chapters, the roots of the technocracy reach deep into our cultural past and are ultimately entangled in the scientific world-view of the Western tradition. But for our purposes here it will be enough to define the technocracy as that society in which those who govern justify themselves by appeal to technical experts who, in turn, justify themselves by appeal to scientific forms of knowledge. And beyond the authority of science, there is no appeal.

Understood in these terms, as the mature product of technological progress and the scientific ethos, the technocracy easily eludes all traditional political categories. Indeed, it is characteristic of the technocracy to render itself ideologically invisible. Its assumptions about reality and its values become as unobtrusively pervasive as the air we breathe. While daily political argument continues within and between the capitalist and collectivist societies of the world, the technocracy increases and consolidates its power in both as a transpolitical phenomenon following the dictates of industrial efficiency, rationality, and necessity. In all these arguments, the technocracy assumes a position similar to that of the purely neutral umpire in an athletic contest. The umpire is normally the least obtrusive person on the scene. Why? Because we give our attention and passionate allegiance to the teams, who compete within the rules; we tend to ignore the man who stands above the contest and who simply interprets and enforces the rules. Yet, in a sense, the umpire is the most significant figure in the game, since he alone sets the limits and goals of the competition and judges the contenders.

The technocracy grows without resistance, even despite its most appalling failures and criminalities, primarily because its potential critics continue trying to cope with these breakdowns in terms of antiquated categories. This or that disaster is blamed by Republicans on Democrats (or vice versa), by Tories on Labourites (or vice versa), by French Communists on Gaullists (or vice versa), by socialists on capitalists (or vice versa), by Maoists on Revisionists (or vice versa). But left, right, and center, these are quarrels between technocrats or between factions who subscribe to technocratic values from first to last. The angry debates of conservative and liberal, radical and reactionary touch everything except the technocracy, because the technocracy is not generally perceived as a political phenomenon in our advanced industrial societies. It holds the place, rather, of a grand cultural imperative which is beyond question, beyond discussion.

When any system of politics devours the surrounding culture, we have totalitarianism, the attempt to bring the whole of life under authoritarian control. We are bitterly familiar with totalitarian politics in the forms of brutal regimes which achieve their integration by bludgeon and bayonet. But in the case of the technocracy, totalitarianism is perfected because its techniques become progressively more subliminal. The distinctive feature of the regime of

experts lies in the fact that, while possessing ample power to coerce, it prefers to charm conformity from us by exploiting our deep-seated commitment to the scientific world-view and by manipulating the securities and creature comforts of the industrial affluence which science has given us.

So subtle and so well rationalized have the arts of technocratic domination become in our advanced industrial societies that even those in the state and/or corporate structure who dominate our lives must find it impossible to conceive of themselves as the agents of a totalitarian control. Rather, they easily see themselves as the conscientious managers of a munificent social system which is, by the very fact of its broadcast affluence, incompatible with any form of exploitation. At worst, the system may contain some distributive inefficiencies. But these are bound to be repaired . . . in time. And no doubt they will be. Those who gamble that either capitalism or collectivism is, by its very nature, incompatible with a totally efficient technocracy, one which will finally eliminate material poverty and gross physical exploitation, are making a risky wager. It is certainly one of the oldest, but one of the weakest radical arguments which insists stubbornly that capitalism is *inherently* incapable of laying golden eggs for everyone.

The great secret of the technocracy lies, then, in its capacity to convince us of three interlocking premises. They are:

1. That the vital needs of man are (contrary to everything the great souls of history have told us) purely technical in character. Meaning: the requirements of our humanity yield wholly to some manner of formal analysis which

can be carried out by specialists possessing certain impenetrable skills and which can then be translated by them directly into a congeries of social and economic programs, personnel management procedures, merchandise, and mechanical gadgetry. If a problem does not have such a technical solution, it must not be a real problem. It is but an illusion . . . a figment born of some regressive cultural tendency.

2. That this formal (and highly esoteric) analysis of our needs has now achieved 99 per cent completion. Thus, with minor hitches and snags on the part of irrational elements in our midst, the prerequisites of human fulfillment have all but been satisfied. It is this assumption which leads to the conclusion that wherever social friction appears in the technocracy, it must be due to what is called a "breakdown in communication." For where human happiness has been so precisely calibrated and where the powers that be are so utterly well intentioned, controversy could not possibly derive from a substantive issue, but only from misunderstanding. Thus we need only sit down and reason together and all will be well.

3. That the experts who have fathomed our heart's desires and who alone can continue providing for our needs, the experts who *really* know what they're talking about, all happen to be on the official payroll of the state and/or corporate structure. The experts who count are the certified experts. And the certified experts belong to headquarters. . . .

Why should it be the young who rise most noticeably in protest against the expansion of the technocracy?

There is no way around the most obvious answer of all: the young stand forth so prominently because they act against a background of nearly pathological passivity on the part of the adult generation. It would only be by reducing our conception of citizenship to absolute zero that we could get our senior generation off the hook for its astonishing default. The adults of the World War II period, trapped as they have been in the frozen posture of befuddled docility—the condition Paul Goodman has called "the nothing can be done disease"—have in effect divested themselves of their adulthood, if that term means anything more than being tall and debt-worried and capable of buying liquor without having to show one's driver's license. Which is to say: they have surrendered their responsibility for making morally demanding decisions, for generating ideals, for controlling public authority, for safeguarding the society against its despoilers.

Why and how this generation lost control of the institutions that hold sway over its life is more then we can go into here. The remembered background of economic collapse in the thirties, the grand distraction and fatigue of the war, the pathetic if understandable search for security and relaxation afterwards, the bedazzlement of the new prosperity, a sheer defensive numbness in the face of thermonuclear terror and the protracted state of international emergency during the late forties and fifties, the red-baiting and witch-hunting and out-and-out barbarism of the McCarthy years . . . no doubt all these played their part. And there is also the rapidity and momentum with which technocratic totalitarianism came rolling out of the war years and the early cold war era, drawing on heavy wartime industrial investments, the emergency centralization of decision making, and the awe-stricken public reverence for science. The situation descended swiftly and ponderously. Perhaps no society could have kept its presence of mind; certainly ours didn't. And the failure was not only American. Nicola Chiaromonte, seeking to explain the restiveness of Italian youth, observes,

> . . . the young—those born after 1940—find themselves living in a society that neither commands nor deserves respect. . . . For has modern man, in his collective existence, laid claim to any god or ideal but the god of possession and enjoyment and the limitless satisfaction of material needs? Has he put forward any reason for working but the reward of pleasure and prosperity? Has he, in fact, evolved anything but this "consumer society" that is so easily and falsely repudiated? [3]

On the American scene, this was the parental generation whose god Allen Ginsberg identified back in the mid-fifties as the sterile and omnivorous "Moloch." It is the generation whose premature senility Dwight Eisenhower

[3] The "falsely" in this quotation relates to Chiaromonte's very astute analysis of a doctrinaire blind spot in the outlook of Italian youth—namely their tendency to identify the technocracy with capitalism, which, as I have suggested, is a general failing of European youth movements. This very shrewd article appears in *Encounter*, July 1968, pp. 25–27. Chiaromonte does not mention the factor of fascism in Italy, but certainly in Germany the cleavage between young and old has been driven deeper than anything we know in America by the older generation's complicity with Nazism.

so marvelously incarnated and the disease of whose soul shone so lugubriously through the public obscenities that men like John Foster Dulles and Herman Kahn and Edward Teller were prepared to call "policy." There are never many clear landmarks in affairs of the spirit, but Ginsberg's *Howl* may serve as the most public report announcing the war of the generations. It can be coupled with a few other significant phenomena. One of them would be the appearance of *MAD* magazine, which has since become standard reading material for the junior high school population. True, the dissent of *MAD* often sticks at about the Katzenjammer Kids level: but nevertheless the nasty cynicism *MAD* began applying to the American way of life —politics, advertising, mass media, education—has had its effect. *MAD* brought into the malt shops the same angry abuse of middle-class America which comics like Mort Sahl and Lenny Bruce were to begin bringing into the night clubs of the mid-fifties. The kids who were twelve when *MAD* first appeared are in their early twenties now—and they have had a decade's experience in treating the stuff of their parents' lives as contemptible laughing stock.

At a more significant intellectual level, Ginsberg and the beatniks can be associated chronologically with the aggressively activist sociology of C. Wright Mills—let us say with the publication of Mills' *Causes of World War III* (1957), which is about the point at which Mills' writing turned from scholarship to first-class pamphleteering. Mills was by no means the first postwar figure who sought to tell it like it is about the state of American public life and culture; the valiant groups that maintained radical journals like *Liberation* and *Dissent* had been filling the wilderness with their cries for quite as long. And as far as the end of the war, Paul Goodman and Dwight Macdonald were doing an even shrewder job of analyzing technocratic America than Mills was ever to do—and without relinquishing their humanitarian tone. But it was Mills who caught on. His tone was more blatant; his rhetoric, catchier. He was the successful academic who suddenly began to cry for action in a lethargic profession, in a lethargic society. He was prepared to step forth and brazenly pin his indictment like a target to the enemy's chest. And by the time he finished playing Emile Zola he had marked out just about everybody in sight for accusation.

Most important, Mills was lucky enough to discover ears that would hear: his indignation found an audience. But the New Left he was looking for when he died in 1961 did not appear among his peers. It appeared among the students—and just about nowhere else. If Mills were alive today, his following would still be among the under thirties (though the Vietnam war has brought a marvelous number of his academic colleagues out into open dissent—but will they stay out when the war finally grinds to its ambiguous finish?).

Doing What Comes Scientifically and Technologically

ROBERT M. HUTCHINS

Science began as a search for understanding. It is becoming part of the search for power.

. . . Science began as part of the search for understanding. Now it is part of the search for power. President Johnson and his predecessor recommended large expenditures on scientific objects

Reprinted, by permission, from the January 1969 issue of The Center Magazine, Vol. II, #1, a publication of the Center for the Study of Democratic Institutions in Santa Barbara, California.

in the name of the power and prosperity of their country. In doing so they did not invent a new idea; they followed what has become a global fashion. What the fashion means is that science has become engineering. It is studied not because it is worth knowing in itself but because of its applications. John Wilkinson has pointed out that the time between a "scientific" discovery and its application is steadily diminishing; he estimates that by 1990 the interval will have shrunk to 5/1000 of a second. This means that the application is in the mind of the scientist from the beginning of his work; it also means that the scientist has become an engineer. He becomes the servant of a society that has almost exclusively technological preoccupations. Assisting in this process is what is called the "moral neutrality" of science. The scientist is not a check on the modern preoccupation with power but simply an adjunct to it.

Preoccupation with power, technology, and innovation has led to something new in the world—Big Science. The enormous costs associated with this phenomenon are met by persuading corporations and governments of the commercial and political value of science. Big Science is therefore a propaganda machine for more Big Science. In the United States Big Science is carried on principally in the universities. They thus become the instruments of corporations and the government: they seek to achieve the objects that those who put up the money have in view. Big Science changes the role of the professor. Instead of being a teacher and a man interested in understanding some aspect of nature, he becomes an executive, a money-raiser, a businessman, organizing and "selling" the work of others.

These tendencies have been intensified by the Cold War. Almost every technological outrage of recent years has been perpetrated under the protection of the slogan, "We have to do it because the Russians will." When I asked Arthur Compton, the Nobel Laureate who had directed the research at Chicago leading to the atomic bomb, what terrible thing he proposed next,

he said, "Well, we *could* probably do something with hydrogen, but we really don't need to, because we can do so much damage with what we've got already." But the United States manufactured the hydrogen bomb because "We had to."

No wonder it is sometimes suggested that technology is autonomous. We do things not because we need to or want to, but because we can. Even if it were possible for one country to do what none has yet been able to accomplish, to guide and control the development of technology within its own borders, such control could be at best only temporary and illusory as long as the country remained convinced that it could not fall behind its present or potential enemies, that is, behind any other country in the world. The seabed struggle is one illustration. The unseemly space race that is now going on has in the United States an aim that is obviously idiotic, to put a man on the moon this year. In this frenzy the lives of three brave men have already been sacrificed and many millions of dollars and much scientific and engineering skill have been wasted; but the frenzy appears to be an inevitable accompaniment of international competition for power and prestige.

When prosperity, power, and prestige come through science, it is natural that everybody should want to be "scientific." To this there could be no objection if science were still regarded as the pursuit of truth or the attempt to understand the natural world. The universal desire to be scientific has swept over us, however, while we are oppressed with crude misunderstandings of the scope and method of science. In some way or other the report has gone round the world, and is widely believed, that only science is careful, accurate, honest, and objective. Anything that cannot be called science must therefore be careless, inaccurate, dishonest, and biased. The philosopher, for example, must either regard his subject as superstition or he must make it look as "scientific" as possible.

Since scientists do not judge the laws of nature, a social scientist cannot judge the laws of his society. I once asked a great expert on the American system whether the decision of the United States Supreme Court desegregating the schools was good or bad. He replied, "As a social scientist I do not make value judgments." He indicated that he had personal, unscientific views about the question I had asked but he exhibited no confidence in them, appearing to think that they were the accidental, and indefensible, product of his early environment.

Since physics, the most popular of all sciences, rests on mathematics, we are easily led to the conclusion that nothing without a mathematical base can be worth knowing, and that everything that might have a mathematical base achieves intellectual dignity by virtue of this possibility alone. Hence the tremendous effort to count that goes on in American social science, the greatest triumph of which is the public-opinion poll. The slogan is, If you can't count it, it doesn't count. It is not surprising that attempts have been made to understand love by measuring the increases in temperature and pulse rate that are said to occur under its influence.

In some circles in America the notion has gained ground that only science can give us the truth and that the only true science is laboratory science. It follows that nothing is true unless it can be experimentally verified in the labora-

tory. Thus a dean of the division of biological sciences of the University of Chicago once informed me that the truths of theology and metaphysics, if any, could be accepted only provisionally as substitutes for real truths. Natural science would discover these as soon as it had developed experimental techniques adequate to the purpose. Such an attitude must leave the laborers in disciplines other than experimental science with the uneasy feeling that at any moment they may have their foundations shot out from under them. . . .

I have referred previously in *The Center Magazine* to the articles on Political Science and on Political Philosophy in the current edition of the Encyclopaedia Britannica. The first is written by a political scientist and the second by a political philosopher. The political scientist says that his subject is descriptive and as quantitative as possible, whereas political philosophy is "strongly normative." The political philosopher instantly repudiates this offensive remark. He says the normative elements of political philosophy have been driven back into ethics, and "ethical principles in their turn have been removed from the field of rational discussion." All that remains of political philosophy, the author says, is linguistic analysis. The result is that neither political science nor political philosophy contains any normative elements. In this case neither one can show us how to guide and control science and technology. They are both "value-free."

Science and technology cannot judge themselves. The scientist can judge an experiment as an experiment; the engineer can judge a weapon as a weapon. But, when they decide to conduct the experiment or manufacture the weapon, they are, whether they know it or not, entering the realm of moral and political philosophy. They have abandoned their moral neutrality.

The decay of political philosophy means that politics is nothing but the exercise of power. Harold Lasswell's *Politics: Who Gets What, How, and Why* is the title of one of the most popular American works in this field. Politics so conceived cannot help us find the means of guiding and controlling science and technology. On the contrary, the conception of politics as power has produced and will continue to reproduce the situation we have today, in which science and technology are being exploited for the purposes of power in such a way as to threaten the existence of the race.

Politics is and ought to be the architectonic science. It is the science of the common good. Good is a moral term. The common good is a good that accrues to every member of the community because he belongs to it; it is a good he would not have if he did not belong to it. The task of politics is to define the common good and to organize the community to achieve it. The task is to find the means, as Harvey Wheeler has said, of constitutionalizing the intellectual enterprise and in particular, since science is now an untamed power, of constitutionalizing science. We have to find out how to direct science to the service of the common good.

And the community we are bound to consider is not simply that of the nation-state. We have seen that science and technology have become a threat to the survival of the race largely because no nation-state can contemplate the possibility that any other can surpass it in acquiring the power science gives.

The *furor technologicus* cannot be allayed unless science and technology can be constitutionalized on a world basis and made to serve the common good of the whole human community. This is the great political task of the future. The right to think, speak, and write must be inalienable. So must the right to inquire and investigate. But the common good now requires that the application of scientific knowledge be regulated in the common interest.

Some of the more absurd consequences of international competition could be obviated without further international organization. For example, Linus Pauling has proposed that space investigation be a joint venture of those nations which want to engage in it. There is no reason why there should be a race, with all the dangerous and irrelevant pressures that the notion of such a contest brings with it. The object must be to bring science and technology under the rule of law. Law is an ordinance of reason directed to the common good.

The redefinition and restoration of liberal education, the redefinition of the university, the redefinition and restoration of the professional idea, the revival of philosophy, and the restoration of and resort to politics may have to be the work of countries that have not yet felt the full force of the technological fever, or that have not yet succumbed to it. Such countries are, of course, eager to get going. They can easily deceive themselves into thinking that vocational training and the multiversity, in a society dedicated to power and unrestrained by professional and philosophical standards, will give them the affluence and influence they desire. History suggests, however, that the unrestrained pursuit of power is suicidal, and not merely murderous. We may hope that this is a lesson our country will not have to learn from experience.

My theme is that science must once more be regarded as a branch of knowledge and that its uses must be regulated in the public interest. On these principles, nothing that science can give us would be lost except those applications of it which are destructive of both science and society.

two

ALIENATION: LONELY IN THE CROWD

Protean Man

ROBERT JAY LIFTON

I would stress two historical developments as having special importance for creating protean man. The first is the world-wide sense of what I have called *historical* (or *psychohistorical*) *dislocation,* the break in the sense of connection which men have long felt with the vital and nourishing symbols of their cultural tradition—symbols revolving around family, idea systems,

Reprinted from History and Human Survival by Robert Jay Lifton. Reprinted by permission of Random House, Inc.

religions, and the life cycle in general. In our contemporary world one perceives these traditional symbols as irrelevant, burdensome or inactivating, and yet one cannot avoid carrying them within or having one's self-process profoundly affected by them. The second large historical tendency is the *flooding* of *imagery* produced by the extraordinary flow of post-modern cultural influences over mass communication networks. These cross readily over local and national boundaries, and permit each individual to be touched by everything, but at the same time cause him to be overwhelmed by superficial messages and undigested cultural elements, by headlines and by endless partial alternatives in every sphere of life. These alternatives, moreover, are universally and simultaneously shared—if not as courses of action, at least in the form of significant inner imagery.

We know from Greek mythology that Proteus was able to change his shape with relative ease—from wild boar to lion to dragon to fire to flood. But what he did find difficult, and would not do unless seized and chained, was to commit himself to a single form, the form most his own, and carry out his function of prophecy. We can say the same of protean man, but we must keep in mind his possibilities as well as his difficulties.

The protean style of self-process, then, is characterized by an interminable series of experiments and explorations —some shallow, some profound—each of which may be readily abandoned in favor of still new psychological quests. The patterns in many ways resembles what Erik Erikson has called "identity diffusion" or "identity confusion," and the impaired psychological functioning which those terms suggest can be very much present. But I would stress that the protean style is by no means pathological as such, and, in fact, may well be one of the functional patterns of our day. It extends to all areas of human experience—to political as well as sexual behavior, to the holding and promulgating of ideas and to the general organization of lives. . . .

To be sure, one can observe in contemporary man a tendency which seems to be precisely the opposite of the protean style. I refer to the closing off of identity or constriction of self-process, to a straight-and-narrow specialization in psychological as well as in intellectual life, and to reluctance to let in any "extraneous" influences. But I would emphasize that where this kind of constricted or "one-dimensional" self-process exists, it has an essentially reactive and compensatory quality. In this it differs from earlier characterological styles it may seem to resemble (such as the "inner-directed" man described by Riesman, and still earlier patterns in traditional society). For these were direct outgrowths of societies which then existed, and in harmony with those societies, while at the present time a constricted self-process requires continuous "psychological work" to fend off protean influences which are always abroad.

Protean man has a particular relationship to the holding of ideas which has, I believe, great significance for the politics, religion, and general intellectual life of the future. For just as elements of the self can be experimented with and readily altered, so can idea systems and ideologies be embraced, modified, let go of and re-embraced, all with a new ease that stands in sharp contrast to the inner struggle we have in the past associated with these shifts. Until relatively recently, no more than one major ideological shift was likely to occur in a lifetime, and that one would be long remembered as a significant individual turning-point accompanied by profound soul-searching and conflict. But today it is not unusual to encounter several such shifts, accomplished relatively painlessly, within a year or even a month; and among many groups, the rarity is a man yho has gone through his life holding firmly to a single ideological vision.

In one sense, this tendency is related to "the end of ideology" spoken of by Daniel Bell, since protean man is incapable of enduring an unquestioning allegiance to the large ideologies and utopian thought of the nineteenth and early twentieth centuries. One must be cautious about speaking of the end of anything, however, especially ideology, and one also encounters in protean man what I would call strong ideological hunger. He is starved for ideas and feelings that can give coherence to his world, but here too his taste is toward new combinations. While he is by no means without yearning for the absolute, what he finds most acceptable are images of a more fragmentary nature than those of the ideologies of the past; and these images, although limited and often fleeting, can have great influence upon his psychological life. Thus political and religious movements, as they confront protean man, are likely to experience less difficulty convincing him to alter previous convictions than they do providing him a set of beliefs which can command his allegiance for more than a brief experimental interlude.

Intimately bound up with his flux in emotions and beliefs is a profound inner sense of absurdity, which finds expression in a tone of mockery. The sense and the tone are related to a perception of surrounding activities and belief as profoundly strange and inappropriate. They stem from a breakdown in the relationship between inner and outer worlds—that is, in the sense of symbolic integrity—and are part of the pattern of psychohistorical dislocation I mentioned earlier. For if we view man as primarily a symbol-forming organism, we must recognize that he has constant need of a meaningful inner formulation of self and world in which his own actions and even his impulses, have some kind of "fit" with the "outside" as he perceives it.

The sense of absurdity, of course, has a considerable modern tradition, and has been discussed by such writers as Camus as a function of man's spiritual homelessness and inability to find any meaning in traditional belief systems. But absurdity and mockery have taken much more extreme form in the post-World War II world, and have in fact become a prominent part of a universal life style.

In American life, absurdity and mockery are everywhere. Perhaps their most vivid expression can be found in such areas as Pop Art and the more general burgeoning of "pop culture." Important here is the complex stance of the pop artist toward the objects he depicts. On the one hand he embraces the materials of the everyday world, celebrates and even exalts them—boldly asserting his creative return to representational art (in active rebellion against the previously reigning nonobjective school), and his psychological return to the "real world" of *things*. On the other hand, everything he touches he mocks. "Thingness" is pressed to the point of caricature. He is indeed artistically reborn as he moves freely among the physical and symbolic materials of his environment, but mockery is his birth certificate and his passport. This kind of duality of approach is formalized in the stated "duplicity" of Camp, a poorly-defined aesthetic in which (among other things) all varieties of mockery coverage under the guiding influence of the homosexual's subversion of a heterosexual world.

Also relevant are a group of expressions in current slang, some of them derived originally from jazz. The "dry mock" has replaced the dry wit; one refers to a segment of life experience as a "bit," "bag," "caper," "game," (or "con game"), "scene," "show" or "scenario"; and one seeks to "make the scene" (or "make it"), "beat the system" or "pull it off"—or else one "cools it" ("plays it cool") or "cops out." The thing to be experienced, in other words, is too absurd to be taken at its face value; one must either keep most of the self aloof from it, or if not one must lubricate the encounter with mockery.

A similar spirit seems to pervade literature and social action alike. What is best termed a "literature of mockery" has come to dominate fiction and other forms of writing on an international scale. Again Günter Grass's *The Tin Drum* comes to mind, and is probably the greatest single example of this literature—a work, I believe, which will eventually be appreciated as much as a general evocation of contemporary man as of the particular German experience with Nazism. In this country the divergent group of novelists known as "black humorists" also fit into the general category—related as they are to a trend in the American literary consciousness which R. B. W. Lewis has called a "savagely comical apocalypse" or a "new kind of ironic literary form and distrubing vision, the joining of the dark thread of apocalypse with the nervous detonations of satiric laughter." For it is precisely death itself, and particularly threats of the contemporary apocalypse, that protean man ultimately mocks.

The relationship of mockery to political and social action has been less apparent, but is, I would claim, equally significant. There is more than coincidence in the fact that the largest American student uprising of recent decades,

the Berkeley Free Speech Movement of 1965, was followed immediately by a "Dirty Speech Movement." While the object of the Dirty Speech Movement —achieving free expression of forbidden language, particularly of four-letter words—can be viewed as a serious one, the predominant effect, even in the matter of names, was that of a mocking caricature of the movement which preceded it. But if mockery can undermine protest, it can also enliven it. There have been signs of craving for it in major American expressions of protest such as the Negro movement and the opposition to the war in Vietnam. In the former a certain chord can be struck by the comedian Dick Gregory, and in the latter by the use of satirical skits and parodies, that revives the flagging attention of protestors becoming gradually bored with the repetition of their "straight" slogans and goals. And on an international scale, I would say that, during the past decade, Russian intellectual life has been enriched by a leavening spirit of mockery— against which the Chinese leaders are now, in the extremes of their "Cultural Revolution," fighting a vigorous but ultimately losing battle.

Closely related to the sense of absurdity and the spirit of mockery is another characteristic of protean man which can be called "suspicion of counterfeit nurturance." Involved here is a severe conflict of dependency, a core problem of protean man. I first began to think of the concept several years ago while working with survivors of the atomic bomb in Hiroshima. I found that these survivors both felt themselves in need of special help, and resented whatever help was offered them because they equated it with weakness and inferiority. In considering the matter more generally, I found this equation of nurturance with the threat to autonomy a major theme of contemporary life. The increased dependency needs resulting from the breakdown of traditional institutions lead protean man to seek out replacements wherever he can find them. The large organizations (government, business, academic, and so forth) to which he turns, and which contemporary society more and more holds out as a substitute for traditional institutions, present an ambivalent threat to his autonomy in one way; and the intense individual relationships in which he seeks to anchor himself in another. Both are therefore likely to be perceived as counterfeit. But the obverse side of this tendency is an expanding sensitivity to the unauthentic, which may be just beginning to exert its general creative force on man's behalf.

Technology (and technique in general), together with science, have special significance for protean man. Technical achievement of any kind can be strongly embraced to combat inner tendencies toward diffusion, and to transcend feelings of absurdity and conflicts over counterfeit nurturance. The image of science itself, however, as the ultimate power behind technology and, to a considerable extent, behind contemporary thought in general, becomes much more difficult to cope with. Only in certain underdeveloped countries can one find in relatively pure form, those expectations of scientific-utopian deliverance from all human want and conflict which were characteristic of eighteenth- and nineteenth-century Western thought. Protean man retains much of this utopian imagery, but he finds it increasingly undermined by massive disillusionment. More and more he calls forth the other side of the God-devil polarity generally applied to science, and sees it as a purveyor of total destructiveness. This kind of profound ambivalence creates for him the most extreme psychic paradox: the very force he still feels to be his liberator from the heavy burdens of past irrationality also threatens him with absolute annihilation, even extinction. But this paradox may well be—in fact, I believe, already has been—the source of imaginative efforts to achieve new relationships between science and man, and indeed, new visions of science itself.

I suggested before that protean man was not free of guilt. He indeed suffers from it considerably, but often without awareness of what is causing his suffering. For his is a form of hidden guilt: a vague but persistent kind of self-condemnation related to the symbolic disharmonies I have described, a sense of having no outlet for his loyalties and no symbolic structure for his achievements. This is the guilt of social breakdown, and it includes various forms of historical and racial guilt experienced by whole nations and peoples, both by the privileged and the abused. Rather than a clear feeling of evil or sinfulness, it takes the form of a nagging sense of unworthiness all the more troublesome for its lack of clear origin.

Protean man experiences similarly vague constellations of anxiety and resentment. These too have origin in symbolic impairments and are particularly tied-in with suspicion of counterfeit nurturance. Often feeling himself uncared for, even abandoned, protean man responds with diffuse fear and anger. But he can neither find a good cause for the former, nor a consistent target for the latter. He nonetheless cultivates his anger because he finds it more serviceable than anxiety, because there are plenty of targets of one kind or another beckoning, and because even moving targets are better than none. His difficulty is that focused indignation is as hard for him to sustain as is any single identification or conviction.

Involved in all of these patterns is a profound psychic struggle with the idea of change itself. For here too protean man finds himself ambivalent in the extreme. He is profoundly attracted to the idea of making all things, including himself, totally new—to the "mode of transformation." But he is equally drawn to an image of a mythical past of perfect harmony and prescientific wholeness, to the "mode of restoration." Moreover, beneath his transformationism is nostalgia, and beneath his restorationism is his fascinated attraction to contemporary forms and symbols. Constantly balancing these elements midst the extraordinarily rapid change surrounding his own life, the nostalgia is pervasive, and can be one of his most explosive and dangerous emotions. This longing for a "Golden Age" of absolute oneness, prior to individual and cultural separation or delineation, not only sets the tone for the restorationism of the politically Rightist antagonists of history: the still-extant Emperor-worshipping assassins in Japan, the Colons in France and the John Birchites and Ku Klux Klanners in this country. It also, in more disguised form, energizes that transformationist totalism of the Left which courts violence, and is even willing to risk nuclear violence, in a similarly elusive quest.

Following upon all that I have said are radical impairments to the symbolism of transition within the life cycle—

the *rites de passage* surrounding birth, entry into adulthood, marriage and death. Whatever rites remain seem shallow, inappropriate, fragmentary. Protean man cannot take them seriously, and often seeks to improvise new ones with whatever contemporary materials he has available, including cars and drugs. Perhaps the central impairment here is that of symbolic immortality—of the universal need for imagery of connection predating and extending beyond the individual life span, whether the idiom of this immortality is biological (living on through children and grandchildren), theological (through a life after death), natural (*in* nature itself which outlasts all) or creative (through what man makes and does). I have suggested elsewhere that this sense of immortality is a fundamental component of ordinary psychic life, and that it is now being profoundly threatened; by simple historical velocity, which subverts the idioms (notably the theological) in which it has traditionally been maintained; and, of particular importance to protean man, by the existence of nuclear weapons, which, even without being used, call into question all modes of immortality. (Who can be certain of living on through children and grandchildren, through teachings or kindnesses?)

Protean man is left with two paths to symbolic immortality which he tries to cultivate sometimes pleasurably and sometimes desperately. One is the natural mode we have mentioned. His attraction to nature and concern at its desecration has to do with an unconscious sense that, in whatever holocaust, at least nature will endure—though such are the dimensions of our present weapons that he cannot be absolutely certain even of this. His second path may be termed that of "experiential transcendence"—of seeking a sense of immortality in the way that mystics always have, through psychic experience of such great intensity that time and death are, in effect, eliminated. This, I believe, is the larger meaning of the "drug revolution," of protean man's hunger for chemical aids to "expanded consciousness." And indeed all revolutions may be thought of, at bottom, as innovations in the struggle for immortality, as new combinations of old modes.

We have seen that young adults individually, and youth movements collectively, express most vividly the psychological themes of protean man. And although it is true that these themes make contact with what we sometimes call the "psychology of adolescence," we err badly if we overlook their expression in all age groups and dismiss them as "mere adolescent phenomena." Rather, protean man's affinity for the

young—his being metaphorically and psychologically so young in spirit—has to do with his never-ceasing quest for imagery of rebirth. He seeks such imagery from all sources: from ideas, techniques, religious and political systems, mass movements and drugs; or from special individuals of his own kind whom he sees as possessing that problematic gift of his namesake, the gift of prophecy. The dangers inherent in the quest seem hardly to require emphasis. What perhaps needs most to be kept in mind is the general principle that renewal on a large scale is impossible to achieve without forays into danger, destruction and negativity. The principle of "death and rebirth" is as valid psychohistorically as it is mythologically. However misguided many of his forays may be, protean man also carries with him an extraordinary range of possibility for man's betterment, or more important, for his survival.

A Revolutionary Consciousness

RICHARD JOHN NEUHAUS

The phenomenon is undeniable, what it means is subject to interpretation. It is the growth of a revolutionary

From Richard John Neuhaus, "The Thorough Revolutionary," in Peter Berger and Richard J. Neuhaus, Movement and Revolution. Copyright © 1970 by Richard J. Neuhaus and Peter L. Berger. Reprinted by permission of Doubleday & Company, Inc.

consciousness in American life, and the Movement is its prophet. The revolutionary consciousness is in part a mood, to a lesser extent a program. It is the feeling that the times have brought things to a head, things cannot go on as they are.

The political significance of this consciousness is frequently dismissed.

Psychologists note that the feeling of historical uniqueness, the intuition of impending events of unprecedented impact, is endemic to youth. Only the young, it is said, have not been ravaged by cynicism. They alone hold dreams inviolate. The hope for radical change is an indulgence that only the innocent can afford. But the Movement is more than the young. And, even with regard to the youth sector, the psychological explanation fails to do justice to the phenomenon. A St. Louis professor was explaining, and explaining away, the campus insurrection in terms of "youthful rebellion." "That's exactly what we're talking about," interrupted a student, "that's your way of making it seem like the problem's with us instead of the university. That's what you call rational explanation, but it's just clever evasion. In fact it's not even very clever any more, it's just standard hypocrisy dressed up like objectivity."

Whether the hypocrisy is standard or redesigned in response to a new situation, it has lost its power to discredit the radical conviction. Few young people and fewer over thirty deny the impact of hidden and overt psychological dynamics shaping the Movement. But they protest those analyses that distract from and tend to dissipate the emphatically political character of radicalism. Any explanation of the Movement is suspect as "reductionist" that does not first take seriously the Movement's professed intent to bring about radical change. No matter how skilled the explanation, it cannot evade the self-evident fact that hundreds of thousands of Americans believe this society needs revolution. That is in itself of momentous political significance, regardless of its alleged dynamics. Nor can even the most evasive explanation

credibly claim that radical protest can be explained by forces emanating from the Movement itself. Revolutionary consciousness is not a creation ex *nihilo* nor is it immaculately conceived.

The failure to permit the fulfillment of black identity and potential, the militarization of the society, the unresponsiveness of the political system, the inability even to conceive of an American role in stemming world famine, the decay of urban areas, the emptiness of technological success in space and affluence in the suburbs, Vietnam, Vietnam, and Vietnam—these are not the inventions of the Movement. They are not ghostly apparitions conjured for the purpose of radicalizing the society. They are part of a long list of failures that compel people to the conclusion that this is a failing social order. Some black Americans may be spared the feeling of deep disillusionment, of which James Baldwin wrote in *The Fire Next Time:*

> The American Negro has the great advantage of having never believed that collection of myths to which white Americans cling [when this was written, 1963]; that their ancestors were all freedom-loving heroes, that they were born in the greatest country the world has ever seen, or that Americans are invincible in battle and wise in peace, that Americans have always dealt honorably with Mexicans and Indians and all other neighbors or inferiors, that American men are the world's most direct and virile, that American women are pure.

There are enclaves in which James Baldwin's description of white America's self-understanding seems plausible, in American Legion halls and among the "new" Republicans of the South.

Perhaps the majority of Middle America, what conservatives like to call "the heartland," still accepts the description. But an "enclave" attitude is not defined by a nose count that determines it is held by a minority of Americans. The attitudes of an intellectually and culturally sterile majority can be reshaped by an aggressive and creative minority. It is not so much a matter of *how many* are disillusioned with the existing order as of *who* is disillusioned.

An inordinate influence in how a society understands itself is exercised by the intellectuals who mint the metaphors and those in the media who promulgate them. The same weight in the scales of social effectiveness cannot realistically be assigned to the young and activist, on the one side, and to the old and indifferent on the other. It is true that in the existing order the latter often outweigh the former. But the fragility of the existing order is increased in exact ratio to the frequency with which that truth is demonstrated. The more blind and brutal the response to change, the more naked the display of power, the less real power possessed by the existing order. This observation is supposedly a commonplace, but it is clearly not common in the places where decisions are made. The bloodied clubs of frenzied police continue to be an effective organizing instrument for the Movement.

Less than a decade ago, but it seems in another epoch, John F. Kennedy announced that citizens should ask themselves, What can I do for my country? Incredibly enough, it seemed credible then, and millions of Americans, young and old, spoke without embarrassment about service to American purposes in the world. Eight years later, Senator Robert Kennedy evoked hopeful response with his call to "seek a newer world." The assumption of national righteousness had become implausible, but the hope was extended that perhaps United States power could be switched to the right side of the world revolution.

The loss of confidence grows among a large and influential sector of the American public who choose not to close their eyes to the oppressive uses of American power. In their eyes America is not the breaker but the welder of the chains of enslavement. They doubt that all the reform movements combined can do little more than sustain false hope for the healing of an irredeemably corrupt system. By congressional criticism of the military budget one or two of the Pentagon's more outrageous programs are less lavishly funded than the generals wish. Foreign aid builds a handful of schools in Latin America, which results in conditioning bourgeois counterrevolutionaries in lands that cry for revolution. The reformists applaud more black "firsts" in public life, business, and the entertainment world (soon there may be four blacks with their own network program), for all of which the black masses should feel a pride that takes the mind off degrading schools, housing, medical care, and welfare systems that conspire to deprive them of their humanity. And if you are troubled by conditions that imperil planet Earth, find patriotic comfort in America's mature acceptance of its world responsibility, symbolized by napalm, torture, and the presence of U.S. counterinsurgency teams in more than thirty countries where we insure political stability against the subversive impatience of the wretched of the earth. Albert Camus yearned for a country that an honorable man could love and love justice too. The most lively and socially committed sector of our population is persuaded that the United States is not such a country.

THIS TIME THINGS ARE DIFFERENT

This is not the first time there has been a widespread disillusionment among Americans about America. Already in 1914, Walter Lippmann wrote about the sense of drift that pervaded American life. We dignified this sense of drift, this feeling that we are victims and not masters of historical circumstance, he said, by terming it liberalism. There had been the Revolutionary period, succeeded by the National period, in both of which there was a plausible and encompassing rationale for the American experiment. The Civil War came in time to distract attention from troubling doubts, but the doubts emerged again through industrialization, urbanization, and other fundamental changes for which history supplied no ideological framework.

By 1914 the doubts seemed inescapable, but again we escaped by closing ranks for war. Critical reflection stood little chance of getting a hearing during the "high" of the nineteen twenties exhilarated by a sense of peace and unaccustomed prosperity. The collapse of the thirties opened the floodgates of radical criticism and hungry people were treated to an infinite variety of Utopian ideas and revolutionary programs in lieu of bread. As the popular and radical critique approached the nerve center of the system, however, a partially revived economy was strengthened by war, which again came to the rescue. Since 1947 and the Truman Doctrine ("It must be

the policy of the United States to support free peoples who are resisting attempted subjugation by armed minorities or by outside pressures.") the prevailing order has been sustained by a state of permanent warfare. Now Vietnam has not ended the Cold War but it has decisively ended the Cold War as a politically plausible context for the definition of national purpose.

We are back again with the "drift" of 1914. There is no war, and it is inconceivable that there can be a war which will solidify more than it divides the American people. Unlike the nineteen twenties and thirties, economic prosperity is neither a distracting novelty nor an overriding concern that can answer the questions now raised. The issues, so long sublimated, can no longer be ignored. Liberalism drifts in smug self-satisfaction, preening itself with its pragmatic and value-free cleverness in social problem-solving. In academia and in the councils of public power, political philosophy in the tradition of Western thought is moribund, if not already interred. The time for radicalism has struck. The stage is set and the casting offices have announced auditions for the event of the season, "Revolution."

POLITICS OF ACCOMMODATION

Not everyone who auditions for Revolution can be expected to show up for the manning of the barricades. This is not due only to a failure of nerve. There are within the Movement differing ideas about the appropriate response to radicalism's moment. For each an argument can be made and, no matter which a person chooses, it is good to understand the options he rejects. In what follows we will focus on armed revolution and the questions that attend that option. But first we must understand why some participants are and will be coming out at different points, although they share in the Movement's pervasive revolutionary consciousness.

Some, and this is a probable majority of the Movement, will decide to work, as they say, "within the system." It is both unfair and inaccurate to view this choice as being in every instance a betrayal or cop-out. Sympathy is in order. And not only sympathy, which implies condescension, but an honest evaluation of the forces that compel so many to this choice. The younger radical, for instance, is forced to make a new decision when faced with the new situation of financial responsibility for a family. This situation usually marks the exit door from the youth culture. Critics of the Movement find comfort in their suspicion that the young radical will follow their form and shed his radicalism when he assumes his "responsibilities." There will unquestionably be many instances to confirm the suspicion. Our generation, like other generations, has a greater capacity for security than for adventure. And we have not fully estimated the devious achievement of the American Way, with its lures, rewards, and sanctions, if we are still shocked by people selling out.

Others will maintain their radical critique in spite of formidable pressures to conform. They will conclude that the United States is not in fact in a prerevolutionary stage. They will agree with the judgment of some historians that successful reform can have revolutionary results, while abortive revolutions bring only frustration and repression. They will add that such reforms must be radical reforms, disrupting the values and patterns of convenience.

But the emphasis will be on continuity rather than discontinuity, aimed not so much at bringing to fruition the revolutionary potential of American political history as at simply fulfilling the promises that America has explicitly made. In all this they will be working, and when put to the wall will admit they are working, within the system. To prevent the system from becoming more oppressive, they say, it is necessary to oppose it radically. But the intention is clearly to reform and, if possible, to redeem what is. In the absence of more Vietnams—and even the Pentagon is not likely to re-enact that drama in its universally repulsive form—it is inevitable that many of the radicalized liberals in the Movement will take a kinder view of possibilities for what they will call radical reform of the system.

Those who are now posturing can be expected to revert or progress to another style. The literary stars and denizens of the cocktail circuits will in large part withdraw at the touch of serious repression. Or, if not out of fear, they will act out of boredom, going on to something else when fashionable people agree that "the revolution thing has been done." In short, whether because the cost is too high or the scene unfashionably dull, one should not expect to meet all his Movement friends at the barricades.

TOO RADICAL FOR REVOLUTION

Yet others will not show up at the barricades because they are too radical for revolution. The change they want is not contained in any political ideology of Left or Right nor susceptible to any political program. They are not apolitical so much as anti-political. The goal is personal and communal fulfillment, and politics in all its incarnations is the enemy. The fast-developing cult of encounter groups on the coast, the style of much "guerrilla theater," the spread of experimental communes from Big Sur to Pennsylvania, and Ray and Alice's church up in Stockbridge, Massachusetts, bear witness against the dehumanizing politicization of the whole of life.

This too is part of the Movement. The participant in 1970's commune was more than likely on 1968's picket line. He protested the war and the draft with a fervent "Hell no, we won't go!" and "Not with my life you don't!" But even then these were not so much political slogans in the conventional sense as a protest against politics as such, against an enterprise that presumes to subordinate personal values and relationships to programs, good and bad, of public policy. The suspicion that politics is sordid, exploitative, and humanly unsatisfying is, of course, shared by many Americans who cannot be considered radical. But for the radical who is graduated from the caldron of Movement politics, it goes much deeper.

Anti-politics is comparable to the *via negativa* of those who search for God. That is, the mystic moves beyond the conventional language and practices of religion. He pursues a theology not of God's presence but of his absence. Or it can be compared to what Susan Sontag describes as the "esthetics of silence." Art, she says, tends toward anti-art as the earnest artist becomes disillusioned with the tools, styles, and experiments of his work. They are no longer instruments but obstacles to what he yearns for, until finally he sees art as something to be overthrown. So the radical personalist and communalist

would not change the political system or replace it with another but overthrow the despotic hold of politics on man's hopes. The new man will be brought into being not by politics but by liberation from politics.

There is no politcial program to liberate people from politics. Yet there is something one can do. It is emphatically not "dropping out" but an entering into possibilities of personal and communal experience. The pharmaceutical mysticism of the drug scene is a part of it that looms inordinately large in the minds of critics. The entire personalist and communalist venture is distressingly irrelevant to those who see the Movement solely as a political instrument. But to its devotees it is gloriously, liberatingly irrelevant. In its irrelevance is its guarantee against being captured by some foreigner's program for change. Those involved say they are making a "cultural revolution" or a "revolution in human consciousness." It is beyond politics but not indifferent to society. Some participants believe they are building a refuge to which people from the Movement can resort when they too have seen the futility of political programs and passions. Others have more ambitious and Utopian goals of a society, and perhaps all mankind, turned on to the infinite joys of being human.

The American system has been quick to capitalize on this development. A strong argument can be made that much of the "cultural revolution" is little more than a new faddishness filling the coffers of American business by producing new fashions, musical and literary tastes, and psychedelic styles for the advertising media. Confirmation of this thesis can be found in the teenie-bopper center of any medium-sized city or at the box offices of a dozen New York shows which, while purportedly revolutionizing the culture, must certainly satisfy their distinctly non-revolutionary producers.

The personalist-communitarian direction of part of the Movement may, some argue, be worse than frivolous and delusive. It directly strengthens the most destructive dynamics of American capitalism. In *One-Dimensional Man*, Herbert Marcuse condemns the instrument of "desublimation" by which criticism of the prevailing order is neutralized. The most radical protest, the most bizarre behavior, the most grating screed of the alienated is not repressed or punished. Diverse opinion or behavior when sublimated maintains its integrity and therefore, presumably, its danger to society. So, according to Marcuse, the cleverly exploitative social order encourages de-sublimation, welcomes even the most radical criticism as another factor that enriches the variety of experiences and therefore demonstrates the superiority of the System. Thus toleration is the enemy most to be feared by revolutionaries.

Those in the anti-political sector of the Movement, however, are trying something of significance far beyond what is suggested by the beads, posters, hair, and pot that have been so thoroughly co-opted. And mixed with America's cheap exploitation of the hippie scene is a perhaps unconscious hope that the alumni of politics will succeed. The successful middle-upper-middle-class American is neither so secure nor so satisfied as some Leftist polemics picture him. "The Organization Man,"

"The Gray Flannel Suit," "The Lonely Crowd," "The Status Seekers," enrich his everyday vocabulary of self-disdain. Hoping against hope and in spite of his knowledge of the failures that have gone before, he too yearns for a new community uncorrupted by relentless competition and the making of deals to survive. There is precious little happening in America that witnesses to the possibility of a radically different and liberating life style. There is nothing that provides the referent for judgment and provocation provided, for example, by monasticism in the Middle Ages. So, while some are busy exploiting "the cultural revolution" for selfish gain, others try to protect and nurture it as a tender plant that may yet become the Tree of Life.

The personalist-communitarian sector of the Movement is only now being recognized in its distinctiveness. Thus it does not play a large part in the previous description of the Movement's origins and constituency. In times of dramatic conflict between the forces of good and evil, such as during the protest against the Vietnam war, distinctions are blurred and the personalist-communitarians are inseparable from the radical politicians. Now it seems their numbers are growing. Their social marginality is by design and not necessarily the measure of importance. It is just barely conceivable that these gentle experiments in community may form the creative subculture from which will come the American Revolution of our century. Clearly, there is a growing number of people who are prepared to gamble on that possibility.

6

WHAT DIRECTION:

MOOD OR MOVEMENT?

The French are frequently quoted as saying that the more things change, the more they stay the same. Such a presumption may or may not be prognostic of the fate of the new politics. However the first element of the proposition, ubiquity of change, is certainly apparent. New conditions and new problems are flourishing—population stress and environmental strain, generational pressures with "youngering" and "aging" trends, an increasing productivity in new knowledge (especially in science and technology), and an incipient cultural and psychic revolution.

The exact direction that the reaction to change will take is difficult to delineate, but some kind of a response, planned or unplanned, must occur. Recently a sociologist remarked, "We can predict with considerable precision the number of new cars we will produce next year, also the number of transistor radios, color television sets, four-lane highways, divorces, school dropouts, drug addicts, juvenile delinquents, social deviants." The point the social scientist was trying to make is that drastic technical changes cannot be introduced without having social reverberations.

Already there are massive stirrings and responses to historical discontinuities brought about by technological change. The result is that new aspirations and expectations are pulsating through the nation and the world. Movements arising out of these forces reject the idea that certain problems are rooted in human nature and are beyond amelioration. Despite the apparent discord and disruption, there is a growing feeling of hope and even revolutionary excitement that action can and will be taken now.

Some time ago Alfred North Whitehead wrote, "Mankind is now in one of its rare moods of shifting its outlook. The mere compulsion of tradition has lost its force." The commentary seems more current than when it was written. Almost everywhere is a mood of radicalization and reform that is as much cultural and psychological in its orientation as it is political. While the mood oscillates and is more like a kaleidoscope than a searchlight, the general posture challenges, among other things, time-honored concepts relating to the ethic of work, status based upon material possessions, and the inevitability of war as an instrument of national policy. The approach ranges from thinking "unthinkable" thoughts on foreign policy matters to insisting on a realignment of national priorities. The eventual goal is to create a more humanizing society, one in which more people will have more choice points in their lives and a greater opportunity to develop the full potential of their personalities.

There is still a question, however, whether the feeling for reform and renewal will find a significant and substantial political expression. The energy and effort could easily be dissipated in cute and curious life styles that, in turn, might be scornfully dismissed or commercialized and defused. The sales receipts of books on contemporary revolution at least raise the question of whether certain phases of the movement will be able to maintain their authenticity and integrity.

If the press for change and the impetus for social renewal are channeled into politics, what form will they take? Will the two-party system be strengthened and made more responsive and responsible? The basis of the two-party system is the reconciliation of differences and the creation of compromise. In the end the victorious party is the party better able to bridge differences and to build the largest alignment of voting blocs ("appeals to the faithful the most, disturbs the unfaithful the least"). Can the thrust of the new politics cause the two major parties to modernize their structures, to direct themselves to the critical, unresolved issues, and to become agents of positive action? Or, are the problems too big and too insoluble? Is the force of tradition too great to permit the parties to change? Should the two-party system fail as an effective instrument for bringing about needed change, will there emerge some kind of a multiparty or multifaction system spurred by highly personal and charismatic leadership? If the American political system is unable to accommodate the forces for reform, will there be a movement toward the radical left?

It would be tragic and ironic if our political institutions proved to be inadequate to carry out social renewal programs, and violence became the only alternative. Unfortunately our history in this area is not reassuring. Social change, which one would expect to come easily and naturally in a democracy, as in the case of moderate measures for racial equality and social welfare, has been strenuously resisted. Only after a long struggle, which included the use and threat of violence in the civil rights and labor movements, has progress occurred. The question still to be answered is whether it is possible to bring about peaceful yet radical change in our society. Up until now we have been unable to recognize when radical change is needed and, when it is needed, to welcome rather than to thwart it. Perhaps no country has been more committed to technological change than the United States and has done less to plan for the social consequences that technology creates.

The political system, like all other institutions, must respond to change and in some minuscule ways it already has. The convention nominating system is being slowly modified to make it more responsive, and the use of television in campaigning has altered the role of the political machine. But fundamental change is still elusive in such areas as the development of programmatic political parties and in devising a more broadly based and more relevant political system.

This is the challenge of the new politics. Will the movement be capable of revitalizing American political parties, or will it be simply another passing mood; interesting, dramatic, but lacking the organizational skill, political activism, and electoral strategy to have a lasting impact on American politics?

Specifically, this last section is concerned with several issues, all related to the original question, "What is the new politics?" In answering this question, it can be said that the new politics calls for change, either within the "system" or outside. It is a populist reaction to a number of deep-seated issues and forces in American life—a reaction caused by the apparent failure of the political system, or old politics, to cope adequately with those issues and forces. If one can accept the sincerity of the many groups that now advocate various forms of new political action, the new politics is more than simply a passing mood. On the other hand, it is not a single movement, but a large collection of widely differing movements backed by groups that for various reasons have felt more or less bypassed by the old politics.

One can discern at least two general trends in the new politics—one toward real, substantive changes in the American political system, and the other toward relatively minor adjustments in the present system in order to accommodate some of the most pressing demands. The difference is basically a matter of degree, with the second trend being more attractive to those who now possess political power but who also desire change. An example of this more moderate approach to change would be the recent McGovern Commission proposals for reforms in the procedures and structure of the Democratic party.

There is also another trend in American politics—one that appears as an answer to the demands of the disenchanted and alienated in the direction of a new politics, but which really consists of little more than new kinds of appeals to the old politics. Recently, former Congressman Allard Lowenstein, of New York, suggested that a system of "floating coalitions," or alliances, might be an answer to the desire for political change. "You don't change your views to get these kind of alliances, but neither do you demand that other people agree with you on everything else to work with you on one specific problem." [1]

Although coming from a famous advocate of the new politics, who is also

---

[1] David Hapgood, "Polarize or Persuade: An Interview With Congressman Allard K. Lowenstein," *The Washington Monthly*, I, 11 (December, 1969), 70.

credited with having induced Senator Eugene McCarthy to challenge President Johnson in 1968, this "solution" is really an adaptation of the old political method of compromise or group politics. Many of the so-called old politicians, favor this method, too. John W. Gardner, chairman of the National Urban Coalition, is organizing a national citizens' lobby whose goals will "include reshaping government and party politics at all levels to make the system work." It remains to be seen whether Lowenstein's "floating coalitions" or Gardner's "third force" will fulfill the challenge of the New Politics for fundamental change, either within or outside the system, in order to begin solving the great issues of our times.

Thus, the advocates of the new politics, whether they are radical or moderate in their demands and actions, have succeeded in challenging the old politics at many of its weakest points. To the traditional system's failure to include all major groups of American society, the newcomers have answered with their populism. To the "establishment's" calloused, pragmatic lack of regard for the issues, the new challengers have focused attention on the outstanding questions of this era. And as an alternative to the moderate, muddling, and traditional approach to solving these problems, the new politics offers an appeal to all kinds of direct action. The new politics has thus forcefully demonstrated the hypocrisy of the American political system's refusal to recognize many of the stark realities of American life.

But the new politics also suffers from several great weaknesses. For one thing, its advocates tend to be extremely naïve when it comes to converting some of their demands into action. Their frequent unwillingness to compromise often leads to a total lack of accomplishment. Moreover, their frequent failure to offer more than vague answers to national problems means that they are doomed to suffer frustration in their dealings with the "establishment." It is one thing to criticize and attack, but it is quite another thing to offer constructive alternatives to the present policies and procedures of our political system. The more radical the demands for change, in fact, the greater the frustration. The extreme militancy of some of the new politicians, often leading to violence, has also tended to stimulate the development of a kind of right-wing populism that offers another challenge to the American political system.

Moreover, leaders in both political parties have shown definite tendencies toward encouraging support of the status-quo-oriented "Middle American." American politics may thus tend to become polarized between right and left, with the advocates of the old politics supporting and encouraging the forces of right-wing conservatism. Hence it would seem all the more important for the American political system to play some kind of mediating role and to offer positive and constructive alternatives. In particular, America's political parties might take the initiative in putting before the voting public a new kind of politics than can be both militantly progressive and constructively concerned with the leading issues of our society.

Perhaps the question becomes simply this: "Can the old politics compromise with the new politics in order to revitalize American democracy?" If it can, the American political system might once again become both an instrument for continuity and stability, and an instrument for social change. If it cannot accommodate at least the most reasonable and pressing of the new demands, or if the abolitionist spirit that the disaffected groups currently display does not permit compromise, then we may see some drastic and, perhaps, unfortunate changes in our political and social institutions.

The diversity of the selections that appear in the last chapter reflects the wide diversity of directions of the new politics. If the reader is confused or doubtful at this stage of the analysis, his confusion and doubt are at least matched by that of the editors. But such feelings are perhaps inevitable when one considers the many facets of the "new politics."

The following essays begin with one by James Perry of *The National Observer*, who predicts that we must have "a new order—or no order at all." This is countered with a short statement by the conservative writer, James Kilpatrick, who feels that change must only come very slowly, if it is to come at all. Norman Cousins gives a different point of view. The selections by William Connolly, David Anderson, Bayard Rustin, and John Gardner present different alternatives, or strategies, for change, and Jack Newfield points out that the "new politics" is too committed to supporting the existing Democratic party to be effective in bringing about needed change. Finally, several reactions to the "new politics" are presented, beginning with a statement by President Richard Nixon, who offers a kind of "middle-of-the-road" viewpoint. This is followed with statements by several current public officeholders who appear to belong to that "new breed" of politicians in American life, in both political parties. With this basis for thinking about the future of the new politics, the reader is now asked to form his own opinions to match his own aspirations.

CHANGE IS NEEDED—BUT HOW MUCH?

A New Order—Or no Order at All

JAMES PERRY

The New Deal is dead. The Great Society is prostrate. The cities are in desolate decay, the suburbs are in turmoil. Richard Nixon is in the White House and Edward Kennedy is in trouble.

Millions of whites resent, fear, hate, distrust millions of resentful, fearful, hateful, distrustful blacks. Millions of older Americans are puzzled and embittered by their own children. Millions of young people resent—are even contemptuous of—their parents.

There is a race gap in America. There is a generation gap too.

The decade of the '60s, to repeat an altogether inadequate cliche, has been a time of change. Searing, disabling, destructive change, on the face of it. The change that began in the '60s will lead to a new order in the '70s—or to no order at all.

Most politicians hate change. They especially distrust indescribable, incomprehensible change. Politicians like to know where they've been, where they

Reprinted from The National Observer (September 8, 1969), pp. 1, 14. Copyright 1969 by Dow Jones and Company, Inc. Reprinted by permission of the publisher.

are, and particularly where they're going.

WHERE IS THE SAFE GROUND?

They like to find the safe, high ground, climb up on it, and play king of the mountain. But where today is that safe, high ground?

Over the next rise—into the '70s—who will be the kings of the mountain; who will be the vassals?

It is a vast puzzle, the resolution of which will affect all of us. This much is absolutely, flat-out certain: There will be new mountains and new kings. No more will we see politics as it has been played at least since 1932.

"We have cried wolf so often about the imminent restructuring of American politics that everyone stopped believing," says one thoughtful politician. "But now, finally, way behind schedule, the time is here."

Restructuring is a heavy word. To restructure means to tear down the pieces and put them back together in a new and different way. The restructuring of American politics is an unusual event; it occurs, at best, only every

35 or 50 years. The last restructuring began in Alfred E. Smith's losing Democratic campaign in 1928. The new structure emerged—the New Deal coalition—with Franklin D. Roosevelt in 1932.

What the new structure will be— if it, in fact, holds together, if the whole system doesn't splinter entirely—can be gleaned, in outline, from what the old structure was, and how it has changed.

AN URBAN PHENOMENON

The New Deal was an urban phenomenon. At its heart were those millions of children born in the early 1900s, most of them of immigrant parents, who came to voting maturity as the nation plunged into Depression. Samuel Lubell put it this way in 1952, in his prescient book, The Future of American Politics:

"The really revolutionary surge behind the New Deal lay in this coupling of the Depression with the rise of a new generation, which had been malnourished on the congestion of our cities and the abuses of industrialism. Roosevelt did not start the revolt of the city. What he did do was to awaken the climbing urban masses to a consciousness of the power in their numbers. . . . The big-city masses furnished the votes which re-elected Roosevelt again and again —and, in the process, ended the traditional Republican majority in this country."

There were, of course, other components of the New Deal. The South voted with it, for populist, traditional, and pocketbook reasons. The Civil War, in fact, continued to play a role in American politics. "Vote the way you shot" still had meaning well into the Twentieth Century.

Intellectuals flocked to the New Deal. Labor found a friend and voted that way. Impoverished farmers voted Democratic, to get help. Kevin Phillips, a special assistant to Attorney General John N. Mitchell, has written a controversial and provocative book, The Emerging Republican Majority, in which he outlines how the Republicans will succeed the Democrats as this nation's majority party.

The New Deal, Mr. Phillips says, taxed the few to help the many. An oversimplification, perhaps. But millions of Americans believed that to be so.

Like most political coalitions, the New Deal coalition was an uncomfortable one. Everyone knew it couldn't last forever, but almost everyone misjudged its durability. It held together through Harry S Truman; it held together, basically, during those eight years that Dwight Eisenhower occupied the White House. It largely held together for John Kennedy in 1960, helped a great deal by the fact he was a Catholic.

Then, in 1964, the Democrats won a stunning triumph. Barry Goldwater, the Republican candidate, carried only six states. The electoral vote result: Lyndon B. Johnson, 486; Goldwater, 52.

But 1964 was an aberration. Millions of voters perceived Mr. Goldwater not as a conservative or a moderate, but as a radical. These voters were afraid he would upset the enduring works of the New Deal, which, by 1964, were accepted by almost all Americans; they were afraid he would be itchy on the nuclear trigger. Most Americans voted for what they thought was the lesser of two evils—Lyndon Johnson.

Despite the 1964 returns, immense shifts in the nation's politics were taking place. They continue to take place, and it is these shifts that will determine the emerging politics of the '70s. . . .

INTO THE CONTROVERSY

So, let us leave the familiar landmarks behind and plunge into the thickets of controversy.

There is something happening in American life that is full of anger and uncertainty, and I think (now we lapse into the first person, for this is subjective ground) it may change all the rules.

A great many things are coming together at once—a new generation of kids, nurtured by television, the effects of which no one yet understands; a disintegration of traditional morals, partly made possible by the introduction of the Pill; the discontent, now politicized, of the black man; the continuation of an unpopular war in Asia; the dwindling of a generation that survived a Depression and gave birth to the New Deal; a surging affluence that has permitted the children of the New Deal to stop worrying about where their next pay check is coming from; yet, a persistent inability of millions of Americans to break free of poverty; a technological revolution that puts men on the moon but that, seemingly, cannot deliver the mail, add up a bill, educate a child, or rebuild a slum.

Politics does not live in isolation; it is buffeted by attitudes and changing values. When a revolution occurs in values and attitudes, a revolution is bound to occur in politics. And it almost always starts with the young.

It was young people—the children of immigrants—who formed the New Deal vanguard. Now there is a new generation of young people, reared in the suburbs, reared at the knee of a television tube.

Mr. Phillips, the blueprint-maker of the new Republican strategy, barely mentions young people in his book.

"Youth is important," he concedes, but voters under 25 cast only 7.4 per cent of the nation's ballots in 1968. "And," he adds, "while many Northeastern young people are more liberal and Democratic than their parents— especially the affluent and anarchic progeny of the Establishment—the reverse seems to be true in Southern, Border, Rocky Mountain, Catholic, lower middle-class and working-class areas."

Note Mr. Phillips' caveat—"the reverse seems to be true. . . ." But can we know what the new politics will be if we don't know for sure what the other, the non-Northeastern kids are thinking?

Scientific surveys have been made about the attitudes of youth, notably by the Gallup organization and Daniel Yankelovich, Inc. They make interesting, and provocative, reading.

The Gallup organization, last May, undertook a major examination of the attitudes of *college* youth. That report began:

"Those who comfort themselves that the trouble on the college campuses of America is caused by only a 'handful of students' and that the majority is completely out of sympathy with the goals of the militant few would be disabused of this view if they were to talk to students across the nation. . . ."

The Gallup report continued:

"Attitudes vary from college to college and region to region on specific issues . . . but at the heart of the discontent . . . is the feeling that society as a whole is seriously ill and that changes are imperative."

'BIGGEST GRIPE'

The students were asked to name their "biggest gripe" and these were the responses:

Not enough say in running of colleges—42 per cent

Current inadequacies of society—22 per cent

Adult and governmental authority—16 per cent

The Vietnam War—11 per cent

Want to have their voices heard—7 per cent

Civil Rights—6 per cent

Asked about their political philosophy, 2 per cent said they were "extremely conservative," 19 per cent said they were "fairly conservative," 24 per cent described themselves as "middle of the road," 41 per cent said they were fairly liberal, and 12 per cent said they were "extremely liberal."

But party labels have little appeal. Twenty-three per cent described themselves as Republicans (against 29 per cent in the general population); 33 per cent listed themselves as Democrats (against 42 per cent of the general public), and 44 per cent marked themselves as Independent (against 29 per cent).

"The trend on the campus is strongly toward the left," the Gallup survey reported. The word "conservative," the survey added, "is almost a dirty word on U.S. campuses today."

The Yankelovich survey, commissioned by CBS News, found that "the ideas that have kept colleges in turmoil this year are spreading beyond radical students to the rest of American youth, including those not in colleges."

The Yankelovich survey reported that 3.3 per cent of college youth consider themselves "revolutionary," 9.5 per cent believe in "radical dissent"; 39.3 per cent say they are "reformers," 37.1 per cent describe themselves as "moderates," and 10.8 per cent as "conservatives."

Noncollege youth, Yankelovich found, are less radical, more conservative. But there was a uniformity of response to some of the questions, such as: "Do you think American society is characterized by injustice, insensitivity, lack of candor, and inhumanity?" Fifteen per cent of all the young people strongly agreed and 41 per cent partly agreed. Of the noncollege youth, 13 per cent strongly agreed and 41 per cent partly agreed. . . .

THE WORKING-CLASS YOUTH

This sense of outrage is especially strong among the working-class young. It wasn't these young people who made *The Graduate* the leading money-making movie in 1968. That was a movie for suburban, middle-class kids. The working-class kids, as William Simon, John H. Gagnon, and Donald Carns reported in the Spring of 1969 issue of New Generation, went by the millions to the drive-ins to see John Wayne in *The Green Berets*. They made that movie the second leading money-maker in 1968. In their article, the Messrs. Simon, Gagnon, and Carns write:

"For all the talk of a youth revolution and the constant reminders of the proportion of the total population under 25, we should bear in mind that not all of this swelling tide comes from suburban homes or ghetto tenements. The images of Holden Caulfield and poor Benjamin the Graduate have become commonplace. So has the discovery of Claude Brown. Perhaps what is missing is a portrait of Studs Lonigan, a Studs frustrated, however, not by a depression but by the more ambiguous context of an affluent society."

There is, then, a gap between the kids themselves, and it may grow larger in the '70s. But the future belongs more and more to the suburban kids. The suburbs already are more important than the cities and they will become even more important. What happens in the suburbs—to young and old alike—will tell much about what happens to American politics.

Mr. Phillips argues that the suburbs are growing conservative. The only liberal suburbs are those "silk-stocking" outposts in the Northeast, Scarsdale, N.Y., for example, or Philadelphia's Main Line.

The liberalism of the middle-aged may, in fact, be largely a phenomenon of Northeastern suburbanism. But there is no evidence to show that the children of suburbia in most parts of the country are very much different from the children of the Northeast. On the contrary, the evidence suggests that college youth are remarkably in agreement in all parts of the country, with the almost certain exception of the South. Further, the evidence suggests that what has happened to college youth is happening now to some non-college youth.

If the war continues, if there is no reform of the draft, if there is no social progress by the Nixon Administration, these young children of the suburbs will become increasingly radical. By their actions to date they have touched off a generational backlash. That backlash could grow to a frenzy, and the voting trends would become fiercely conservative. . . .

It is impossible to predict events or personalities. Weeks ago, most people would have predicted that Edward Kennedy would be the Democrat to challenge Mr. Nixon in 1972, and maybe give him a pretty tough fight. Now, most people agree that Chappaquiddick has brought Mr. Kennedy's

national political career to a close. Maybe so. If not Teddy in 1972, who else? Hubert Humphrey would like another shot at it; so would Eugene McCarthy. Sen. Edmund Muskie of Maine, who got so many rave notices in 1968, is one possibility; Sen. George McGovern of South Dakota, who also made a brief run in 1968, is another. Sen. Fred Harris of Oklahoma, the Democratic national chairman, has enough ambition to try.

Somehow, though, one suspects that the Democrats may come up with a surprise. The Kennedy era is over; it's time for new faces. Taking a wild stab, how about Sen. Harold E. Hughes of Iowa as the Democratic candidate for President in 1972? He is big, confident, candid, and intelligent. Young party activists, who really have no candidate now, might well turn to such a man.

It will take more than personality to grapple with the political problems of the '70s. There could be very serious trouble ahead. "I'm not so sure we can survive," says a serious, liberal, young Republican. Others talk about the danger of a kind of political repression that would amount to a barracks state.

COLLAPSE OF THE SYSTEM?

Instead of an orderly restructuring of the American political system, the whole edifice could collapse.

But that kind of Armageddon is somehow hard to visualize. It is not impossible, just improbable.

It is my own opinion that there will be bad times, much worse than we have seen so far, but that we will be spared the anarchy of the doomsdayers.

One day, the dust will settle; these things never last forever. And when the dust settles, I am not sure we will find a neatly restructured two-party system. And that is because I am not sure the two-party system as we have known it, restructured or not, will survive.

Party labels are becoming less and less important. Each time Gallup measures party identification, more and more people identify themselves as Independent. But this is not nearly so significant as the trend to ticket-splitting. Last year, 54 per cent of the American voters split their tickets.

This, of course, is partly because a great number of voters do not trust either party. But it is more than that: It is an expression of voting maturity. Voters are being more careful in measuring issues and men. Because of television and other techniques, they can be much more easily aroused. Sad to say, some of them—because of these new techniques—can also be manipulated.

LESSONS OF '68

George Wallace and Eugene McCarthy taught some basic political lessons in 1968. Mr. Wallace, in a remarkable performance, managed to get on the ballot as a third-party candidate in all 50 states. Until he did it, nobody thought it could be done. Eugene Mc-

Carthy taught politicians that no one —not even the President of the United States—is safe from intraparty rebellion. The brokers are no longer there to protect him.

"Political parties are dead," says Joseph Napolitan, the professional campaign manager who created Hubert Humphrey's advertising in 1968.

That may be a bit of hyperbole. Political parties will continue to be important in the Presidential nominating process, unless that process is changed. They will continue to be significant in other elections too, when the issues, the personalities, and the offices are murky.

But, in a great many elections, candidates will run their own campaigns, appealing directly to the voters. Money and advisers will cluster about these men and they will become partylike instruments themselves. The Kennedys, perhaps, were representative of this kind of politics.

Ideology, to be sure, will shift from left to right, and back again. Events will dictate that.

For now, events dictate a movement to the right. But here come all these kids. Smoking pot. Wearing beards. They'll grow up and they'll vote, by the millions. They may want —and one day may get—their own kind of politics.

two

THE POLITICS OF CHANGE

A Conservative Speaks

JAMES J. KILPATRICK

Dear Norman:

We have been friends a long time now, you and I, almost from the time you took over as editor of Saturday Review; and from opposite poles, liberal and conservative, we have shattered some goodly lances.

Let me saddle up and take aim on the speech you made last week here in Washington.

This was out at American University, where the Assn. for Education in Journalism was meeting, and you spoke to that audience primarily of your magazine and why is has prospered.

One of your main points was that Saturday Review has a basic editorial philosophy—a picture of "the world as it ought to be"—and you went on to outline a few of your convictions.

"The first duty of government," you said, "is to protect the lives and the property of its people. But govern-

The Columbia Missourian, August 25, 1970. James J. Kilpatrick, "An Open Letter From Kilpo," copyright 1970, Washington Star Syndicate. Reprinted by permission of the publisher.

ment no longer is able to do those things that governments historically were created to do. No government anywhere can protect its people from war. National sovereignty no longer is functional; it has become impossible to carry on the business of the human race through 150 to 200 national governments."

Thus, you said, "new institutions" must be devised, capable of protecting the lives and property of all people and creating for them a congenial life.

And this is urgent: the pace of change is accelerating so swiftly that unless great decisions are made by the turn of the century, especially in control of the pollutants that contaminate our planet, man's destiny may slide to a point of no return.

I found myself reflecting, as I drove across Washington, back to the office, that most conservatives would applaud your vision and accept your premises and still disagree with the conclusions you reach.

One of the great differences between liberal and conservative, I suspect, is that you tend to start with men and nations as they ought to be—generous, peaceful, tolerant and wise. We tend to start with men and nations as they are, which is not that way at all.

As a consequense, when you call for "new institutions," we cannot make the ski-jump leap that comes so easily to you.

It is a great and valuable exercise to serve as architect of a world as it ought to be, filled with stately temples, but some of us ask: How do you work the plumbing? What holds up the walls? These are practical questions: How do you demolish the existing structure of sovereignty?

The answer, in my own view, is that you don't. Norman, you are like the Man from La Mancha; you dream the impossible dream.

Oh, it is all very well to say, abstractly and metaphysically, that ours is one world, populated by a single air-breathing species, the land-based mammal, Homo sapiens. Right.

But the commonality that unites mankind, for good or ill, is much less than the differences that divide us. The tribal instinct is fixed in the genes; and there is no such thing as "one tribe."

Can you imagine—seriously imagine—the Soviet Union, Red China and the United States of America entering into some "new institution" that demanded the abandonment of sovereignty?

The men and women who must make such urgent decisions—the decisions of the next 30 years—already are born. Can you believe they will be impelled, by fear or by nobility, to reverse the human currents of ten thousand years? For my own part, I cannot imagine or believe such things.

Two prospects occur.

The first is that over the next 50 to 100 years, man will render himself extinct here on earth by famine, by nuclear war, or by such gross pollution of the ecosystem that the species cannot survive.

This would be regrettable, but our planet is a mustard seed in the universe and God surely has planted His interesting species somewhere else.

The second prospect, which seems to me more likely, is that men and nations will modify old institutions just enough to muddle along.

Wars will continue, but not to Doomsday. Hunger, poverty and sickness will continue, but not in unbearable proportions. Pollution will continue, but not fatally.

Fifty years hence, they still will be hurling bricks in Belfast, for this is how men are, and will be. You and I won't be around, in any event, but perhaps we can break another lance somewhere else.

Best,
J. K.

Norman Cousins: A Liberal Speaks

JAMES J. KILPATRICK

A couple of weeks ago I addressed an "open letter" to Norman Cousins, editor of Saturday Review, following a provocative talk he had made before the Association for Education in Journalism. His theme was the urgent need, as he sees it, for the development of new international institutions with power to hold the disintegration of our planet and to shape a better world.

Mr. Cousins is an old friend. By the generally accepted definitions of our day, he is a liberal, I a conservative. One trouble with his idealism, I said, is that liberals tend to start with a view of men and nations as they ought to be —generous, peace-loving, tolerant and wise—while we conservatives start with men and nations as they are, which is not that way at all.

The column stirred up a gratifying mail, including a long and thoughtful letter from Mr. Cousins himself. He wrote me:

"I am not sure I know how to define liberalism. In any event, here goes: the essence of the liberal philosophy is a belief in the perfectability of man. But the upgrading of the human condition is nothing that proceeds out of

Reprinted from Columbia Missourian, September 22, 1970. Copyright 1970 by Washington Star Syndicate. Reprinted by permission of publisher.

drift. It calls for the finest expression of the human spirit and the most strenuous exercise of the human intelligence. It must be nurtured by hope and all the affirmative gifts and energies within human capability. It calls for the development of those conditions which foster and make human freedom possible.

"Now, having said this, it is also necessary to say that, under certain circumstances and conditions, otherwise decent men can become knaves. Human spirit can turn sour.

"Therefore, the question for all of us—liberal or conservative—is not whether man is basically good or evil, but how best to bring out the good and cope with the evil.

"I am sure you agree that no men understood this problem more thoroughly than the remarkable group of young men who founded the United States. In setting up a government, they wanted to make it possible for good men to hold office, but they also wanted to make it as difficult as possible for bad men in office. They felt that good men became bad when it is too easy for them to conceal their errors. Hence the emphasis on checks and balances. Hence the emphasis, too, on creating machinery that makes it possible for the voters periodically to get rid of the rascals.

"What meaning does all this have in our own time? The entire world has now become a geographic unit. Man, as the lunar astronauts discovered, is a creature of the planet earth even before he is an American or a Russian or a Buddhist or a Presbyterian or an Elk or a lawyer or a newspapermen or a farmer. He lives on the only planet in our solar system that can sustain life. Human life on earth is now endangered by war and preparations for war, by the poisoning of air and water, by depletion of natural resources, by overcrowding, by constrictions on human freedom.

"These dangers are real. These dangers transcend national boundaries. These are world dangers but we lack the world institutions to deal with them.

"What I urged in my Washington talk was that we fix our attention on these dangers and their implications. I am opposed to anarchy in all its forms. I do not think that mankind will solve its present problems in a dominant condition of world anarchy. . . .

"Therefore, I have been urging the development of world institutions to meet world problems. I do not believe that the individual nation is capable by itself of meeting such problems. I recognize the mammoth difficulty of getting enough nations to work together towards essential ends. But I believe that some nations can get moving in the right direction and that the procession will grow.

"Advocacy of ideas creates basic energy. No one can say that this energy will not carry us as far as we have to go . . . What counts are the things we are prepared to do to create a basic situation of safety, sanity, and freedom in our world and in our time. And we can work for what we believe with a spirit of confidence that comes from knowing that any problem created by man is within the reach of man to solve."

The Bias of Pluralism: Strategies of Change

WILLIAM CONNOLLY

Conventional pluralist theory, perceiving a minimal gap between existing arrangements and desired alternatives, fosters only a marginal interest in strategies of institutional change. Indeed,

Reprinted by Permission of the Publishers, Atherton Press, Inc. Copyright © 1969, Atherton Press, Inc. New York. All Rights Reserved. Pp. 26–28.

Myron Hale suggests that the "cosmology" of group theory encourages inquiry into processes of "partisan mutual adjustment," but discourages exploration into possibilities of inducing significant social change.

For those, however, who perceive a significant gap between the processes of a biased pluralism and more desirable alternatives, the problem of strategy becomes central. Many questions are involved here, including identification of places where new information, moral considerations, and pressure are likely to be most effective; development of tactics which promise the most long-run success; location of those societal segments whose position renders them actually or potentially interested in challenging prevailing practice; mobilizing the potential forces, and maintaining pressure over a long haul. The problem of strategy is the most difficult question faced by the critical temper.

Yet, for all its importance, the problem has not received much systematic attention. C. Wright Mills mentioned the "intellectuals" as a possible agency for "radical change." John Kenneth Galbraith has exhorted the "educational estate" to use its increasingly strategic position to challenge existing priorities in the industrial system. Arnold Kaufman has recently explored the range of strategies open to the "radical liberal," seeking to escape the twin dangers of the "realist's" anticipatory surrender to the status quo and the "self indulgent" radical's refusal to use established "pluralist" structures to effect significant change. David Kettler has found the strategies of the responsible party, Presidential leadership, and partisan mutual adjustment to have inherent weaknesses as well as objectives only partially congruent with the critical temper. He seeks to supplement these conventional strategies with new infusions of "outside" pressure which expose privileged elites to the substratum of groups and concerns presently ignored by the prevailing pressure system.

These recent investigations display an awareness that the question of strategy cannot be left to "historical forces"

or resolved by simple recourse to conventional political strategies. They reveal, further, a serious effort to cope with the well-known obstacle stated by Roberto Michels: that the organization required to channel inchoate discontents and unstructured idealism into coherent pressure also tends to generate conservative leadership and to dilute original objectives.

Much more work is needed here, certainly. But it should be noted that the emergence of the critical temper itself can be a contribution to strategy. The articulated temper helps to educate a larger public to the deficiencies of a biased pluralism and to the promise of future achievement; it reopens forgotten debates among social scientists, challenging the complacency of some and activating the latent concerns of others; it exerts constructive pressure on liberals in and around government.

The actual and potential impact of the critical temper is hard to locate precisely. Indeed, it is possible that its positive impact will be swept away amidst the society's repressive reaction to ghetto riots, student unrest, and the uncertainties of international politics. The pluralists are right in contending that no single group can control the shifting sentiments and forces which emerge in times of stress.

But individuals and groups can make some difference. Whichever way the pendulum threatens to swing and whatever amount of influence the critical temper promises to have, its reasoned articulation of criticisms, alternatives, and strategies shows some promise of mobilizing disaffected groups, of driving wedges in the prevailing system of balances, and of undermining attempts to justify a politics of suppression. This is no mean contribution in a period when the politics of complacency has failed to speak to those groups and aspirations balanced out of the plural-ist system.

A Strategy of the Right . . . ?

DAVID C. ANDERSON

. . . There is great reason for confusion, of course, for the word "repression" is bandied with increasing carelessness. Its most fashionable use—by various kinds of radicals who assert that American society is repressive by nature—is largely unwarranted.

THE RADICAL IMPRESSION

Repression in the radicals' understanding seems mostly a function of their own alienation, which has incurred the hostility of the larger society. One can argue over the merits of the alienation, and recognize that sometimes the hostility has led to illegal overreaction against the more flamboyantly alienated or those who profess openly to favor the destruction of America. But one cannot say that they are victims of true repression, which would involve the denial of free speech and due process as a matter of official policy.

The argument—or non-argument—fostered by the radical charges, how-ever, too often seems to obscure a more legitimate cause for worry: The *potential* for true repression in America has risen to a troubling level.

The sources of the potential lie in some of the well chronicled changes of the last decade or so, whose long range meanings one can only begin to fathom.

There was the social-political change: Sustained prosperity, demographic shifts, the Vietnam war and other developments, all seemed finally to coincide at the end of the sixties in such a way that huge numbers of Americans began to grow disillusioned with the democratic process.

A new factionalism arose; in the extreme the left turned to militant intolerance and revolutionary violence; the right to overreaction and vigilantism. Though the actual anti-democratic behavior was limited to a very few, they could claim sympathy in some degree from large segments of the population; the situation seemed to be evolving inexorably toward the classic confrontation of an anarchist minority and a majority demanding a return to tranquility at any price.

There was the increased mesmerization of the public by the electronic media. It eroded the traditional insulating time between events and their social impact, distorting perspective and judgment in the process. To some, anyone with long hair became a revolutionary; to others, the local traffic cop became an agent of evil oppressiveness.

And of course, the communications factor also meant that the distortions could begin to fulfill themselves as realities. People like Jerry Rubin and Abbie Hoffman could play for media impact and win large followings. Publicity from a single bombing could set off a rash of bomb threats and more actual bombings.

Beyond communications, other new technologies grew to have an even more direct relevance to the increased threat to democratic freedoms.

Recent advances in electronic miniaturization and other areas vastly increased the range and efficiency of eavesdropping devices for example.

And the uncomfortable implications of such increased capability were hardly diminished by the desire of some public officials to claim broad powers to use it. Attorney General John Mitchell felt free to declare unilaterally and rather formally last year at the opening of the Chicago conspiracy trial that Government agents had a right to eavesdrop on anybody the Attorney General decides is a threat to the national security, without any court review, and without having to disclose what has been overheard.

Computers have also had an impact. Last spring it was reported that the Administration had decided to organize and intensify its surveillance of radicals in the United States because of their increasingly violent activity. Then during the summer it was disclosed that various agencies of Government

had created a computerized data bank to centralize the information the Government collects on citizens and make it available at the punch of a key.

Should an Administration decide that a Quebec-style crackdown on dissidents were in order, presumably, the computers would play a vital role.

STRAINING THE DEMOCRATIC PROCESS

If all of these developments are disturbing in themselves, even more disturbing is the apparent symbiosis between them. If the new political tensions, the communications, and the information and surveillance technology obviously have not yet destroyed the democratic process, they are straining it.

This, indeed, is the nub of the repression issue in its modern sense. Because of the divisive politics and the instant communications, it's suggested with good reason, the moods, prejudices and emotions of men in power, beyond more rational words and carefully framed policies, have a heightened impact both on the public and on the bureaucracies of government. The new, readily abusable powers of information and surveillance make it all the easier for the moods and emotions to play an unhealthy role in practical terms.

Thus, some are tempted to blame the inflammatory anti-student rhetoric of Spiro Agnew for the shootings of students by National Guardsmen at Kent State University. And when New Left journalist Jack Newfield recently asked Ramsey Clark if there is a systematic Justice Department conspiracy against the Black Panthers, the former Attorney General replied:

"It's not so simple as a directive to get the Panthers. It's a mood, a tone, a license. The Justice Department sets a tone toward dissent, toward the Panthers. They circulate profiles of the leaders to the local police, there's a police raid in one city, and then another city gets the idea by example. . . ."

It may be pointed out, of course, that blaming Mr. Agnew for the Kent deaths amounts to gross oversimplification. The complex pot of campus and anti-war unrest was boiling vigorously long before he came along; he is entitled to his freedom of speech along with other Americans; and anyway, whatever his tone, much of what he says is true.

Furthermore, if there is an anti-Panther mood at the Justice Department, it is probably quite justified in the case of an avowedly revolutionary group with open ties to hostile foreign governments. Few, surely, would question an anti-Mafia mood at the Department—though, significantly, some Italian-Americans claim that it too has come to include unwarranted ethnic prejudice.

And, one must recognize, there is also a definite anti-police mood among the Panthers and other militants, a mood which could also be taken as the source of an informal, unconscious, nationwide "conspiracy" to snipe at the police.

But none of this should mean that Mr. Clark's concern is unwarranted. It is justified not because of any idea that the Panthers are unfairly pursued, but because the official mood may be taken by the pursuers as license to ignore the democratic guarantees normally afforded to any citizen, however criminal or revolutionary he may become.

In this light, for example, one may suggest that it is, after all, hardly essential for a well commanded, professional police force to make an arrest by opening fire on suspects who offer little provocation, as seems to have happened in a number of recent incidents between black militants and police. Of course it is true that the average policeman is only human; he may have trouble showing professional restraint because he has strong reasons for feeling contemptuous of the militants. But this is no excuse; rather, it is exactly the point.

Indeed, the tendency of the new politics and the new technologies to magnify the influence of the irrational in the democratic process ought to be taken very seriously by any responsible national leader. For even the appearance of undemocratic behavior sanctioned by official government may have implications as serious as the breakdown in respect for authority, and may even be a source of it.

If the problem is easy to state, however, it is difficult to grasp in practical terms.

How does a government restore a sense of maturity and perspective in an increasingly polarized society, especially when there are substantial arguments and deep feelings at both poles? What should it do about the impact of television, which can't, after all, be eliminated and shouldn't be controlled? How should it handle the use of the surveillance and information processing equipment, which has its essential and legitimate uses and which probably will be used by somebody, no matter what?

More germanely, perhaps, how does a leader keep from giving in to the powerful temptations to seek greater personal power from the polarized politics, or to abuse his access to the powers of communications and information he remains relatively free to command?

The questions are so unprecedented that a reporter bringing them up in a conversation with Richard G. Kleindienst, the Deputy Attorney General, and a man who claims to reflect the Administration's view of repression, finds him somewhat defensive.

Mr. Kleindienst concedes that unaccountable power of the Attorney General to authorize eavesdropping represents some dangers to freedom, especially when the eavesdropping is only for surveillance and not for use in court.

But the point, he contends, is that the Attorney General is a cautious man who is not about to misuse such authority. Indeed, he argues, since Mr. Mitchell is concerned with leaving a good record for the history books, his taking personal responsibility for the eavesdropping actually amounts to a check on his use of the power.

THE PRESIDENT'S BELIEFS

Furthermore, he goes on, the President shares a deep sensitivity to the question of Constitutional liberties; his personal beliefs and attitudes actually are the best bulwark possible to prevent the collapse of American democracy

as the far-out radicals stir up angry feelings of reaction.

And perhaps this reflects more of a policy than it seems at first glance. Whatever its sources or its dangers, the President clearly has concluded that the net result of the new changes is a surge of rightist feeling. And he seems to see his role, as Stewart Alsop suggested recently, as similar to that of Franklin Roosevelt facing a surge of leftist feeling: To accommodate and channel the new passions in ways that keep them from harming America drastically.

Thus the deliberate, rather than precipitate withdrawal from Indochina; the public embrace of the hard-hats; the tough-sounding anti-crime laws; the exhortations to the electorate to get back at the bombers and the "obscenity shouters" by voting for Republicans.

If this is a rational policy, however, one still cannot help a depressing feeling that the drift to repression, very much indeed like economic inflation, is stubbornly larger than government. For it is hard to see how a strategy of the right will do that much to reverse the impact of the technologies or wind down the escalation they abet of terrorism, fear and popular pressure for order. And history has shown, sadly, that the popular pressure will always prevail.

What the Left Needs Now is Politics

BAYARD RUSTIN

We on the democratic left are living through a pervasive crisis.

One aspect is that many people on the left today substitute psychology for politics. Now, I have no objection to a life-style, or how you wear your hair, or whether you eat pig's feet. But to substitute this "how I feel, what my thing is," for politics, is an extremely dangerous attitude.

The second aspect is the tendency to substitute morality, and very often predictions-of-doom morality, for programs. It is fashionable to assume that the United States is going fascist, that there are concentration camps up in the hills, that nothing can work now. This creates a mood of desperation which is extremely dangerous. In this respect I refer back to the abolitionists, who were extremely moral people, who were extremely anxious that black people should be brought out of slavery. But those of them who had nothing but morality disappeared once the Emancipation Proclamation was signed. And when black people cried out, "Give us forty acres and a mule," they did not assist in that struggle because they were purely moralists and did not understand its economic dimensions.

ADA World (Sept., 1970). Reprinted by permission of New America, the newspaper of the Socialist Party, U.S.A.

Just as the abolitionists were a moral movement with no economic and social program, so it is likely that the last people on whom we can depend, when the war in Vietnam is over, are the peace people, because a movement cannot be sustained which is purely moral, but which has no political and economic undergirding.

Blacks are also sometimes guilty of obsessive moralism. Take the question of white racism. Simply telling white people that they're blue-eyed devils or that they are racist is dangerous and counter-productive. It becomes a cop-out for blacks who don't want to develop programs. And it's a cop-out for whites who are titilated and delighted to be abused and called racists. And thus Stokely Carmichael can come back to the United States and demand (and receive) $2,500 a lecture for telling white people how they stink.

The third aspect of this crisis is to substitute slogans for analysis. Thus, many blacks no longer need to think about an unbearable reality. If a debate comes up, you simply stop the discussion by calling the person with whom you are in debate an Uncle Tom. This is exactly what the Ku Klux Klan did in the South, stopping any debate by the center by the use of a nasty term. Thus, it's claimed that only someone who's under 30 can understand a problem, or someone who eats soul food. And in like manner, one can take out his frustrations as a peace person by equating hard hats with fascists and brown shirts.

Now the fact is that if anybody simply uses the word "hard hats" to dismiss a whole mass of people with whom we should be in alliance, he is not thinking. He is failing to see that it is people in the economic circumstances of the "hard hats" who are the only people in the United States saving and borrowing to send their own children to college. These are the people who never had a chance to get an education and who profoundly want one, and who in their perverse manner show their profound appreciation of education by being angry at those whom they think misuse it.

What we must do is analyze the present political situation so that we can know where our strengths lie. Now, a good example of this point is the NAACP. There is no organization that can be called a national organization in the black community except the NAACP. It is the only black group which organizes almost a half-million dues-paying members and which collects almost five million dollars exclusively from black people. The Urban League does not get its money from black people; SCLC does not get its money from black people; CORE never got its money from black people; SNCC never got its money from black people. And yet, today, the one organization which is never discussed, or is called "middle class," is the NAACP. The Panthers do not have one thousand members. Most of the kids you see on the street are not Panthers. They are there to sell the

paper—for every one they sell, they get a dime. There are about one thousand Panther members in the country, half of whom are F.B.I. men watching the five hundred legitimate members. And yet, it is these types, and the SDS types, and the Weathermen types that everybody gives attention to.

Forget the Weathermen, forget, SDS and forget the college kids who are charming, elitist and rich and who probably are not going to contribute very much either to thinking or political action. The average family which has children in SDS makes $23,000 a year while the average American family makes $8,000 a year. That is the injustice which SDS should be protesting.

President Nixon's objective is very clear. It is to destroy that coalition which Franklin Delano Roosevelt established and upon which every important social change in this country has depended. He wants to destroy that coalition and establish one of his own, the same type of alliance which was established in 1876 of Southern conservatives and Northern Republicans. Now his strategy for doing this is to woo the South, and his tactic is a creation of division and polarization. Whatever he has done has been calculated to divide black from white, young from old, hawks from doves, rich from poor, and —in his statement following the Carswell rejection—to separate North from South. That is his tactic.

I maintain that there are two elements in our society which can block Nixon's strategy and they are the labor movement and the minorities, particularly the blacks. Economic progress is the basis for maintaining our coalition—we are going to win because we emphasize the economic issues in this society. There is no possibility for black people making progress if we emphasize only race. You can psychoanalyze every white person in the United States until he comes out pristine pure tomorrow morning, filled with love for black people—and that will not provide jobs or build housing. That is a political task which we must face.

A Lobby of the People

JOHN W. GARDNER

Dear Friend:

I would like to ask you to join me in forming a new, independent, nonpartisan organization to help in rebuiding this nation. It will be known as *Common Cause*. It will not be a third party but a third force in American life, deriving its strength from a common desire to solve the nation's problems and revitalize its institutions of government.

There is so much that needs to be done. There are so few who are properly organized to do it. We must end the war. We must bring about a drastic change in national priorities. We must renew our attack on poverty and discrimination. And we must keep at it until we build a new America.

I know many of you share my concern and my deep sense of urgency. We must act now. We must demand more of ourselves and much, much more of our leaders. We must shake up and renew outworn institutions.

Reprinted from John W. Gardner, Letter to potential members of Common Cause, October, 1970. Reprinted by permission.

Common Cause offers you the opportunity.

Many people today recognize that national priorities must be changed, but they don't know how to go about it. They are shocked by the facts of poverty and pollution and inadequate housing, but they don't know what to do.

The first thing Common Cause will do is to assist you to speak and act in behalf of legislation designed to solve the nation's problems. We are going to build a true "citizens' lobby" —concerned *not* with the advancement of special interests but with the well-being of the nation. We will keep you up-to-date on crucial issues before Congress. We will suggest when and where to bring pressure to bear.

One of our aims will be to revitalize politics and government. The need is great. State governments are mostly feeble. City government is archaic. The Congress of the United States is in grave need of overhaul. The parties are virtually useless as instruments of the popular will. We can no longer accept such obsolescence.

Most parts of the system have grown so rigid that they cannot respond to impending disaster. They are so ill-designed for contemporary purposes that they waste taxpayers' money, mangle good programs and frustrate every good man who enters the system. The solutions are not mysterious. Any capable city councilman, state legislator, party official, or Member of Congress can tell you highly practical steps that might be taken tomorrow to make the system more responsive. But there has been no active, powerful, hard-hitting constituency to fight for such steps. We can provide that kind of constituency.

Skeptics say "But you can't really change such things." The Congress of the United States has changed in dramatic ways since its founding. Why should we assume it has lost the capacity to change further?

The political parties have changed even more dramatically since the birth of the Republic. They can change again.

Common Cause is an outgrowth of the Urban Coalition Action Council. Operating under a governing board of extraordinary diversity (mayors, minority group leaders, and leaders from business, labor and the major religious groups), the Action Council proved to be astonishingly effective. The Council has worked with a variety of allies in the civil rights organizations, the labor movement, the business community, and other groups. It has participated in major legislative victories, including extension of the Voting Rights Act, passage of the Welfare Reform Bill in the House, and defeat of a measure that would have virtually ended nonpartisan voter registration programs.

In short, we *know from first hand* experience *that citizen action can be effective.* We ask you to join us in making it even more so.

I shall not attempt to list here all the issues with which Common Cause will be concerned. We believe there is great urgency in ending the Vietnam War on a scheduled timetable. We believe there must be a major reordering of national priorities. We believe the problems of poverty and race must be among our first concerns. We will call for new solutions in housing, employment, education, health, consumer protection, environment, family planning, law enforcement and the administration of justice.

As our membership grows, we will ask members to help in identifying priority issues.

We do not expect every member to agree with every detail of our agenda. But our governing board has learned in three years of experience that it is possible to arrive at significant proposals that will be agreed on by Americans of widely differing backgrounds.

We take the phrase "Common Cause" seriously. The things that unite us as a people are more important than the things that divide us. No particular interest group can prosper for long if the nation is disintegrating. Every group must have an overriding interest in the well-being of the whole society. It follows that our agenda must be an agenda for *all* Americans —for the poor, the comfortable and those in between, for old and young, for black and white, for city dweller and farmer, for men and women.

Many of you who will receive this letter share my anger at institutions and individuals that have behaved irresponsibly. But, if we're going to focus our anger, a good place to begin is with ourselves.

We have not behaved like a great people. We are not being the people we set out to be. We have not lived by the values we profess to honor.

America is not the nation it set out to be. And we will never get back on course until we take some tough, realistic steps to revitalize our institutions. That won't be easy or comfortable. Institutions don't enjoy the process of renewal. But we had better get on with it.

In recent years we have seen altogether too much complacency, narrow self-interest, meanness of mind and spirit, irrational hatred and fear. But as I travel around the country, I see something else. I see great remaining strength in this nation. I see deeper reserves of devotion and community concern than are being tapped by present leadership. I see many, many Americans who would like to help rebuild this nation but don't know where to begin.

I invite you to be among the first to join us in *Common Cause.* . . .

With a large and active membership we can begin to remake America.

Sincerely yours,
John W. Gardner

three

THE NEW POLITICS vs. NEW APPEALS
TO THE OLD POLITICS

New Politics: More Mood Than Movement

JACK NEWFIELD

The new technology or the new politics—call it what you will—has arrived.
—James M. Perry, *The New Politics*

The New Politics is becoming a huckster's phrase, invoked by plastic politicians, to con what they think is a gullible electorate. It is as much a cliché as the New Journalism or the New Theatre. It has become like Silly Putty, bent and twisted into dozens of distorted and unnatural shapes by careerists trying to redefine it to their particular advantage.

Jacob Javits, who campaigned last autumn for Richard Nixon, proclaims himself a partisan of the New Politics because "it means problem solving." Theodore Sorensen, who tried to convince Robert Kennedy not to speak out against the war in Vietnam, says he is for it because it "means participation, like giving 18-year-olds the vote." Or-

ganization men like Jesse Unruh and Stanley Steingut claim to be part of the New Politics. James Perry and Penn Kimball have written whole books defining the New Politics exclusively in terms of manipulative technology, computers and mass communications. Hubert Humphrey and Fred Harris say they are "for" the New Politics. But then Albert Shanker *says* he is for decentralization and Mayor Richard Daley *says* he is for civil liberties. It all makes one recall George Orwell's prophetic quote:

"In our time, political speech and writings are largely the defense of the indefensible. . . . Political language has come to consist largely of euphemism, question-begging and sheer cloudy vagueness. . . . The inflated style is itself a kind of euphemism. A mass of Latin words falls upon the facts like soft snow, blurring the outlines and covering up all the details."

The sociologist Daniel Boorstin has written perceptively about "pseudo events" and "pseudo personalities," but the New Politics just might be the first pseudo movement. It has no program, no money, no leadership, no power, a weak national organization and almost nothing for its citizen supporters to do. An Albany meeting of the cannibalistic New York group in May broke up in petty bickering. Candidates running in the name of the New Politics—Tom Bradley, Henry Helstoski and Herman Badillo—all lost important elections within the last month. Instead of an issues convention, the New Democratic Coalition (NDC) spent its energies last spring organizing a fundraising dinner in Washington.

At this point, the New Politics is still more mood than movement, more desire than reality, more label than program. I hope in this exploratory and fraternal article to suggest a few reasons why the New Politics groups have been ineffective, and why, since the Chicago convention, they have lost the political initiative to the Nixon Administration, and to the old politics, machine Democrats, corporate managers, union bureaucrats and senior Southern Congressmen.

One reason is that most of the organizational leaders of the New Politics seem wedded to the notion that incremental change should come exclusively through electoral politics. They have geared their state groupings toward the 1970 elections, and are already preoccupied with the personalities of 1972. At their conferences they talk at length about taking over irrelevant, hollow shells like the Young Democrats and the Democratic National Committee. This parochial electoral vision has tended to flood the local organizations with anal technicians and power-tripping hustlers, while turning off the younger activists, who prize ideas

and confrontations more than candidates and campaigns.

Up to now, the orators of the New Politics have sounded much too optimistic and impatient. They recall 1968 in shades of victory, and see the Democratic convention of 1972 as a final vision of Armageddon. They are not mentally preparing for a movement that will span a decade or more of hard work in local communities. They have a furtive eye fixed on a short cut. And they see the Democratic Party as the only possible vehicle for reform, even though it was the Democratic Party that involved us in fighting the Vietnamese, ruined the poverty program and sanctioned the police violence during the Democratic convention.

Although I shall speak here primarily of cooperation with grass-roots movements to the left of the Democrats, I also believe that an excessive preoccupation with the Democratic Party is causing the New Politics to ignore the progressive wing of the Republican Party: the Ripon Society, Senators Goodell, Aiken and Percy and Mayor Lindsay.

The Democratic Party still houses the worst institutionalized elements in our national politics: the Meany-Lovestone-CIA complex; the Dixiecrats, the missile contractors and the Mafia. We should try to think of the New Politics as historically ten minutes old, and still view the idea of a new political party, including Ripon Republicans, as an open option. The endless talk of "capturing" the Democratic Party is both elitist and delusional. And much harder than folks think.

This narrow electoral bias seems based on a bad misreading of the history of this decade in America. Since the sit-ins of 1960, history has been pushed forward by insurgent movements rather than by political candidates. The black movement, the student movement, the anti-war movement and the dump LBJ movement should be the models of a new participatory politics. These were—and are—long-term, issue-oriented movements, on the margins of parliamentary politics, that engage thousands of ordinary citizens. At the necessary moment these movements invented their own leader—Eugene McCarthy—and entered the electoral process. By emphasizing infighting over nominations and positions within the Democratic Party now, the New Politics groups are cutting themselves off from the generators of energy and imagination on the campuses and in the ghettos. If the New Politics becomes a broad enough movement, it will once more have the power to create its own leaders at the right time.

The electoral strategy also neglects two of the most significant lessons to be extracted from the events of 1968. One is that *the basic institutions of liberal politics—the unions, the convention system, the mass media and the Democratic Party itself—are undemocratic.* Only by exposing and reforming these institutions—and by building alternatives to them—can citizen politics be made to work. One must remember that Vice President Humphrey lost every primary where his name was on the ballot, and was still nominated because of the power of three men—Mayor Daley, Governor Connally and George Meany. And the convention adopted a hawkish Vietnam plank, even though the policy had been repudiated by 80 per cent of the primary voters.

The other lesson of 1968 is that you can no longer base mass movements on charismatic heroes in this country, because those heroes get assassinated. Any American insurgent movement must be anchored on participation and commitment in order to survive the gunmen.

The New Politics will have to root itself in issues that move masses of people: an end to the endless war in Vietnam, a drastic reduction in military spending; community control, citizen participation, and opposition to the general over-centralization of American life; reform of the draft; democratization of the rules and structures of the Democratic Party; a guaranteed annual income, socialized medicine and the closing of tax loopholes for corporations and the very rich. And possibly most urgently, it must devise a program that addresses the legitimate needs and frustrations of the powerless white working class. Robert Kennedy won the votes of the steelworkers, farmers and cops in Indiana, Nebraska and California, and they can be won again by men who speak in plain Populist language against remote experts and bureaucracy; against big business and the war; and against the casual hypocrisy of programmed politicians.

This should be the agenda of a New Politics, not the small maneuvers for small positions within the existing Democratic hierarchy.

Another shortcoming of the New Politics has been its inability to win the trust—or even the curiosity—of the high school and college activists, a group of about 3 million. I don't mean to suggest that this is an easy thing to do these days. The young today quite properly believe in no adult authority in the country. With Dylan they sing, "I've got nothin', ma, to live up to." But if there is any New Politics, in the sense of ideas and constituency, it is the radical, activist students, from Mc-Carthy volunteers to draft resisters. They are the one authentically new element in the body politic of the country since the union movement of the 1930s.

No current national political leader now expresses the feelings or demands of the students. Worse, none even adequately defends them against the swelling backlash of repression. Yet, they all covet the students as volunteers in their future campaigns to climb the greasy pole.

Rep. Edith Green, who was Robert Kennedy's Oregon campaign manager, is emerging as the major draftsman of the vicious new and anti-student bill in the House Committee on Education and Labor. Eugene McCarthy, the man for one inning, refused to testify on behalf of his own delegates when they were on trial in Chicago last spring. Theodore Sorensen tells the National Book Association that the enemy is equally Herbert Marcuse and Ronald Reagan, neglecting to mention John Mitchell, Melvin Laird and Richard Nixon, who hold actual raw power, but whose names lack the same symmetry of the two cited. No Senator as yet has called illegal the indictments of the eight New Left leaders in Chicago, or dared suggest that Mayor Daley should have been indicted instead, if the grand jury had only read the Walker Report. What Senator has spoken out against the systematic roundups of Black Panthers, or the Congressional probe into SDS? There is a new McCarthyism in the land, and the New Politics has hardly noticed it, much less fought back.

One thing the liberal politicians can do is understand the cultural root of the generational alienation. The kids hate the environment most of them grew up in—impersonal split-level sub-urbs, homogenized religion, dull 9-to-5 jobs, sex by the marriage manuals, a mass media that promotes banality and suppresses the Smothers Brothers. The young just can live in that world.

They are in revolt against the most traditional values of the middle class—God, money, status and the family. One small way in which the New Politics can begin to relate to these kids would be to develop a cultural analysis of America that takes the adversary culture of the young seriously.

To summarize: the New Politics seems too committed to the Democratic Party as the one historical agency of renewal. It seems too remote from the para-political movements at the base of the society: blacks, students, the poor, women. It has not begun to raise the idea of redistribution of wealth and income. It is white and elite.

The New Politics should be more activist, more radically concerned with institutions, more concerned with cultural issues, more like a social movement than a political campaign. For example, it should now be leading the opposition to the war in Vietnam, organizing a new March on Washington, or perhaps a national strike. It should lend its support to the basic demands of the campus movements, and not contribute further to the paranoid backlash against the young. It should try to strike alliances with low-income whites on issues of economic self-interest, possibly through the new Alliance for Labor Action. It should be able to grasp the enormity of the present crisis, and realize that the business-as-usual ritual of making good speeches and nominating assemblymen is insufficient as long as 350 Americans are dying each week in Vietnam.

Right now the New Politics hardly exists, except as a simplistic slogan easily appropriated by hacks and hucksters. What we do have, out of the ashes of 1968, are some *excellent new politicians:* Sam Brown, Adam Walinsky, Paul Schrade, Don Peterson, Julian Bond, Channing Phillips, Representatives Chisholm, Koch and Lowenstein. But we do not yet begin to have a *new politics* that can generate a new majority for radical reform. I will end by quoting the candid and passionate speech Adam Walinsky delivered to the founding meeting of the National Democratic Coalition in Minneapolis last October:

We are a rump faction of a party which is sliding—indeed, rolling—into an abyss of ruin.

It would be easy and comforting to attribute this failure to the sins of Humphrey, Richard Daley, or John Connally, to a killer five years ago or a killer more recent. It would be easy—and it would be self-deluding and self-defeating and wildly, catastrophically wrong. . . .

These men, the current villains in the liberal demonology, have played their full part in these events . . . [*but*] there is no hope for this coalition, no hope for a regeneration of our politics, unless we are prepared to learn from the errors and illusions that have brought us to our present pass; not the errors of others, though they have been more than plentiful, but our own. It is time to face our truth. . . .

This is not only a matter of the war in Vietnam—where we promised peace in 1964 and then stood silent for too long as that pledge was broken and our Administration went to war. It is a matter, sadly, of almost all the great social legislation of the last four years.

We promised education—but our education programs have not taught the children. We promised new cities—but our housing programs have gone far toward destroying the ones we have. We promised health—and our vaunted medicare program has shot the cost of medical care up while doing little or nothing to improve the quality of care for which we now pay so much. We promised help to the farm—and nearly eliminated the farmer.

We promised blacks that patience would bring justice. We promised whites that justice would bring order. We have achieved neither. We promised and promised, passed laws and appropriation bills, taxed and spent. And when it was all over, who is there to say that life is truly better than it was before?

four

RESPONSES TO THE NEW POLITICS

Freedom: A Condition and a Process

PRESIDENT RICHARD NIXON

We live in a deeply troubled and profoundly unsettled time. Drugs, crime, campus revolts, racial discord, draft resistance—on every hand we find old standards violated, old values discarded, old precepts ignored. A vocal minority of the young are opting out of the process by which a civilization maintains its continuity: the passing on of values from one generation to the next. Old and young shout across a chasm of misunderstanding—and the more loudly they shout, the wider the chasm grows.

As a result, our institutions are undergoing what may be their severest challenge yet. I speak not of the physical challenge: the force and threats of force that have wracked our cities, and now our colleges. Force can be contained. We have the power to strike back if need be, and to prevail. The nation has survived other attempts at insurrection. We can survive this. It has

Reprinted from Address at the dedication of the Karl E. Mundt Library at General Beadle State College, Madison, South Dakota, June 3, 1969, by permission.

not been a lack of civil power, but the reluctance of a free people to employ it, that so often has stayed the hand of authorities faced with confrontation.

The challenge I speak of is deeper: the challenge to our values, and to the *moral* base of the authority that sustains those values.

At the outset, let me draw one clear distinction.

A great deal of today's debate about "values," or about "morality," centers on what essentially are private values and personal codes: patterns of dress and appearance; sexual mores; religious practices; the uses to which a person intends to put his own life.

These are immensely important, but they are not the values I mean to discuss here.

My concern today is not with the length of a person's hair, but with his conduct in relation to his community; not with what he wears, but with his impact on the process by which a free society governs itself.

I speak not of private morality, but of public morality—and of "moral-

223

ity" in its broadest sense, as a set of standards by which the community chooses to judge itself.

Some critics call ours an "immoral" society because they disagree with its policies, or they refuse to obey its laws because they claim that those laws have no moral basis. Yet the structure of our laws has rested from the beginning on a foundation of moral purpose. That moral purpose embodies what is, above all, a deeply humane set of values—rooted in a profound respect for the individual, for the integrity of his person and the dignity of his humanity.

At first glance, there is something homely and unexciting about basic values we have long believed in. We feel apologetic about espousing them; even the profoundest truths become clichés with repetition. But they can be like sleeping giants: slow to rouse, but magnificent in their strength.

Let us look at some of those values —so familiar now, and yet once so revolutionary:

- Liberty: recognizing that liberties can only exist in balance, with the liberty of each stopping at that point at which it would infringe the liberty of another.
- Freedom of conscience: Meaning that each person has the freedom of his own conscience, and therefore none has the right to dictate the conscience of his neighbor.
- Justice: recognizing that true justice is impartial, and that no man can be judge in his own cause.
- Human dignity: a dignity that inspires pride, is rooted in self-reliance, and provides the satisfaction of being a useful and respected member of the community.

- Concern for the disadvantaged and dispossessed: but a concern that neither panders nor patronizes.
- The right to participate in public decisions: which carries with it the duty to abide by those decisions when reached, recognizing that no one can have his own way all the time.
- Human fulfillment: in the sense not of unlimited license, but of maximum opportunity.
- The right to grow, to reach upward, to be all that we can become, in a system that rewards enterprise, encourages innovation and honors excellence.

In essence, these all are aspects of freedom. They inhere in the concept of freedom; they aim at extending freedom; they celebrate the uses of freedom. They are not new. But they are as timeless and as timely as the human spirit, because they are rooted in the human spirit.

Our basic values concern not only what we seek, but how we seek it.

Freedom is a condition; it also is a process. And the process is essential to the freedom itself.

We have a Constitution that sets certain limits on what government can do, but that allows wide discretion within those limits. We have a system of divided powers, of checks and balances, of periodic elections, all of which are designed to ensure that the majority has a chance to work its will —but not to override the rights of the minority, or to infringe the rights of the individual.

What this adds up to is a democratic process, carefully constructed and stringently guarded. It is not perfect. No system could be. But it has served the nation well—and nearly two centuries of growth and change testify to its strength and adaptability.

They testify, also, to the fact that avenues of peaceful change do exist. Those who can make a persuasive case for changes they want can achieve them through this orderly process.

To challenge a particular policy is one thing; to challenge the government's right to set it is another—for this denies the process of freedom.

Lately, however, a great many people have become impatient with the democratic process. Some of the more extreme even argue, with curious logic, that there is no majority, because the majority has no right to hold opinions that they disagree with. Scorning persuasion, they prefer coercion. Awarding themselves what they call a higher morality, they try to bully authorities into yielding to their "demands." On college campuses, they draw support from faculty members who should know better; in the larger community, they find the usual apologists ready to excuse any tactic in the name of "progress."

It should be self-evident that this sort of self-righteous moral arrogance has no place in a free community. It denies the most fundamental of all the values we hold: respect for the rights of others. This principle of mutual respect is the keystone of the entire structure of ordered liberty that makes freedom possible.

The student who invades an administration building, roughs up the dean, rifles the files and issues "non-negotiable demands" may have some of his demands met by a permissive university administration. But the greater his "victory," the more he will have undermined the security of his own rights. In a free society, the rights of none are secure unless the rights of all are respected. It is precisely the structure of law and custom that he has chosen to violate—the *process* of freedom—by which the rights of all are protected.

We have long considered our colleges and universities citadels of freedom, where the rule of reason prevails. Now both the process of freedom and the rule of reason are under attack. At the same time, our colleges are under pressure to collapse their educational standards, in the misguided belief that this would promote "opportunity."

Instead of seeking to raise lagging students up to meet the college standards, the cry now is to lower the standards to meet the students. This is the old, familiar, self-indulgent cry for the easy way. It debases the integrity of the educational process. There is no easy way to excellence, no short-cut to the truth, no magic wand that can produce a trained and disciplined mind without the hard discipline of learning. To yield to these demands would weaken the institution; more importantly, it would cheat the student of what he comes to a college for: his education.

No group, as a group, should be more zealous defenders of the integrity of academic standards and the rule of reason in academic life than the faculties of our great institutions. If they simply follow the loudest voices, parrot the latest slogan, yield to unreasonable demands, they will have won not the respect but the contempt of their students. Students have a right to guidance, to leadership, to direction; they have a right to expect their teachers to listen, and to be reasonable, but also to stand for something—and most especially, to stand for the rule of reason againts the rule of force.

Our colleges have their weaknesses. Some have become too impersonal, or too ingrown, and curricula have lagged. But with all its faults, the fact remains that the American system of higher education is the best in this whole imperfect world—and it provides, in the United States today, a better education for more students of all economic levels than ever before, anywhere, in the history of the world.

This is no small achievement.

Often, the worst mischief is done in the name of the best cause. In our zeal for instant reform, we should be careful not to destroy our educational standards, and our educational system along with them; and not to undermine the process of freedom, on which all else rests.

The process of freedom will be less threatened in America, however, if we pay more heed to one of the great cries of the young today. I speak now of their demand for honesty: intellectual honesty, personal honesty, public honesty. Much of what seems to be revolt is really little more than this: an attempt to strip away sham and pretense, to puncture illusion, to get down to the basic nub of truth.

We should welcome this. We have seen too many patterns of deception:

- In political life, impossible promises.
- In advertising, extravagant claims.
- In business, shady deals.

In personal life, we all have witnessed deceits that ranged from the "little white lie" to moral hypocrisy;

from cheating on income taxes to bilking insurance companies.

In public life, we have seen reputations destroyed by smear, and gimmicks paraded as panaceas. We have heard shrill voices of hate, shouting lies, and sly voices of malice, twisting facts.

Even in intellectual life, we too often have seen logical gymnastics performed to justify a pet theory, and refusal to accept facts that fail to support it.

Absolute honesty would be ungenerous. Courtesy compels us to welcome the unwanted visitor; kindness leads us to compliment the homely girl on how pretty she looks. But in our public discussions, we sorely need a kind of honesty that has too often been lacking: the honesty of straight talk; a doing away with hyperbole; a careful concern with the gradations of truth, and a frank recognition of the limits of our knowledge about the problems we have to deal with. We have long demanded financial integrity in public life; we now need the most rigorous kind of intellectual integrity in public debate.

Unless we can find a way to speak plainly, truly, unselfconsciously, about the facts of public life, we may find that our grip on the forces of history is too loose to control our own destiny.

The honesty of straight talk leads us to the conclusion that some of our recent social experiments have worked, and some have failed, and that most have achieved something—but less than their advance billing promised. This same honesty is concerned not with assigning blame, but with discovering what lessons can be drawn from that experience in order to design better programs next time. Perhaps the goals were unattainable; perhaps the means were inadequate; perhaps the program was based on an unrealistic assessment of human nature.

We can learn these lessons only to the extent that we can be candid with one another. We face enormously complex choices. In approaching these, confrontation is no substitute for consultation; passionate concern gets us nowhere without dispassionate analysis. More fundamentally, our structure of values depends on mutual faith, and faith depends on truth.

The values we cherish are sustained by a fabric of mutual self-restraint, woven of ordinary civil decency, respect for the rights of others, respect for the laws of the community, and respect for the democratic process of orderly change. The purpose of these restraints is not to protect an "establishment," but to establish the protection of liberty; not to prevent change, but to ensure that change reflects the public will and respects the rights of all.

This process is our most precious resource as a nation. But it depends on public acceptance, public understanding and public faith.

Whether our values are maintained depends ultimately not on the government, but on the people.

A nation can be only as great as its people want it to be.

A nation can be only as free as its people insist that it be.

A nation's laws are only as strong as its people's will to see them enforced.

A nation's freedoms are only as secure as its people's determination to see them maintained.

A nation's values are only as lasting as the ability of each generation to pass them on to the next.

We often have a tendency to turn away from the familiar because it is familiar, and to seek the new because it is new.

To those intoxicated with the romance of violent revolution, the continuing revolution of democracy may seem unexciting. But no system has ever liberated the spirits of so many so fully. Nothing has ever "turned on" man's energies, his imagination, his unfettered creativity, the way the ideal of freedom has.

Some see America's vast wealth, and protest that this has made us "materialistic." But we should not be apologetic about our abundance. We should not fall into the easy trap of confusing the production of things with the worship of things. We produce abundantly; but our *values* turn not on what we have, but on what we believe.

We believe in liberty, and decency, and the process of freedom. On these beliefs we rest our pride as a nation; in these beliefs, we rest our hopes for the future; and by our fidelity to the process of freedom, we can assure to ourselves and our posterity the blessings of freedom.

The New Politics

SENATOR GEORGE McGOVERN

The need for a new approach to politics and political problems is as obvious as it is urgent. Everywhere we see irrefutable evidence of the failure of conventional politics, the tragic results of politics as usual and the consequence of "benign neglect" toward particular groups, issues and problems. If we really believe, and I do believe, that our political system can work, we must make it work and work now.

In addition to making the political system work, I think we must introduce into American politics a new emphasis upon sincerity. It is time that we brought honesty, integrity and personal commitment back into politics, and this is what the new politics is attempting to do. We must say what we believe, and believe what we say. We must close the credibility gap between the people and their elected officials. The place to begin is on the national level, since this is the focal point of the nation. We must say less and do more. Certainly there should be much less stress on rhetoric and much more positive action. Nowhere is this gap between rhetoric and action more striking than in the realm of foreign affairs. Here we must trim our pronouncements

Amplified telephone interview with seven colleges, January 8, 1969.

to our resources; our promises to our ability to fulfill them; and our commitments to priorities here at home.

This leads into the second characteristic of the new politics, and that is the pressing need for a new list of national priorities. Currently we are spending over $70 billion for arms and armaments, while at the same time 10 million people in this country are hungry and malnourished. The idea of spending $4 billion on a supersonic air transport which will permit a few people to travel to Paris two hours quicker than they can today is almost unthinkable when one considers the problems of our cities, our schools, and our poor. We need to put first things first in our country—to create a national agenda of our problems and to enact programs for solving these problems. We need then, both to examine the pressing issues of our society and to reexamine our present foreign and domestic policies in terms of what is most urgent and what is realistically possible to achieve.

Finally, we need to open up the political process to large numbers of submerged individuals in our society. The disadvantaged minorities need to be brought into the policymaking process. At the present time there are large, relatively unorganized groups which are without their proper share of repre-sentation in the government and with-out political influence. Youth, blacks, Indians, Chicanoes, women; these groups are not participating fully in decision-making, particularly in the

making of those decisions which vitally affect their fate and fortune. We must restore the confidence and the com-petence of these groups by increasing their participatory role in the govern-mental process.

Politics: The Old and the New

ADLAI STEVENSON III

I think some things are rather ob-vious. I don't think that the old politics is going to work very well any more for a variety of reasons. The patronage system, the paid political worker, the person who is on the public payroll in return for working in the precincts—this system doesn't seem to be produc-tive any more. The plain unvarnished fact is that there are too many more attractive alternatives to political pa-tronage. It is not the same as it was back in the days of the 19th century when there were waves of immigrants who were terribly dependent on the local political boss for jobs, for turkeys at Christmas and for all sorts of hand-outs. Consequently, these people be-came indebted to the precinct captain and the machine. They helped the party and the party helped them. Many worked their way up in the party.

Today, of course, we have immi-grants—both from the South and from rural areas. Generally, these new ar-

Amplified telephone interview with seven col-leges, January 10, 1969. Senator Stevenson's comments were spontaneous and unrehearsed.

rivals are Blacks and Puerto Ricans, and concentrate in the cities. They are frequently unskilled and forced to live in the ghettoes and do not have the opportunity to work up the ladder in or out of the party. The "older immi-grants" of the 19th century climbed their way up the ladder and when they reached the top they often drew up the ladder and closed the doors behind them. In many urban communities, eco-nomic, political, and social injustices have incited a great deal of unrest among black people. However, the same conditions apply to Puerto Ricans, Latin Americans, and other disadvan-taged groups who live in the larger cities. What I am saying, I suppose, is that one aspect of the old politics was reliance on massive ethnic voting blocs. Well, you cannot rely on these coali-tions to quite the same extent. They are becoming a little more shaky all of the time. Moreover, the groups which formed the basis of the Democratic party from 1932 to 1964 are not the same—labor, the social reform groups, the intellectuals. The cities are not the same. People are continuously moving not only to cities from the rural areas, and from the South into the North, but also from the cities to the suburbs. We find so many cities like Chicago where the traditional Democratic base in the central city is remaining pretty static; but this citadel of power is not getting any larger. On the other hand, the Republican base in the suburbs is expanding continuously. Added to all of this, we have the news media, especially TV, which provides new opportunities for the candidate to reach the people directly, to bypass the middleman, the power broker, the organized political leader, the local county boss, the ethnic leader who used to ply back and forth between his people, and the politicians. These individuals are becoming less important. The citizens are exercising judgments for themselves. They do it through public opinion polls, as well as election polls. They see the candidates on TV.

All of this is changing politics and changing it very rapidly. It is making it very hard for the old politics and the old political leaders to survive. The problem is, as I see it, that we really haven't come up with the right answers, the alternatives to the old politics. This means institutional reform, reforming the electoral process, direct election perhaps of all party officials. It means all kinds of structural reforms. These reforms take time. Right now, it seems to me, that we're caught in the middle—between the old politics and the new politics.

In this time of transition, there is tension between the individuals who have come up through the old politics and the individuals who are trying to come up through the new politics; the public figures who are reaching out directly to the people, who not only understand the techniques of the new politics but who are also aware of the new issues, the new problems of urban America; the environmental problems of air and water pollution, the regional problems, and the conflicts between races and generations.

The old politicians have failed to grasp many of the new issues. Right now we're in a real period of conflict between the old and the new. The "new" forces are going to win, but there may be a period of agonizing conflict in the immediate future. Certainly there can be a great deal of self-destructiveness and demoralization for young people who become involved in a purely negative way. If young people participate constructively they can really help the country get through this transitional period.

As soon as you engage in the language of violence and coercion, and self-righteousness, you invite the same kind of response from the other side and your efforts can become counterproductive. Violence is not the language of a free society. We are just not going to make this transition without citizen participation. I think it's really going to take very painstaking, patient, hard work in the precincts and at every level. It is going to require good will, the putting aside of violence, and recriminations and abuse, and all the rest.

And those who undertake it will find out that hard work year in and out pays off. They will also discover that much of that work is in a sense "old" politics—the best of the old. It means canvassing in the precincts, not from compulsion but from the heart. It means door bells and postage stamps. It means opening the doors to the disadvantaged

—not with turkeys at Christmas—but with candidates and issues relevant to their needs. And it requires that we recon- cile the minor differences which shouldn't divide us and recognize the real dif- ferences that should divide us.

The Challenge of Change

EDWARD BROOKE

The Republican Party cannot reverse its decline by thinking of its own needs. It must think primarily of the needs of the country. As Governor Nelson Rockefeller has said, "The Republican Party stands today at the crossroads of its destiny—its destiny is to save the nation by first saving itself." For political parties are not ends in themselves. They are meant to be agencies for promoting the national welfare, for expressing and shaping the general will.

Yet in a real sense, the fate of the Republican Party itself has become a national issue of major proportions. Ordinarily the interests of the nation far outweigh the interests of any of its political parties. But under present circumstances, the nation has no greater interest than the rebirth of a dynamic Republican Party.

This proposition is illustrated by one of my favorite political stories. It took place in 1933 when Republican

Reprinted from Edward W. Brooke, The Challenge of Change: Crisis in Our Two-Party System (Boston: Little, Brown and Company, 1966), pp. 259–66. Copyright 1966 by Edward W. Brooke. Reprinted by permission of the publisher.

fortunes and prospects seemed even more gloomy than they do now. After President Franklin Roosevelt's extraordinary congressional successes during the period known as the Hundred Days—a period in which Republicans all but ceased to function as a party—the President asked the late Felix Frankfurter, on the eve of Mr. Frankfurter's trip abroad, for some parting advice. "Get yourself an opposition," Mr. Frankfurter replied.

Get yourself an opposition—it was sage advice, for the country more than for President Roosevelt. No doubt President Lyndon Johnson would not agree that he or the country now need a stronger Republican Party. But in this respect at least, President Johnson is outside the American consensus. For the very foundation of American politics, the two-party system, has been undermined by present Republican weakness. And even the most partisan Democrat agrees that America suffers in every respect when it lacks a strong two-party system.

The two-party system was not established by the Constitution or even by law, but it has become so integral to the workings of American government that any serious damage to it is by the nature of things damage to our entire political structure. We do not now enjoy the benefits of genuine two-party competition. And unless Republican strength is restored, there is no guarantee that we will enjoy those benefits in the foreseeable future.

Do I exaggerate? I fear not. Republican representation in the federal government and in many states is now too meager even to sustain an effective and responsible opposition. It is not so much one-party rule in the totalitarian sense that we must fear, as the breakdown of the checks and balances—the principal advantages—of competition. Our government, like our trials at common law, is grounded in the adversary system. Just as a fair trial in the common law presupposes conflict between two sides roughly equal in skill and resources, good government presupposes conflict between two political parties roughly equal in numbers and influence. When one side is palpably weaker than the other, the system loses its balance, its logic, and soon thereafter, its integrity and effectiveness.

More than fifteen years ago, when Republican fortunes were considerably brighter than they are now, an ardent Democrat, Arthur Schlesinger, Jr., warned that "while Democrats may gain short-run benefits from the present absence of competition, thoughtful members of that party understand the long-run dangers from absence of competition. An essential function of a party in our system is to secure the concurrence of that part of the community which it represents, and if a party becomes so feeble and confused that it turns into an object of public pity or contempt, it can no longer assist in se-

curing that concurrence. As a result, our whole political fabric suffers."

It suffers in a dozen ways. At the local level, the absence of competition encourages wrongdoing by public officials. I have had to spend too much of my time as Attorney General of Massachusetts fighting corruption of elective and appointive officials at state, county and local levels. While I cannot say that one-party government is the sole cause of corruption, my experience has consistently confirmed what is commonly assumed about corruption in government: one-party government provides a climate in which all forms of dishonesty and unethical behavior flourish in the conduct of the public business. I am often chided by people who say I enjoy prosecuting wrongdoers because I am "only getting rid of the Democrats." My answer has been, "There is no one here but Democrats." Actually, I have had to prosecute Republicans and Democrats—but more Democrats, logically enough, because Massachusetts is fast becoming a one-party, Democratic state.

Neither political party has a monopoly on corruption or a monopoly on virtue. But voters are creating a Democratic monopoly of public office in Massachusetts and in the nation. A climate therefore exists in which the tendency toward virtue struggles unevenly against the tendency toward corruption.

But the effects of corruption under one-party government cannot be measured simply in terms of stolen dollars, of bought jobs, of conflict of interest. In a larger sense, our very political atmosphere is corrupted by the absence of serious competition. In state capitals and in Washington as well, the conflict of political principles is reduced to a sham battle. Meaningful debate becomes rhetoric for the record. Controversial proposals and decisions lose their sense of controversy. Legislative and administrative policies are no longer hammered out and put to the test of a strong, self-confident opposition, but are handed out, untested, by an overconfident majority party. Effective investigations, careful review in committees, minority reports on legislative proposals, the sharpening and dramatizing of issues in floor debates —these crucial functions are feebly discharged by a feeble minority. The opposition itself, recognizing its impotence, loses its sense of responsibility. And inevitably, the members of a party enjoying a lopsided majority become arrogant and lazy. A system theoretically based on competition between near-equal partners becomes a caricature of that system.

If I were starting in politics today, without question I would join the Republican Party. For here is where the great challenges and opportunities lie. If one wants to participate in the political process and is serious about improving America, here is the opportunity to channel political energy where it will do the most good. Equal work will produce far more results in the Republican Party than in the Democratic Party.

I honestly believe that as the Republican Party goes, so goes the nation. he restoration of the two-party system is but one of many national objectives directly dependent upon the rebirth of a strong, self-confident Republican Party. Beyond this, America's future will be determined largely by the Republican future. If the country continues to be led by an overwhelmingly victorious and complacent Democratic

Party which is traditionally oriented to temporary solutions and relief, we will continue to make only agonizingly slow progress toward solving our great underlying problems and encouraging excellence in our national life. We will limp along, hesitant, temporizing, protesting and poorly led.

For the restoration of two-party government in America, I make a plea for active support to intellectuals, to members of minorities, to young voters and to those who have, through family ties and background, through labor-union affiliation, through habit and emphathy, always considered themselves Democrats.

The Republican Party must attract intellectual talent and youthful energy. The Republican Party must broaden its overall base. The Republican Party must not accept the outmoded proposition that the Democratic Party is the logical and natural political home of first-, second-, and third-generation Americans. The Republican Party must, by person-to-person contact, work with people who live in America's cities and demonstrate to them a genuine and sincere concern for their problems and aspirations. This is the only road to Republican recovery. It will be long and the obstacles formidable, but that is all the more reason for intellectuals, minorities, and young people to join the march.

I am well aware that the present leadership of many Republican organizations may not encourage intellectuals, minorities and eager young people to join the Republican Party. But that should not dissuade them, for American intellectuals have always loved challenge and here is an opportunity for them to respond with meaningful political activity to a clear-cut challenge vital to the nation's stability. Here is a chance for them to channel their zeal for improving the country into direct action. It has been all too easy for the nation's intellectuals to stand aside and criticize the Republican Party without committing themselves to its improvement. But those intellectuals who have refused to make the commitment, who have reserved their skills and energy for deriding our condition are no less responsible for that condition than the Republican Party they criticize. To allow the Republican Party to "stew in its own juice" is as irresponsible as some of the positions Republican leaders have taken in the last thirty-five years, and for which intellectuals have most criticized our party.

The same reasons that have disaffected the intellectuals have caused young people to avoid the Republican Party. Since the advent of Franklin D. Roosevelt, members of minority groups have, rightly or wrongly, believed that the Democratic Party would best serve their interests. And immigrants, their children and grandchildren have, by and large, shared that belief. Because of this, the composition of the Republican Party has lacked that pluralistic quality which has benefited the Democratic Party so much. The voices of these groups have not been heard in Republican Party Councils. We learn about their problems secondhand. We have not had the advantages of their thinking or their suggestions for solutions to their problems. Worse, their absence has left an intraparty political void— they have not been present as participants to influence the direction in which the Republican Party should move.

They have maximized their philosophical differences with the Republican Party and minimized their philosophical differences with the Democratic Party. They have put practically all of their political eggs in the Democratic Party basket to the detriment of the two-party system and to their own detriment, for they have been taken for granted by the Democratic Party. The leverage they could assert by a better distribution of their strength between the two great political parties in America has never been fully utilized.

I have tried not to minimize the difficulties facing the Republican Party. I realize the enormous efforts which will be required to overcome our inertia and to infuse Republicanism with the qualities necessary for leadership. I know that the very people who avoid us are precisely the people we need most in order to help us overcome our grave handicaps in popularity and dynamism. But I am fully aware that a welcome may not be extended by party leadership for some time. And because of this, I urge them to force their way into the Republican Party. I urge them to join Republican city, town, ward and precinct committees. I urge them to *participate*. I ask them to intensify their efforts. And I say to them that even though it may not be apparent, the great majority of Republicans in this country welcome them with open arms.

It is no secret that an intense ideological struggle within the Republican Party can probably not be avoided —a struggle which, I trust, will be waged without rancor and bitterness. But the Republican Party is not going to wither away; it is an established American institution with enormous resources for survival. The question is, which direction will it take? Its future, and the future of the country and perhaps the future of the world, hang in the balance. No political activity can have more immediate and direct effect on American and world politics as a whole than participation in the struggle within the Republican Party. For those who yearn to do something constructive for America, to commit themselves to a worthwhile cause and to engage in meaningful political activity, the challenge is clear. I urge the skeptical, the critical, the fearful and the disillusioned to put aside the crutch of noninvolvement and join *this* good fight.

I end this book with high optimism and with a prediction that the Republican Party will soon become the majority party. I believe that there is a great future in store for us. I have faith in our determination to govern. I have faith in our ability to govern. I have faith in the intelligence of the American people to give us the opportunity to govern. And, above all, I have faith in the wisdom and willingness of the Republican Party to respond to the challenge of change so essential if we are to govern.

The New Politics

THOMAS F. EAGLETON

Every so often, the obvious is discovered anew with much fanfare. It was in this political year—1970.

In the *Real Majority*, Richard Scammon and Ben Wattenburg argued persuasively that victory in American politics is won in the moderate middle —albeit one that changes in time—not at the extremes of the American political spectrum.

That has, is, and I believe, will continue to be the case for a long time to come. The American system of government was designed to blur issues in search of consensus, rather than sharpen them through confrontation.

The politics of confrontation and polarization are not the winning combination for the 1970's. But to say so is not to deny that the way politics is

conducted has changed and will continue to change.

Today, more people are better educated with more time and perhaps more reason to be concerned about issues. This has raised the level of political debate and should continue to do so.

Better communications, most notably television, have played an important role in increasing voter awareness. At the same time, the ever expanding technology that brought us television also provides us with increasingly sophisticated methods of practicing politics. Computors, advanced management techniques, and motivation research coupled with increased voter awareness have changed the very dynamics of campaigning. Citizens concerned about specific issues or specific candidates have replaced ward heelers in the precincts doing what professional managers map out.

This, it seems to me is the "new politics."

The battleground has remained the same—the political middle—but there are new political leaders, followers, and tactics.